# The Voice of the Century

INDIANA UNIVERSITY PRESS

INGEBORG SOLBREKKEN

TRANSLATED BY ANNE BRUCE

# The Voice of the Century

# KIRSTEN FLAGSTAD

*This book is a publication of*

Indiana University Press
Herman B Wells Library 350
1320 East 10th Street
Bloomington, Indiana 47405 USA

iupress.org

First published in Norway as Århundrets stemme by
Opera Forlag Jon Otterbeck AS, 2021
First published in USA by Indiana University Press, 2025
Copyright © Ingeborg Solbrekken and Jon Otterbeck
English translation copyright © Anne Bruce, 2025

𝄢 OPERA FORLAG

All rights reserved
No part of this book may be reproduced or utilized in any form or
by any means, electronic or mechanical, including photocopying
and recording, or by any information storage and retrieval system,
without permission in writing from the publisher.

First printing 2025

Cataloging information is available from
the Library of Congress.

ISBN 978-0-253-07201-6 (hdbk.)
ISBN 978-0-253-07202-3 (pbk.)
ISBN 978-0-253-07204-7 (ebook)
ISBN 978-0-253-07203-0 (web PDF)

# CONTENTS

Introduction  1
Post Festum  5

**PART 1** The Making of a Singer (1895–1935)  11

**PART 2** The Voice of the Century (1935–41)  63

**PART 3** The Years of Struggle (1941–51)  140

**PART 4** Postlude (1951–62)  263

*Acknowledgments* 289
*Sources* 291

# The Voice of the Century

# Introduction

KIRSTEN MALFRID FLAGSTAD (1895–1962) was undoubtedly the greatest voice of her age and the most outstanding interpreter of Richard Wagner's music. Famous across the entire American continent and throughout Europe, she was less well known in her homeland, Norway. Wagner's biographer and music critic Ernest Newman heard Flagstad sing as early as 1936 at the Queen's Hall, London, and wrote in the *Sunday Times* that her voice was exceptional, a combination of purity and warmth—like bright sunlight on snow. He was astonished that it sounded so natural. She never seemed to have to reach for a high note but simply glided into it like a bird in flight.[1] Others compare her sound to sunshine on hillsides, mountaintops, and glaciers. Jessye Norman associated it with molten gold on black velvet, while Elisabeth Schwarzkopf felt it had the dimensions of a cosmic mother, embracing the universe.[2]

Flagstad was born with musical genius and perfect pitch, but on the other hand, she was rather tone deaf when it came to the world around her and the times in which she lived. Her life and career largely unfolded during a dark time for Europe—before, during, and after World War II. This biography places her life and those of her musical contemporaries in this historical context, caught in the tension that arose between art and politics.

Flagstad's fate often coincided with the content of the Wagner operas she sang, something this text sheds light on from an in-depth psychological perspective. She came close to being trapped by Nazism's politicization of Wagner's works and characters. The composer used ancient Nordic myths as the raw material for his operas. What do these myths convey, exactly, and how could their archaic wisdom be reinterpreted and exploited in the service of

Nazi ideology? What were the consequences for Jewish singers and musicians in Germany from 1933 onward? And what were the consequences for culture in general? These questions are explored in this book.

In 1934, a contact at the Metropolitan in New York saved Flagstad from continuing her career at Bayreuth. She was under contract at the Metropolitan from 1935 until 1941, and it is claimed that she rescued the opera house from bankruptcy and also renewed opera as an art form in America. In 1934, Bayreuth regarded her as the next generation's Isolde and Brunhild. However, continuing to work there could have had disastrous consequences. The dazzling, supernatural character of the Valkyrie was idolized by the Hitler regime as a war goddess in the cause of Nazism, and it proved difficult to separate the performer from the message.

In the US, from 1935 until 1940, Wagner was not politicized in the same way. The American public experienced his operas beyond the bounds of a German and Nazi context as purely mythological dramas dressed in spectacular music.

Through the genius of Wagner, his works were rooted in a universal plane. At the same time, they were clouded by the man's ideological shadow, which Hitler and his collaborators sensed and incorporated into their project. Flagstad was first caught up with this shadow in 1940, when her Wagner repertoire was construed as treason by the Norwegian ambassador in America and the Norwegian Ministry of Foreign Affairs. German now sounded like the language of the enemy in the ears of representatives of occupied countries. She had a more calamitous encounter with this in 1941, when she left America and returned home to occupied Norway. Waiting for her there was a husband who was a member of the National Samling Party (NS), and to make matters worse, he engaged in extensive business dealings with the occupying power.

All the same, Flagstad never lived up to this image of her as the enemy, created by leading men in the Norwegian diplomatic service, with Wilhelm af Munthe von Morgenstierne, the Norwegian ambassador in the US, at the forefront. They unfairly accused her in public of being a Nazi sympathizer and war profiteer who sang for Hitler and entertained the Third Reich's occupying forces.

She was also drawn into a conspiracy theory alleging that an underground organization called "the Economic Ring" had been formed in Norway in 1945. Flagstad was suspected of assisting this group by holding the organization's funds, camouflaged as her own personal wealth. She was apparently intending to withdraw and transfer them when she moved abroad after the war. This was part of the reason that her assets were illegally frozen until as late as 1950

# Introduction

and that she was refused a passport and permission to leave Norway until December 1946.

A subsequent police investigation, led by the Norwegian director of public prosecution, Andreas Aulie, in 1950, concluded that there was no evidence of the existence of the Economic Ring. The idea had been invented by two former Gestapo agents used by the Norwegian secret police as informants and collaborators from 1945 to 1948.[3] These revelations cast serious doubts on the credibility of both the prosecuting authorities and the police.

The systematic postwar persecution of Norway's premier vocal artist is documented in detail in a series of letters marked "confidential," in the archives of the Norwegian Foreign Office. Their express aim was to prevent her from leaving Norway and from working professionally in Europe and America. Her accusers misinformed the American authorities, gave false information to the Norwegian royal family, planted fake news stories in the foreign media, and had corrupt dealings with elements of the Norwegian press.

The campaign was successful and led to the most extensive controversies that any artist has faced in the US since World War II. It stirred up thousands of Americans who believed what they read in the papers about Kirsten Flagstad. The management of the Metropolitan Opera House also believed it, and they did not invite her back onstage until 1951. For several years, Flagstad lived in constant fear of physical attacks by furious individuals and demonstrating crowds and sometimes even required police protection.

The harassment failed to break her as an artist, but the prolonged victimization did irreparable damage to her, both body and soul. Her bitter legal will, in which she sought to erase her own memory from Norwegian society, sends a clear message. All the same, no doubt she knew that her numerous recordings would leave an enduring, brilliant legacy in global music history.

This book is written with an international audience in mind. Since it tells of musical life in different countries, opera lovers and music institutions around the world will find a great deal of useful information. The biography now available is the result of more than twenty years of research and includes pioneering work in previously unexplored and overlooked archives. Flagstad's life and career challenge a number of well-established narratives, and her life story is at times woven into events and circumstances that run counter to Norwegian collective cultural memory. However, her reputation is gradually being restored in Norwegian society, where she features as a monument, on street names, and even on banknotes. In her birthplace of Hamar, a museum has been set up in her honor in the house in which she was born.

The publication of such an international biographical work will serve to redress the lack of knowledge about Kirsten Flagstad in the music history of the world. This biography's account of her persecution by the Norwegian authorities is substantially taken from two of the author's previous books, *The Post-war Settlement's Secret History* (2015) and *The Conspiracy against Kirsten Flagstad* (2016), in which her persecution is thoroughly documented.

*Etnedal, October 6, 2020*
*Ingeborg Solbrekken*

## Notes

1. Gunnarson (1985), s. 91.

2. Kirsten Flagstad documentary—1994, https://www.youtube.com/watch?v=qf40j5NQRyM&t=3515s.

3. Parliamentary report no. 64 (1950), Attacks on the Postwar Treason Trials, https://www.stortinget.no/no/Saker-og-publikasjoner/Stortingsforhandlinger/Lesevisning/?p=1950&paid=2&wid=c&psid=DIVL1190.

# Post Festum

"ONLY THOSE WHO unravel the spool to the very end can understand my words," sings the Woodbird in Richard Wagner's opera *Siegfried*. On Friday, December 14, 1962, Kirsten Flagstad's funeral took place in Oslo. She was, without a doubt, the greatest voice of her age, a singer who had been singled out as early as 1936 by English music critics as the voice of the century, "a shining button on the world's waistcoat," to use Henrik Ibsen's famous phrase from *Peer Gynt*.[1] Immediately after her death, several major newspapers in Europe and America published articles paying homage to this unique artist. Admittedly, her will stated that she did not want her death made public until after her cremation. Nor did she want anyone to attend her funeral or preserve her ashes.[2]

It was a very cold day. So cold that many people shivered as they walked down the aisle of the Vestre Crematorium to the organ playing "In Lonely Moments," a Norwegian folk song written down by Ole Bull in around 1850. When they had all left the chapel, the undertakers took over. The candles were blown out and the abundant floral tributes and wreaths cleared away.

The next day, the newspapers reported that everyone of any significance had been present and that a wreath sent by the king had lain majestically in front of the coffin. They described the graceful tendrils of carnations, the vivid trumpets of amaryllis blooms, and the snow-white splendor of lilies and lilacs, but by then it had all been removed.

The coffin was lowered into the basement, where a small team organized the incineration of coffins and filling of urns. The flames flickered around the body, the instrument of a voice no orchestra had ever been able to drown out, and turned it to ashes. How often it had sung:

> Fly home, ye ravens!
> Tell your lord the tidings
> That here on the Rhine ye have learned!
> To Brünnhilde's rock first wing your flight!
> There burneth Loge.[3]

The ashes were collected and placed in an urn marked "Kirsten Flagstad," which remained on a shelf in the basement of the new crematorium for three years. Perhaps "In Lonely Moments" was played many hundreds of times in the chapel above before the urn was at last moved to an anonymous memorial garden with five others.

All these arrangements violated her last wishes, but they gave the impression that everything was just fine. It was business as usual, and Norway had given a fitting farewell to a world-famous Norwegian artist.

What was the life story behind the decision she made, that she wished for no publicization of her death until after her cremation, no mourners at her funeral, and no preservation of her ashes?

## Beethoven and Flagstad under Attack

Kirsten Flagstad is especially famous for her interpretations of Richard Wagner's characters, such as Isolde and Brunhild. However, there is one composer even closer to her heart: Ludwig van Beethoven. In the spring of 1802, Beethoven had left Vienna. He was in the midst of a desperate inner crisis, and it had become a matter of life and death, which is why he sought refuge in nature. Previously he had obtained some relief in this maternal element, but now there was no peace of mind to be found there, no shelter where he could recover a sense of calm. Beethoven was a sensitive individual with a subtly developed inner and outer ear to guide him. The landscape was now silent, the world around him was about to close down for him, and the goatherds' songs would soon become only a vague memory. Progressive hearing loss had driven him away from humans and out of the sensate world. He realized that he would end up incurably deaf. The pain and desperation this prompted were almost unbearable, and they drove him to contemplate suicide.[4]

Somewhere out there on the sheer edge of the mind's darkest cliff, a sense of resolve may have taken hold of him. The external world disappeared, but by some miracle a new reality opened up. He was increasingly deaf to the world, but his inner ear captured new vibrations from the harmonies of the spheres. The Greek mathematician and mystic Pythagoras is said to have been able to hear these too, although he believed they had to be transmitted. As Beethoven's hearing reached them, he rediscovered the lyre of Orpheus, which, with its music, could bring humanity's soul up from the underworld. He moved from a geocentric to a heliocentric position and so made a deeper connection with his spiritual center, his original true self. From here, Beethoven could appreciate that the perceptible world was an empty vessel. But behind form and emptiness, he found the absolute.

During this period, he was working on Gellert's devotional poems, which became Opus 48. These songs convey his insights and occupy a special place in Beethoven's collected works. They express his deepened spirituality and are the fruit of the great life crisis he survived.

Kirsten Flagstad had included two of these songs in her concert program on April 22, 1947, in the venerable old opera house, the Academy of Music in Philadelphia. She was to start with the last and longest song, "Busslied" (Song of penitence). The concert was one of her first in the US after the war. The police had warned her that it would be eventful. Someone had told her that one of the city's millionaires had pledged more than $100,000 to oppose her if she showed herself on the American stage. She could not quite believe this, but, with her safety in mind, she had traveled to the opera house under police escort early that afternoon. The pianist who was to accompany her looked pale and seemed frightened, as if he expected the worst.

They were told that the box office had accepted a suspicious booking of a large number of tickets, in small groups scattered throughout the hall. This was so unusual that the office had noted the seat numbers and handed a list of them to the police. Outside the opera house, a group of students had gathered, walking in some kind of protest march. Flagstad's agent went out to speak to them, and several reported that they had received fifteen dollars to demonstrate, as well as free tickets to the concert. The number of protesters increased in the course of the afternoon. A car drove around with a megaphone, shrieking that a Nazi was giving a concert, that Americans who had fought against Nazism had been killed by Kirsten Flagstad's friends, and that the fallen could no longer be present—so everyone else should stay away from the concert.

Outside the hall, a woman walked back and forth brandishing a large placard that compared Flagstad to Adolf Hitler. Journalists scurried about with cameras and notepads as an increasing number of demonstrators joined in. Police cars arrived with officers who were then strategically placed both outside

8       THE VOICE OF THE CENTURY

and inside the building. Kirsten Flagstad peered out to count fifteen police officers guarding the stage from every direction and positioned throughout the auditorium. The pianist passed on a message from the police asking her to leave the stage if a dangerous situation arose inside the hall.

She was not sure whether she would want to comply, as right there and then she felt no anxiety. Her fearlessness arose from a conviction that she had done nothing wrong, and she did not recognize herself in any of the things people were screaming and shouting outside the opera house. That was not Kirsten Flagstad, and so she refused to let the mob win.

Courageously, she walks onto the stage, but her shoulders slump at the sight of such a sparse audience in the hall since she is used to attracting thousands. Then she hits the first note of "Busslied," the lyrics of which contain a recognition that the sins we have committed in our lives are, first and foremost, offenses against our higher selves. "An dir allein, an dir hab'ich gesündigt" (And you alone, you have sinned). She gets no further than the first note, played on the piano beside her, before booing erupts in the auditorium. The sound is shocking and puts her off tempo, but at the same time, she also hears applause that encourages her to continue. The amazing thing is that Beethoven and this huge dramatic voice are able to captivate even a mob. No booing is heard while the song is performed. Only once the last strains of "Busslied" have died out does the rabble remember what they are being paid for, and they boo throughout the applause from the music-loving audience.

Just before the next item, "Wonne der Wehmut" (The bliss of melancholy), in which Beethoven conveys something of the sweetness of sadness, silence reigns in the auditorium. She is listening for the pianist's opening note when a voice from the balcony breaks the stillness and sings a word in two chords: "Na . . . zi."

A response is yelled up to the balcony from the orchestra: "You wouldn't dare repeat that." Again the refrain comes from the balcony, "Na . . . zi." The words become burning arrows attacking her nervous system. She is seething inside, her heart has received warnings of danger and is pounding, her adrenaline is pumping, she is ready for flight, but she stands her ground.

A dozen male voices from the auditorium begin singing the American national anthem, "The Star-Spangled Banner," but the audience vigorously claps them into submission. From the stage, she watches a violent commotion break out—not only are people screaming but they are also attacking one another with their fists. The whole rumpus appears unreal, and she steps back slightly but remains onstage. Stubbornness and strength keep her there, even though her body is racked with pain.

The police intervene, throwing the troublemakers out and hauling the worst of them to the station for questioning. It takes some time before there is a hush in the auditorium again. When the dust has settled, she steps forward once more and sings "Wonne der Wehmut." With an almost superhuman ability to concentrate, she manages to convey the sentiment of the song, refusing to allow the distressing experience to affect her performance. An unfamiliar odor spreads around her, a smell she does not recognize. Later she learns that it came from a stink bomb someone had thrown at her.[5] She remains onstage and performs the next song, "Die Ehre Gottes aus der Natur" (The glory of God in nature), with supreme conviction and strength.

Behind the stars, behind the spheres, lay a power. Beethoven found his home there, his spirit and inspiration. She follows him there, seemingly undisturbed.

> Mein ist die Kraft, mein ist Himmel und Erde;
> An meinen Werken kennst du mich.
> Ich bin's, und werde sein, der ich sein werde,
> Dein Gott und Vater ewiglich.[6]

> (Mine is the power, heaven and earth are mine;
> By my works you know me.
> I am, and shall be, that which I am:
> your God and Father for eternity.)

After these verses, there was no further unrest in the auditorium, but when the concert had ended, the police stepped in again. Flagstad had actually intended to leave Philadelphia by train, but after a search of the railway station, the police advised her to drive back to New York instead.[7]

## Notes

1. Henrik Ibsen, "Peer Gynt," akt 5. In: Henrik Ibsens samlede verker, bind II, s.277, Gyldendal Norske forlag, Oslo, 1941.

2. Kirsten Flagstad's will, April 13, 1962, Helge Atle Rønningsens personal archive.

3. "Richard Wagner: Götterdämmerung," Brünnhildes ending scene: Fliegt heim, ihr Raben.

4. Ludwig van Beethoven, "The Heiligenstadt Testament," October 6, 1802.

5. Biancolli (1952), pp. 178–80.

6. Gellert (1757), p. 11.

7. Biancolli (1952), pp. 178–80.

# PART 1

# The Making of a Singer
# (1895–1935)

### A Daughter and a Silver Voice

She is twenty-four and happy to be married. Her husband has promised to provide for her, and she no longer needs to go onstage to sing. On May 17, 1920, she gives birth to a daughter, Else-Marie, and does not sing a note for four months, apart from a few lullabies. She is happy taking care of the baby and has no thought of anything else. Her husband, Sigurd, is besotted with the child too; Else and her father form a strong early bond. And so the days pass until Kirsten Flagstad's mother, Maja, decides that her daughter's life as a housewife now has to end. Kirsten has not sung a single note all summer, to her mother's great dismay. Maja is almost desperate to make her daughter return to singing.[1]

With misgivings that the marriage was no longer happy, Maja suspected that her son-in-law was not as affluent as they had first thought and that her daughter could not base her life on the marriage. The manager of the Opera Comique in Oslo had often asked her whether Kirsten would be coming back soon. Maja was wise enough to realize that she should proceed with caution as her daughter had already turned down a number of previous requests to return to the opera. "The child," as Maja still called Kirsten, had clearly got it into her head that her little daughter and her husband should be her whole world, and this was why she had abandoned her professional career.

One day, Maja arrived carrying sheet music under her arm and sat down at the piano. "Here is a role that was made for you. You should at least take a look at it. It really is meant for you and no one else," she said, making sure there was

12            THE VOICE OF THE CENTURY

no hint of pressure behind the offer. "It's Franz Lehár's *Zigeunerliebe* [Gypsy love], a really beautiful piece." Kirsten allows herself to be tempted, and they look through the music together. Then, just for fun, she sings a cadenza with a high C but stops after a while from sheer astonishment at what she is hearing. "I sang that with a new, fuller sound," she says. Her mother, also taken aback, exclaims, "But, child!"

Her mother leaves the apartment with her daughter's promise that she will return to work. Kirsten regrets this as soon as Maja has gone. She does not really want to leave her six-month-old child—it goes against her nature. A nanny will now look after Else in the mornings, and Sigurd has promised to take care of the baby on the evenings Kirsten is performing. From this time on, the two of them become family while Kirsten becomes a professional singer, working away from home. Her dream of domesticity and a husband who will provide for her becomes a thing of the past: now she is the one who has to go out and earn money.

## A Very Unusual Mother

Maja was pleased. She herself had been a child prodigy, far more musically gifted than most. Her father had begun lifting her up to the organ stool when she was around the age of three. She learned to read music before the alphabet and over time developed great skill on both the chamber organ and the piano. Her parents had lost as many as four infant daughters before she arrived, which left them fearful that their daughter would not do well in life. They passed this anxiety on to her, and it endowed her with a restless nature. Maja's upbringing had emphasized the importance of learning a trade and supporting herself, something that was quite unusual for a girl in Norway at the end of the nineteenth century. This is the background to her intervention in the household of her daughter, Kirsten.

As soon as the child Maja had mastered the chamber organ at home, she was allowed to practice on the organ at Langset Church. When she was nine years old, she played so well that she could fill in for her father, who was an organist blessed with perfect pitch. Eventually, she took over playing for church services and was formally hired as a permanent stand-in. At eleven, she was sent to Christiania, as Oslo was then known, to study under the famous organist and music teacher Peter Lindeman. After three months, he wrote her a reference, stating that Maja played chorales with a serenity that mature organists might envy. Her skills on the keys and pedals were so well developed that she could, without difficulty, work as an organist at public church services.

Part 1: The Making of a Singer (1895–1935)          13

By the age of twelve, she was appointed acting organist at Langset Church, with an annual salary of 150 Norwegian kroner. She kept this position until 1889, when her father decided it would be best for her to travel to Christiania to continue her studies at the music conservatory there. He urged her to practice diligently, as she would soon need to provide for herself as a musician and teacher. She worked hard and was eventually able to take on pupils.

In 1891, she was offered a permanent position at Christiania Theatre as choir tutor and pianist. Female orchestral musicians were unusual in Norway at that time, so this neat woman with red hair and sparkling eyes caused quite a stir as she went about with a sheaf of music under her arm. However, the fact that she was a woman prevented her from pursuing a career as a concert pianist.

Kirsten Flagstad's father, Michael, had wide-ranging talents, but his gifts were not exceptional. Flagstad relates that her father was a good conductor but not a very good violinist. Her mother was horrified as he scraped away with the bow. She, with her perfect pitch, was fanatically meticulous when it came to accurate tone. Kirsten Flagstad was the only one of Maja's children to inherit this ability. When her mother practiced with students who struggled to hit the right notes, Kirsten would be called in. Experienced singers were very surprised when a child, coming straight in from play, could hit the exact note or sing perfectly the parts her mother requested of her. Maja could command her daughter, "Kirsten, please could you sing this duet by Puccini with this gentleman? It's easier for him to sing it correctly when he hears how it should sound." When Kirsten was eleven, her mother called her in to sing Senta's role for a man who was studying Richard Wagner's opera *The Flying Dutchman*. The girl sang it perfectly from the sheet music, to the student's great consternation. When her father changed the strings on his violin and needed to tune them, he asked Kirsten to sing, an A for example, and tuned his instrument accordingly.

## Financial Ruin

The ambition belonged to Maja rather than Kirsten Flagstad. Somewhat reluctantly, she returned to the Opera Comique in 1920, and now a more mature singer entered the stage to sing the part of Zorika in *Zigeunerliebe*. The newspapers reported that Flagstad sang better than ever. The critics noticed the transformation and wrote that her voice had benefited from rest. It rang out, bigger and more beautiful than ever before, her vocal abilities multiplied many times over by the period of respite. She could take on larger roles, such

14       THE VOICE OF THE CENTURY

as Desdemona in *Othello* and Amelia in *Un ballo in maschera* (A masked ball), and she made money. This final point was of vital importance, as the economic downturn in the 1920s had hit hard. Unemployment was high, and many had declared bankruptcy. In the summer of 1921, the Opera Comique also went into liquidation. This was catastrophic for the entire Flagstad family, who had made their living from the opera house.

But the downturn was good news for lighter entertainment, and soon a variety theater, Mayol, where both Flagstad and Maja obtained work, was resurrected. This theater existed from 1922 until 1924, when it became insolvent after running for only two years. A new enterprise, the Casino, took over from 1924. Flagstad worked tirelessly on both these stages and between 1922 and 1927 made her debut in as many as twenty-seven different roles.[2]

Her frantic work rate was driven by material necessity. From March to September 1925, the value of the Norwegian kroner increased by as much as 35 percent. This led, among other things, to rising debt, while the cost of goods collapsed. Prices plummeted, half the country's commercial banks went into liquidation, and many depositors lost their savings. Flagstad's parents were declared bankrupt and left drowning in debt. Her childhood home was repossessed and auctioned off in 1924. This made a terrifying impression on Flagstad, who took out loans to help her family; she qualified for credit with the bank because she could demonstrate a regular income.

Problems had also piled up in her marriage. Her husband's business ventures were going badly, and his moods were becoming more and more unpredictable. There was talk in the Flagstad family that he drank and hit her.[3] They separated, and Flagstad lived for a time as a single mother with her parents in a small apartment in Universitetsgata in Oslo. The family took care of her daughter while she took all kinds of work at the variety theater, simply to service debts. Her proud nature rarely revealed signs of despair, but in later years she would tell her American biographer that she found herself in a desperate financial situation, one that forced her into many roles she would have preferred to avoid.[4]

## Skimpily Dressed Belly Dancer

Flagstad was very shy and reserved by nature, and as a result, she found the operetta *Die Bajadere* (The dancing girl) especially challenging. She wore a sequin or rhinestone in her navel and performed the bayadère dance, a type of temple dance reminiscent of belly dancing. To the audience, it looked as if she were naked from the waist up. Maja sat in the auditorium, following the score, the audience cheered, and the show ran as many as 141 times to packed

Kirsten Flagstad pictured in the role of Countess Mariza.
*Source: Flagstad Museum.*

houses. In the middle of it all, they encountered some unpleasantness with the city's police chief, Christian Grundt. On inspection, he had judged that the ladies onstage were far too skimpily dressed, and Flagstad found this terribly embarrassing.

Her evenings began on the revue stage. Dressed in long ostrich feathers, she sang with high-kicking chorus girls in the background. Even before the audience had finished applauding, she raced to the dressing room, jumped into her concert gown, and dashed to the city's concert hall, the Aula, to sing of exalted human kindness in Beethoven's Ninth Symphony. Then she dashed back to the Casino again, where she once more donned her ostrich feathers to sing of fickle love of the clichéd kind in "Can You Forget?" Afterward, she would sit at her dressing table, staring into space; she felt wretched, on the brink of a breakdown.

Her daughter, Else, saw little of her mother in these years. During the season of 1925–26, she danced as Rosalinde in sixty-five performances of *Die Fledermaus* (The bat). Then she was back in the feathered costume again, drowning in 141 performances of *The Carnival Fairy*, which ran well into the new year. It all ended with what she called a "nervous heart"—in other words, it brought on a stress-related illness—but she had no choice. This was the kind of entertainment people wanted, and she could earn money from it. The press constantly raised objections to her lack of vivacity and frothy Hungarian passion, but they all agreed that she sang wonderfully.

## Struggle for the Soul

After she had sung and acted through seventy-nine performances of Emmerich Kálmán's *The Circus Princess*, all to packed auditoriums, the management at the Casino decided they wanted to stage something serious. They chose the opera *Faust* by Charles Gounod, with the premiere set for December 7, 1926. The libretto is based on a legend from the Middle Ages to which Goethe later gave eternal life in his work of the same name. Flagstad was given the role of Marguerite, a female character who in many ways can be said to be the personification of Faust's soul. The drama explores the great cosmic theme—the salvation or damnation of the soul. The Swedish bass singer Åke Wallgren was to sing the part of Mephistopheles. He was considered one of Stockholm Opera's great singers, perfect to inhabit the devil's resonant bass, which filled the house with the great outburst: "Farewell, nights of passion. Marguerite—your soul is damned!"

A grave opened up, and with an anguished cry, she fell into it, abandoned, night after night. It did her good at last to be able to express some of the desperation and pain that life had heaped upon her. The production became a breakthrough. She was praised in the press for building the character of Marguerite, who was treated so cruelly by fate. A reviewer wrote that he would never forget her song of madness in the prison scene. He had seen the opera in Paris and Berlin but had never heard the role performed so movingly. The clouds were lifting after all her suffering. This was great, genuine art. Another reviewer deeply regretted the absence of an opera house in the capital where Flagstad's talent could be showcased in a more opulent setting.

Flagstad followed up on a similar theme, singing Euridice in a production of Christoph Willibald Gluck's *Orfeo ed Euridice*. Several critics who heard her lamented that so many of her best years had been spent on operettas. One wrote that Kirsten Flagstad in this role sang with scintillating beauty while still possessing the classically metaphysical as she followed Orpheus like a sleepwalker up from the underworld.

## Songs of Substance Given More Prominence

In the summer of 1928, Flagstad's separation from her husband, Sigurd Hall, became a reality. He traveled to Canada, and from then on, Flagstad took Else with her wherever she was performing. The child, now eight years old, was not very happy. Else, who had grown up in a family riddled with conflict, had a traveling entertainer for a mother and a father who had gone to a different continent. All of this gnawed at Flagstad's conscience: she wanted to try to make it up to her daughter as far as she could within her personal circumstances. She desperately sought more stable, secure work now that she had sole parental responsibility.

As a result of Maja's exhortations, she had contacted the Norwegian conductor, Olav Kielland, who was leader of the orchestra at the Stora Teatern in Gothenburg, Sweden. This institution had been in operation since 1859, and with just over six hundred seats, it was a celebrated stage for both opera and theater and was unlikely to go bankrupt in the near future. Sweden had a solid theatrical tradition, and the Stora Teatern was known for the quality of its stagecraft. The theater presented four major opera productions a year, with lighter entertainment in between.

A proposition arrived for Flagstad from the Stora Teatern. Could she come for an audition? The theater was short of a permanent dramatic soprano, whose first part would be that of Agathe in Carl Maria von Weber's opera *The Marksman*, to be performed in the autumn of 1928. She quickly learned some of the role for the audition. If she could convince the management in Gothenburg, it would mean freedom at last from the world of operetta, as well as the opportunity to leave Oslo. Both of these had become of urgent importance to her. The vocal artist she had developed into had long since smashed the confines of what her home country could offer.

In Gothenburg, she wandered restlessly for a few hours, terribly tense after her audition. She felt it had gone well. A heavy burden was lifted from her shoulders when she discovered they were keen to take her on for a whole year. As she traveled home on the train with her daughter, who had accompanied her, she felt relieved and happy. Now she waited for autumn in a state of almost bliss. Flagstad knew that this contract for six roles would provide for both her and her daughter as well as enable her to help her hard-pressed parents.

### *The Marksman*

Flagstad and Else rented a couple of rooms with a family in Gothenburg who also had young children. Their hosts looked after Else while Flagstad was at the theater. Else would start a new academic year at a Swedish school, in a foreign country, with no friends. Her mother would be absent for four nights a week and would give concerts on some weekends. The language was different from the one she was used to. She felt like an outsider, and the only person she knew was her extremely busy mother.

Flagstad, on the other hand, had at last found manageable working conditions. She enjoyed her new workplace, which, in line with Swedish theatrical tradition, invested a great deal of time and effort into making its productions as perfect as possible. This was a luxury for an artist who had often had to learn a role in only a matter of a week or two. The Stora Teatern offered her an opportunity she had never had before to immerse herself in the theatrical world. Flagstad's limited abilities as an actor, which had always lagged behind what her voice could achieve, were now given room to develop.

*The Marksman* is regarded as the masterpiece of the German Romantic Carl Maria von Weber. The opera plays out in a world of myths, legends, and fairy-tale romance, inspired and enriched by the German Romantic school. The composer summons the innate mystical nature of things—adventure, dreams, and the mood of night. It was such a joy for her voice to negotiate the emotional appeals, harmonies, and vibrant orchestration. Flagstad's vocal capacity was finally on full display. After she had sung her first aria at the

## Part 1: The Making of a Singer (1895–1935)

orchestra rehearsal, the musicians, as one, laid down their instruments, got to their feet, and applauded. Apparently the theater had never before seen anything like it.

She is well prepared on opening night, October 4, 1928. In her excitement, she paces back and forth on the stage carpet, wearing Agathe's long white gown, with flowers in her hair. She looks like a true German nymph, a creature from nature's summer night, as she enters the stage and opens her mouth to let her sonorous voice pour out into the auditorium. A critic remarks that the first notes reveal a voice of such nobility that the audience is entranced. She has been endowed with a magnificent soprano of volume and radiance as well as an unusual Nordic timbre that brings azure skies to mind. She has already bewitched the audience through her song, and they are almost rooted to the spot. When the technique is of such excellence that it can no longer be discerned, when it transforms the simplest phrase into a vision in notes, the sound becomes truly exquisite.

The audience was astounded by her vocal artistry. Her voice had everything. It was clear as a bell and strong enough to swell to a volume that knew no bounds. She was also exceptionally musical. Critics found that Flagstad's Agathe belonged among the greatest performances ever on the stage of the Stora Teatern. Her flawless voice lacked for nothing. She brilliantly interpreted the second act's demanding solo and triggered spontaneous applause that went on and on. In her, the theater had discovered the quality of soprano they had been missing for so long, a singer who could really carry the great dramatic roles.

Kirsten Flagstad may have allowed herself to become intoxicated by the newspaper reviews that she read the next day at the breakfast table. She became a star overnight. After the newspapers reported that she was a sensation, people began nodding to her in recognition out on the street. Perhaps Else read the reviews before heading to the school where she had not settled, but she was not quite sure what the description *sensation* entailed. Continually, pictures of her mother in costume appeared in the press. None of her classmates had mothers like hers, and it is possible that Else was bullied as a result. Besides, she had reached an age when mothers seem quite embarrassing anyway. They cannot have spent many evenings alone together as mother and daughter, since Flagstad also gave many concerts while continuing her permanent employment at the opera. One of these was a performance of Schubert's Mass in G Major, and a separate lied, "Die Allmacht" (The Almighty). Her performance became a hymn to the omnipotence of song, the expansive

Kirsten Flagstad and Else-Marie. *Source: Flagstad Museum.*

closing phrase shattering the parameters of the music without detracting from its beauty. A magnificent singer, the critics concluded.

## Painful Separation

Flagstad was able to travel back to Oslo for a well-earned Christmas holiday with her daughter. She must have noticed how unhappy and lonely Else was in Gothenburg; now she could not avoid seeing how her daughter blossomed, and Else refused to return to Gothenburg. Parting from your mother is not an easy thing at the age of only eight, but closeness had not proved easy either. There had been several painful leave-takings in their lives before this, and their relationship would continue in this vein until Else started her own family.

Flagstad handed Else into the care of her brother and sister-in-law. Grandmother Maja would also play a part in looking after her. Later, Flagstad would describe her separation from Else as painful.[5] It reopened her own old wounds—she had not had a mother to whom she could form a close attachment either. Else must have felt she had once more lost the competition for her mother's time and attention. To a certain extent, Flagstad was repeating Maja's way of relating to her. A deep-seated pattern had been laid down within her: mothers do not prioritize their children over their careers, and they do not enter into a close, symbiotic relationship with their young children. Flagstad did not reflect on this conflict until her daughter left her for good in 1937. She was unaware of the nature of their relationship, just as much as she was unthinking about the nature of society outside the world of opera and theater, but she confessed that she suffered greatly as a result of this.

## Childless and Famous

It was with mixed emotions that she returned, alone, to fresh triumphs in Gothenburg in the new year of 1929. She avoided the pain and loneliness by throwing herself into a mountain of work, not only at the theater. She accepted most of what she was offered and made some recordings. Flagstad was probably only at her lodgings when she was asleep or in the early mornings, and she transferred the drama of her own life to the roles she sang. She did not enjoy auditions, which always challenged her shyness. She preferred the auditorium filled with an audience, when the lights had been dimmed and no one could stop or disturb her. Then, left entirely to herself and the music, she could let herself go.

The distance from Norway and the fact that she was alone now made her more liberated onstage, and she developed as an actor. Living vicariously through Aida's and Tosca's drama and passion brought her relief from internal pressure. Her repressed emotional life became a resource for her interpretations: from now on the roles would be her alter egos and the stage her homeland. Aida had been one of her favorite roles ever since she first heard an excerpt on piano as a ten-year-old. In the spring of 1929, she got to sing the role in reality.

The composer, Giuseppe Verdi, was, like Maja Flagstad, employed as an organist in his village church at the early age of twelve. Verdi is often compared to Wagner. Both composers invite their singers to make grand vocal displays, but they have different starting points. Wagner focuses on the orchestra,

## THE VOICE OF THE CENTURY

whereas for Verdi, the voices form the central plank of a work. In Wagner's compositions, voices are constituent parts of a coherent whole, but in Verdi's operas, they carry the melody.

Flagstad's interpretation of Verdi's Aida set audiences alight. The critics declared that her performance would have received universal approval at any of the major opera houses abroad. She went through the whole score with no obvious effort and intensified the orchestra's fortissimo accompaniment, with a touch of perfection in her voice.[6] The wonderful reviews attracted large audiences, and the opera was performed as many as twenty-seven times.

### Was It Fate?

On March 29, 1929, Flagstad gave a concert with the Gothenburg Symphony Orchestra, in which she performed a Wagner aria. She had rehearsed Elisabeth's prayer from *Tannhäuser.* She could not account for why she chose a piece by Wagner. She offered no rational explanation other than that it was a tuneful aria and a good concert number. She speculated to her American biographer that singing Elisabeth's prayer in particular might have had something to do with fate. She performed it with such sensational harmony and intensity that the critics wanted to hear her perform in a production of the entire opera. Because of the dramatic leanings of her voice, they now wholeheartedly directed her to the Wagnerian repertoire. And so a destiny that would lead her to both international fame and persecution was sealed.

Her immense work rate resulted in a rising reputation as an artist. Furthermore, she earned so much money that she could pay off her remaining debts. While she was touring with *Tosca,* she received an inquiry from the Norwegian Opera Singers' Association. Would she consider singing Elsa in Wagner's *Lohengrin?* The opera was being staged at the National Theatre in Oslo in June. She agreed—after all, she had been familiar with Elsa's role since she was ten years old.

In May 1929, Flagstad traveled down through Europe with an Austrian friend but without Else. They stopped first in Berlin, where her friend managed to arrange an audition with the Kroll Opera House. At first, Flagstad had protested—she was on vacation. But her friend took the lead, and Flagstad followed like an obedient lamb. Before the audition, she was allowed to rehearse in a music shop where there was access to a piano. In the hall during the audition, a highly qualified man sat listening: the German conductor and composer Otto Klemperer. In 1907, Klemperer had obtained his first appointment, as conductor at the Provincial German Theatre in Prague, with the

Part 1: The Making of a Singer (1895–1935)                    23

help of his friend Gustav Mahler. On Mahler's recommendation, he went on to conduct at the Hamburg State Opera and other opera houses throughout Germany until, in 1927, he was appointed conductor at the Berlin State Opera.

Flagstad had heard of him and was rather dreading being on view to such a leading authority. After the audition he adopted a fatherly, positive attitude toward the slightly nervous singer. Patting her on the head, he said that he thought she showed great talent. He was keen to hire her at the opera house, but Flagstad's contract bound her to the Stora Teatern for another year, until 1930. After that, Klemperer said, he would be willing to welcome her back to Berlin. It seemed far in the future.

Flagstad and her friend traveled on to Dresden and Munich, and while her friend began her studies in bacteriology, Flagstad began studying Elsa's part. It must have been inspiring to immerse herself in the *Lohengrin* score while she was in Dresden. In the summer of 1845, an exhausted Richard Wagner had been ordered by his doctor to spend time at a curative spa just outside the city. He took Wolfram von Eschenbach's cycle of poems, entitled *Lohengrin*, with him to the countryside. It was in this part of the world, where Flagstad was now on her travels, that the poems began to obsess the composer. Wagner, who experienced visions and had an incredibly vivid imagination, recalled that the dramatic structure of *Lohengrin* came to him all of a sudden. He fought for some time to stick to his doctor's instructions—the composer was not to do any writing during the cure—but his visions grew too powerful. They drove him away from the baths. His imagination took possession of him, and he raced to his room to write down what was forcing its way in, the scenography for *Lohengrin*. And while Wagner wrote, his doctor gave up on him—hydrotherapy was entirely wasted on such a patient.

Flagstad did not waste any time, either, despite being on vacation. She practiced wherever she found herself. They traveled to Italy, which opened up a new world for her. She loved the little Catholic church where she was permitted to sing. The next day, the children sent her flowers, and she delighted in their beauty. Rome was overwhelming, and the small convent where her friend had grown up appealed to her religious soul. She was engrossed in Elsa's life now, constantly hearing the prelude in her inner ear, filled with longing, and she empathized with Elsa's insistent prayers for God's help.

## Arrival of the Grail Knight

Since the dawn of time, stories have been written about heroes coming to the rescue of damsels in distress. Myths have always existed about swans from

24 THE VOICE OF THE CENTURY

far distant places and children and people transformed into swans. There are the stories of Leda, whose lover took the form of a swan, and of heroes from remote lands who were flown or carried by swans. Lohengrin is a Swan Knight of that kind, a dazzling figure from the interior, archaic world where the Holy Grail is the central symbol of the innermost true self.

Flagstad hurries home to Norway, where another Else is waiting, one who in her heart of hearts is desperate for her mother to spend more time with her. They do not have much time together on this occasion, either, because the curtain will rise on *Lohengrin* at the National Theatre as early as June 16, 1929. Flagstad is backstage, dressed like a fairy-tale princess in a golden-haired wig and a white dress with a long train. There is some restlessness in the orchestra pit while the audience members take their seats, because it is not every day that the National Theatre stages such a demanding work. Flagstad is excited ahead of her first major Wagnerian role, but, knowing the part as well as she does, she remains calm. Maja and Michael Flagstad arrive at the theater and take their places in the orchestra along with the rest of her siblings. There is also an unknown man in the theater that night, a man who will have a deep impact on Kirsten's life.

There is a hush in the auditorium as the lights dim, and the orchestra strikes up the first notes of the overture. The curtain has not yet risen. Flagstad concentrates on the music, which tells the story of the opera through its main themes. Here Wagner is working on the interior structure. The central motif is the mystical nature and vision of the Grail and its gradual, growing appearance. First, from a distance, the concept of the Grail is introduced by top register A-minor chords from the strings. Then, the flutes and oboes carry it into the air until the violins come in with the Grail theme itself. The next bars relate to the swan, the Grail's emissary who delivers the Grail Knight, Lohengrin, to the distressed Elsa. Then comes the decrescendo, drawing a measured calm over the music before it settles into a tranquil pool of soaring violins and flutes as the curtain rises.

A highlight of the first act is the aria "Elsa's Dream." This section is characterized by the timbre of woodwind as an oboe plays, carrying Elsa out onto the stage. She sings that in her distress and loneliness she has prayed to God for help. In her dreams, a knight in shining armor has appeared and promised to plead her case. Kneeling, she prays desperately for God to send the knight she has dreamed of. By some miracle her prayer is answered—Lohengrin's theme is heard softly in the trumpets, giving the impression that he is on his way from somewhere far in the distance. At the riverbank a boat, pulled by a swan, comes into sight. Lohengrin announces that he has arrived to fight for her.[7]

Part 1: The Making of a Singer (1895–1935)          25

When the curtain falls after the first act, applause breaks out. Amid great excitement, Kirsten Flagstad is called back onstage nineteen times. Her parents and siblings stand applauding in the orchestra pit for what seems like an eternity. The unknown man is also impressed. He goes out to the restaurant and, as usual, lights a cigar and drinks a glass of cognac. But he is filled with a strange sensation, one he himself does not really understand. There is something about this Elsa and the intensity of her prayers for a knight to come to her rescue. The leitmotif is working within him, and he responds absentmindedly in his conversations with his business colleagues. He may even be in some kind of trance, when at last the bell rings for the second act.

It is only when Elsa steps out onto the gallery that he understands how captivated he is by her. He wants to come to her aid. Quite simply, he has fallen in love with her at first sight. It may have entered his head that, by good fortune, the singers will be going to the Grand Hotel afterward. The Grand is as good as his, as he is the main shareholder, and he will also be making his way there after the performance—that is sure and certain.

## The Knight's Shadow

The third act is extremely lyrical in its orchestration, and it begins in Elsa and Lohengrin's bridal suite, where they sing the long and heartfelt love duet. To the sound of the Grail theme, Lohengrin tells his story. He comes from a distant land, beyond the imagination of earthly eyes. Inside its shining temple, lies the most holy object, the Grail, brought there by angels.

To cut a long story short, in the end, Elsa's faith fails her, and she betrays her promise not to ask him who he really is. And so the swan comes swimming downriver with the boat to carry Lohengrin away. She is left in despair. The Swan Knight is her animus, her spirit, and now he is leaving her behind. Unwittingly, she has shone a light on him when he had to remain in the shadows. She looked upon him in the cold light of rationality, and so his true self has disappeared back to its origins and back into her deep unconscious mind. We find the same motif in the Norwegian folktale "King Valemon, the White Bear," for example. The swan takes Lohengrin away, the curtain falls, and the Grail theme concludes the opera. It comes as a reminder of the deep meaning of the story, the materialization of the original, true self.

When the members of the audience are able to catch their breath, they break into applause. Flagstad is happy that the performance has been such a success. They all feel that everything has gone smoothly. In high spirits, everyone who has taken part in the opening night walks over to the Grand Hotel, where they have reserved a side room for a little party. At 1:00 a.m., one of her friends comes to tell her that there is a man who would like to meet her in the Mirror Room. When she arrives, a tall man, dressed fashionably in black, stands up, takes her hand, and kisses it.

"Your singing this evening has made a profound impression on me," he says as he looks into her eyes. Blushing, she mumbles her thanks. She is unused to anyone being so deferential toward her. They stand there, gazing at each other, unsure of what to say.

## Mutual Fascination

The stranger was the businessman Henry Johansen. He was no Grail Knight but a man of this world and one of the production's main sponsors. Forty-six years old, he was a widower with four children, two daughters and grown-up twin sons. Johansen was a well-known industrialist and timber exporter. For many years, he was a principal shareholder in the Grand as well as the Hotel Bristol in Oslo. He had his own office in Stockholm—Nordiska Handelskompani (the Nordiska Trading Company)—and his business interests extended far across northern Europe. Henry Johansen was decorated with the King's Medal for Meritorious Services for his contribution to Norwegian industry. He was a feared and ruthless entrepreneur, accustomed to being obeyed. The industrialist smoked around twenty fat cigars a day and, with his friends and guests, consumed a considerable amount of wine and spirits. His wine cellar was famous far beyond the borders of Norway.

A number of artists from the production were invited to his home later that night. His spacious villa on Tidemands gate in the well-to-do West End of Oslo must have made a great impression on Kirsten Flagstad. The villa was a mansion, nowadays a private residence for the Belgian ambassador to Norway. The house sits like a luxurious swan—and Flagstad flopped down on a chair in the library normally reserved for Johansen. He came over and sat on the armrest to chat with her and invited her to dinner the very next day.

At the time, there was a lot happening in Flagstad's life. At breakfast the following morning, she read some of the newspaper reviews of the premiere, all of them effusive about her voice. Several pointed out how well she had portrayed Elsa's quiet, dreamy nature. The critics all agreed that the performance would have attracted attention at the most distinguished opera houses around the world.

After breakfast, she sat down and wrote to her estranged husband, asking for a divorce and telling him openly that she had fallen in love with another man. Many times in the course of her miserable marriage, and since then too,

## Part 1: The Making of a Singer (1895–1935)

she had vowed never to fall in love again. Her parents and sister, Karen-Marie, had merely laughed at her. And now here she was, jumping in with both feet, head over heels in love with a man she had met only once.

A short while after the letter was posted, she went on her dinner date with the industrialist. It must have been a success; the next day, they had dinner together again. They sat at a table at the Bristol Hotel, not yet on first-name terms, conversing in rather formal tones, when Johansen suddenly stretched out his hand. "Well, Madame Flagstad, it seems you are in love with me?"

"Yes," she replied, and with that, it was all settled.[8]

The couple decided to keep their cards close to the chest, but Maja Flagstad quickly understood how the land lay, and Henry Johansen was welcomed with open arms into the Flagstad family. Maja and Michael were thrilled with him and presumably also with his wealth and powerful position in Norwegian society. When Flagstad met Johansen, she was living with her bankrupt parents in a cramped apartment. At the age of thirty-four, she was a single mother who dreamed of all this becoming hers. The dream came true. Her future husband had no wish for her to continue singing. For the rest of her life, she could simply be fru Kirsten Johansen, or so she thought.

When Flagstad later told her biographer about this meeting with Johansen, it was his beautiful home, his many directorships, and all his possessions that she highlighted. She may have been infatuated with Henry the man, but it was the industrialist who captured her. The relationship quelled the existential angst she felt for the future. Johansen had an abundance of what she and the rest of her family lacked—material security. At the same time, this underlying motivation made her blind to his darker sides. Her more or less unconscious need to ensure financial security for herself and her parents came at a high price. It later drew her into his economic and political treason after the occupation of Norway and Vidkun Quisling's coup d'état in 1940.

Johansen anxiously followed the fluctuations in the economy. In October 1929, the New York Stock Exchange catastrophically collapsed, leading to a global depression that hit America harder than any other country. Johansen instinctively understood the way things were heading—the banks were facing insolvency. And so he went straight to the bank and came home with two heavy suitcases full of banknotes. Johansen was a businessman, now with an extended family. In Norway, there was increased hostility toward all foreigners, and the politicians were keen to close the borders to anyone who might put a strain on the Norwegian welfare budget. After Johansen's arrival on the scene, the Flagstad family would no longer be a burden on the state.

Henry Johansen took on the role of protector of the artistic Flagstad family. Here photographed with Kirsten's parents. *Source: Flagstad Museum.*

## Life as a Housewife

From the perspective of the present day, Kirsten Flagstad's attitude toward her role as a woman and partner is old-fashioned and difficult to understand. She said she wanted to be subservient to her husband; for a marriage to be happy, the husband had to be in charge. However, that presupposes that he was capable of doing so. If her husband required her to stop singing in public, then that was what she would do. It was her primary duty to please her husband, as he meant more to her than any audience. Being happily married mattered most of all to her.

This attitude was in tune with the ideal prevalent at the time of the bourgeois wife: she gave up her identity and appeared in public as the consort of the manager, the shipowner, or the industrialist. At the same time, Kirsten Flagstad was as stubborn as a mule and set herself against the prominent male

Part 1: The Making of a Singer (1895–1935)          29

authority figures who wanted something from her. Her personality possessed a remarkable mixture of dominance and submission.

Maja Flagstad now feared that housewifely passivity would once again descend on her gifted daughter. To keep the pot boiling during this period of infatuation, she had arranged for a little extra concert before Kirsten's return to Gothenburg, where she still had a contract to fulfill, with Maja by her side at the piano. The newspapers reported rapturous ovations and described Flagstad as the equal of the most outstanding singers in the world.[9]

Else was still living with her aunt and uncle when her mother returned to Gothenburg. Next in line for Flagstad was the role of Eva in Wagner's *The Mastersingers of Nuremberg*. She found great joy in singing this part, and her interest in Wagner's music and characters continued to develop throughout the run. The press in Gothenburg called her a revelation, an unforgettable symbol of the whole Mastersinger cycle's unconscious longing. The critics deployed phrases such as "Germanic Gretchenesque beauty," "fair Germanic," "beautiful Germanic," and "Germanic blue." These expressions unmistakably hinted at the ominous political tendencies of the era.

In the summer of 1930, Kirsten and Henry traveled south in Europe and married at the Norwegian Consulate in Antwerp. From this time on, she wanted only to be fru Johansen. The newly established little family, Kirsten, Henry, and Else, were to live in Tidemands gate but would also go on vacation to Kristiansand, a small town on the south coast of Norway where the businessman owned a large, beautiful second home. In addition, Johansen bought Kirsten's childhood home, and her brother Ole and his family moved in there.

## Fly in the Ointment

Ten-year-old Else looked upon the changes in their lives differently. She, too, moved into Tidemands gate but was unhappy there. Her mother had a new husband who was not her father, and the house was a large and unfamiliar mansion. She was accustomed to a snug, cozy home and simple circumstances. Else would never grow to like Henry Johansen, whom she viewed as an intruder. In addition, her mother intended to do nothing but stay at home, which had never happened before either.

Once again, mother and daughter faced the task of repairing their relationship. They were to live in the same house and see each other every day. Else had spent more of her life apart from her mother than by her side. She missed her father, who had promised to return home soon. Besides, Henry and her mother were often out gallivanting. In the end, Else yet again turned to her aunt and uncle, saying she would prefer to live with them. Kirsten almost certainly tried to get close to her daughter, but Else had been disappointed and abandoned so many times that she resisted intimacy. Moreover, her mother had recently fallen in love, and it was hard for Else to adjust to the fact that she had a new husband. The exceedingly strict and moral Kirsten Flagstad had probably never, during the time she lived on her own, allowed any man to spend the night. Her daughter was not used to other men. All the same, Else did apply to take her mother's surname, and there may have been some attempt at reconciliation in this gesture.

Flagstad left the Gothenburg stage on April 22, 1930, and did not perform in public again until June 6, 1931. This was the longest break she had taken since the start of her career. On December 1, 1930, Michael Flagstad died suddenly of a heart attack. A calm and steady husband and father, this was a great loss for the family. For Flagstad, his death came as a shock. It strengthened her bond with her husband, who became her only refuge in life.

The villa on Tidemands gate was eventually converted into a concert hall. With his mother-in-law in mind, the industrialist installed an organ in the great hall and had plans to acquire a larger pipe organ. Maja worked on church music with Kirsten, and Johansen enjoyed the house being filled with the notes and sounds of musical instruments. There had been conversations—negotiations—between him and his mother-in-law on the subject of Kirsten's future. It might not be such a bad idea for her to take on a new project now and again, they felt.

## Isolde—Transcendental Passion

There is little to suggest that Flagstad made any connection between her next major role, Isolde, and her own life. Even so, she must have been able to identify with the Irish princess's outrage and fury at being abducted and forced to marry a rich, powerful old king. Isolde would far rather die than be regarded merely as a sexual being and sold as a piece of merchandise. Flagstad, who would sing the role a total of 188 times, has said that she only liked Isolde in the first act, when she rebels against being treated as an object.[10] This is an interesting snippet of information. Despite identifying with Isolde here, she could not see that anything similar was taking place in her own life. Her choice was made in the name of security, the opposite of the obsessive, erotic

Part 1: The Making of a Singer (1895–1935)                    31

passion that arises in the second act of *Tristan and Isolde*, when the lovers have left their homes to find each other. As they gaze longingly into each other's eyes, they are vulnerable to every storm.

In 1932, Flagstad was asked to sing the role for the first time. A Norwegian producer had taken it into his head to try to bring the whole of the Bayreuth ensemble up to Oslo. Gunnar Graarud, a leading Norwegian tenor at Bayreuth, in the final years of his career, had agreed to perform. The Norwegian bass Ivar Andresen belonged to Flagstad's generation. He sang at Bayreuth and had studied under the composer's son, Siegfried Wagner. The producer persuaded them both on board. The Swedish soprano Nanny Larsén-Todsen, a famous Isolde of the time, also signed up.

The Opera Fund made their support conditional on Kirsten Flagstad singing the part of Isolde for the final three performances, with Larsén-Todsen undertaking the first seven. Larsén-Todsen was a sought-after Wagnerian soprano in the world's greatest opera houses and one of the most eminent Wagnerian interpreters of the twentieth century, from the generation before Frida Leider and Kirsten Flagstad.

An offer came from the National Theatre in Oslo, and at first, Flagstad turned it down. The role was far too substantial and so demanding that she shrank back from it in fear. However, when she discovered that Larsén-Todsen would sing at the first seven performances, she accepted. She would buckle down, almost as Isolde's understudy, and have her own little premiere on June 29, 1932.

Maja had never rehearsed roles with her daughter before, even though she had helped hundreds of other singers. Awareness that her own career would now only advance through that of her daughter motivated her in the task. They practiced for two hours every day, taking it scene by scene. Flagstad sang with her lungs filled and felt her voice amplify as a result. A great flow of air is needed to carry Isolde's volley of sound. Her lung capacity and back and abdominal muscles gradually expanded. One day, the back of her dress ripped open as she took a deep breath. The language was complicated, and she pedantically jotted down all the difficult phrases and words in a notebook and looked them up in the dictionary, one by one. Then she made an extensive glossary, which she memorized until she knew it by heart. This became a habit she repeated when preparing for all her Wagnerian roles. There are huge amounts of text to learn, and the melody, tempo, and stress on each word must be placed correctly.

It was akin to performing a daredevil stunt, learning Isolde in six weeks flat. In comparison, it is said that after Larsén-Todsen learned the music for Isolde, she spent five years working on the dramatic presentation before she felt she had fully grasped the intricacies of the role. Flagstad would later spend considerably more time on it. Wagner makes almost inhuman vocal demands of Tristan and Isolde, and we do not know how much Flagstad, at that point, understood of Isolde, especially in the second and third acts. She continued to improve and immerse herself in some of these scenes throughout her lengthy career.

The Irish princess Isolde would rather die than surrender to a humdrum, comfortable life with someone she does not love. She asks her maid, Brangäne, to mix a drink of poison that will kill both her and Tristan. His death will be her revenge on him for kidnapping her. He is meant to deliver her to his old uncle, King Marke of Cornwall. But Brangäne swaps the poison for a love potion, which Isolde takes with her. The concoction may be compared to a narcotic elixir, a psychedelic liquor that strips away the mind's veils and boundaries. It arouses Tristan and Isolde's sexual desire, and they dissolve from their individual selves to meld into each other. For those with a "realistic" outlook, it may seem that they are propelled toward death as their only chance of deliverance. A more philosophical interpretation sees them driven to emptiness, toward a void that is aware of its vacuity.

When Wagner created the work, he was engrossed in studies of Arthur Schopenhauer and Buddhist literature. In his increasing melancholia, Wagner experienced the outside world as a tragic illusion.[11] To liberate from this illusion, man had to conquer the categorical orientation of concepts. Reason had to be shut down, ideally through narcotic substances that open the brain to love and transcendental consciousness. Wagner's music has a hypnotic effect that leads Tristan and Isolde into nothingness and Isolde to cosmic orgasm.[12] At the moment of her death, she experiences the highest form of desire.

Flagstad was undoubtedly in touch with the deeply philosophical, expressed through an unconventional religious sensibility. And so the metaphysical damnation experienced by Isolde must at least have satisfied Flagstad's religious instinct. After singing the final note of "Liebestod" (Erotic death), an F-sharp on the fifth octave, she was met with enormous applause from the audience. The tumult overcame her as the stage curtain fell and rose again; there was no end to the curtain calls at the National Theatre that evening. Admittedly, the critics noted that Flagstad had not yet reached the

Kirsten Flagstad as Isolde at the National Theatre, Oslo. *Source: Flagstad Museum.*

heights the role demanded. Larsén-Todsen had a greater inner maturity, but everyone agreed that Flagstad's performance was brilliantly and beautifully executed.[13]

Ellen Gulbranson, the great Valkyrie of Bayreuth and Covent Garden, was in the auditorium that night, and Flagstad's Isolde had made a great impression on her. Gulbranson was significant as the most famous Brunhild of her day. She sang the role in Copenhagen in 1891, under the direction of Johan Svendsen, the first time *Die Walküre* (The Valkyrie) was performed in Scandinavia. The production was such a huge success that reports of her interpretation reached Wagner's widow, Cosima. Gulbranson went on to sing the role at Bayreuth from 1896 until she stood down at the dress rehearsal in 1914, when World War I broke out. Male soloists and orchestral musicians were immediately called up, and the festival had to be canceled. Gulbranson

34 THE VOICE OF THE CENTURY

never again returned to Bayreuth. She was also Edvard Grieg's favorite singer and protégé, and she was the soloist at the Grieg concert in Paris in 1903, when the composer was booed because of his intervention in the Dreyfus affair.

Gulbranson visited Flagstad in her dressing room and told her it was scandalous that she was performing only at home in Norway. She had to go to Bayreuth. Flagstad had no such ambitions, and so Gulbranson took matters into her own hands by writing to Winifred Wagner. Some time later, she sought out Flagstad again, this time to hand her a letter from fru Wagner, asking her to go to Bayreuth for audition in July, when the following year's festival singers would be selected. "Oh, I hope you know what an invitation like this implies" were the imperious old Valkyrie's parting words. Flagstad obediently headed to Bayreuth.

## Richard Wagner and Bayreuth

Wagner is the only composer in music history who managed to build an opera house in his own lifetime for the performance of his music. In 1875, the festival theater, a temple to the composer's works and vision, was completed high on a ridge in Bayreuth. Wagner's own residence, Villa Wahnfried, had been ready to move into a few years earlier. On November 21, 1874, *Der Ring des Nibelungen* (The Ring of the Nibelung) was finalized. Wagner dedicated it to King Ludwig II of Bavaria, who had taken care of the composer, financing his life's work. The first festival took place in 1876, but it was such a financial disaster that Wagner had to go on tour to cover the losses. The next festival was launched in 1882, and Wagner himself conducted the final act of the concluding performance. He declared with satisfaction that his vision had become reality, and with this knowledge he died six months later.

His widow, Cosima Wagner, who personally embodied Wagner's spirit, took over the festival. Cosima was the daughter of the French duchess Marie d'Agoult and the Hungarian composer Franz Liszt. She oversaw the festival with a steady, intelligent hand from 1883 until 1906, and it was thanks to her that the Bayreuth Festival achieved such prestige. Cosima believed, as did her husband, completely and utterly in the superiority of the Germanic peoples. This was subsumed into the notions of Pan-Germanism, but for Cosima, her reverence for all things German resulted from a childhood filled with the hatred between a Germanic-inclined father and a French mother. Cosima viewed anything French with condescension and looked up to Germany as the spiritual and paternal ideal. Jews and Catholics must, in her opinion, bear much of the blame for what was wrong in the world, but she made use of them

Part 1: The Making of a Singer (1895–1935)          35

anyway to advance Wagner's art. Wagner and Cosima claimed that a Jew could redeem his character by devoting himself to Bayreuth. Wagner's antisemitism developed into an aggressive driving force, a transference of evil that is particularly expressed in the pamphlet *Das Judenthum in der Musik* (Judaism in music), published in 1850 and reprinted in 1869.

Cosima and Wagner's son, Siegfried, was known to be homosexual. There had been reports about him in the newspapers, and many people considered him unsuitable to inherit Bayreuth. An elder sister, Isolde, wanted her son to be the rightful heir. Siegfried was Cosima's favorite of favorites, and so she made a tactical move. She disputed, in writing, that Isolde was Wagner's biological daughter. Isolde was conceived while Cosima was still legally married to the conductor Hans von Bülow. Cosima insinuated that she had had sexual relations with both men in the same time period. On the one hand, this was a scandal, but on the other, it clarified the line of succession. No one could disprove Cosima's claim, and consequently, Isolde was disinherited from Bayreuth.[14]

On September 22, 1915, forty-six-year-old Siegfried married the eighteen-year-old Winifred Klindworth. They set up home in Villa Wahnfried and eventually had four children. The master's son took over the festival from his seventy-year-old mother in 1908 and led it until his death in 1930. He was a competent director of the festival and an able conductor who brought many great artists to Bayreuth. His bond with his mother was so strong that his wife correctly predicted that he would not long outlive her. Cosima died on April 1, 1930, at the age of ninety-two. On August 4 that same year, Siegfried passed away. He left full control of the festival to his now thirty-three-year-old widow, who had already been working alongside him for a number of years.

## Winifred Wagner

Flagstad was due to meet Winifred Wagner, a woman with a remarkable background. Winifred was born in England, and by the time she was two years old, both her parents were dead. The little girl was sent to an orphanage where children were punished by being harshly beaten and having mustard powder put in their mouths. The brutality gradually eroded her health. A doctor recommended a continental climate for the child's skin condition, and that is how, at the age of ten, she found herself living with a distant relative in Berlin. Seventy-year-old Henriette Klindworth was married to the well-known pianist and music teacher Karl Klindworth, who had founded his own music conservatoire in the city and was a friend of the Wagner family. In this way,

36 THE VOICE OF THE CENTURY

Winifred came to grow up in a house that idolized everything Wagnerian. Despite her many years within its tradition, it must have come as quite a shock to her when, in 1930, she became the leader of one of Germany's weightiest cultural institutions. An important reason for her success in this was her ability to surround herself with capable colleagues.[15]

Her first appointment as her husband's successor was Heinz Tietjen. He was, without a doubt, the most influential man of theater in the land, and so he was best qualified to work as Bayreuth's artistic director. The conductor Carl Muck had stepped down in protest against modern times, and so the festival was without a conductor for *Parsifal*. Fru Wagner drove to Milan in an effort to convince Arturo Toscanini to take on the task. To further improve the quality of the festival, she also secured the services of another conductor, Wilhelm Furtwängler, head of the Berlin Philharmonic Orchestra. He was presumably even then regarded as the country's greatest conductor and also an eminent interpreter of Wagner's music. Another Wagner admirer, who had long been connected to both the family and the festival, was Adolf Hitler.

At the end of July 1932, Kirsten Flagstad checked into a hotel in Bayreuth and then went on to the Festival Theatre, situated on a plateau surrounded by trees, towering like a castle high above the town. Winifred and Tietjen were there to greet her. Fru Wagner was very pleasant and chatted to Flagstad about their mutual acquaintance, Ellen Gulbranson. She invited Flagstad to her home to continue their conversation afterward. This made it all easier, as Flagstad was nervous and terribly embarrassed about her poor German. Three singers auditioned before her, and she could not help but notice the hall's splendid acoustics. Unlike all other opera houses, the Festival Theatre had no galleries or boxes to muffle vibrations and smother sound. Everything was focused on the stage, with the orchestra pit far below the stage floor. The conductor's head was only just visible to the audience, and the sound emerged from down there with an eardrum-bursting strength. Wind and percussion players were seated far back beneath the edge of the stage.

This muted the wind and percussion instruments and allowed the more lyrical qualities of the music to come to the fore. The pianissimo of the singers could be amplified more subtly when they did not have to increase the volume to avoid being drowned out. Their voices were intended to flow out over the orchestra like oil on water. Furtwängler was not happy with the orchestra being so far underneath the stage, as he felt it lost its brilliance and sounded as if it had been stuffed into a sack. *Parsifal* was an exception since the work was orchestrated differently.[16]

Professor Kittel went through the score with Flagstad before she auditioned, and she immediately noticed his genuine understanding of the music. She herself did not feel that she had done particularly well at audition and returned sadly to her hotel, convinced that she could now travel back home to Henry and stay in Norway. This was the end of her Bayreuth fairy tale. She was not in especially good spirits later that day either, as she looked down the avenue toward the Villa Wahnfried. With dignity, she walked past the statue of King Ludwig II and rang the doorbell. A servant opened the door and ushered her into the famous hall with its magnificent acoustics. Ever since Wagner's time, until present-day 1930, it had been used for auditions and for rehearsals for festival soloists.

Flagstad's subsequent Danish colleague Lauritz Melchior recalled auditioning for the part of Siegmund here. Wagner's son, Siegfried, stood downstairs listening, while the boss sat up in the gallery. Wearing white and looking pale as a ghost, old Cosima perched in her chair and listened while they worked. Then she rustled her papers, a signal for Siegfried to come up. Her son immediately ran up the stairs and came down again with the message that Mama approved. This meant that Melchior was hired.[17] The prelude to *Parsifal* was performed here for the first time, with frescos from *The Ring* covering the walls and with the piano on which Wagner had composed standing in the center of the room. Every object was viewed with the greatest of reverence because each one had been touched by the master.

Flagstad thought she had come to say a final goodbye to fru Wagner, but the reception she received suggested otherwise. Fru Wagner expressed her enthusiasm for Flagstad's voice and asked her to sing more for them up at the Festival Theatre later that day. Unfortunately, all the major roles had been filled for the next two years, but fru Wagner asked if Flagstad would consider singing some minor parts during that time. In the meantime, she could familiarize herself with the Wagnerian tradition. Of course, Flagstad agreed and gratefully accepted the invitation. After she had sung yet again, Tietjen asked her if she would like to join the State Opera in Berlin. She could play all the Wagner roles there. He received a totally unexpected answer: "No," said the stubborn, unambitious Norwegian singer to Germany's foremost opera director. Taken aback, he asked her reasons for turning down such an offer. "Why should I? I'm happily married and enjoy living in Oslo," she replied.

As an experienced director, he was familiar with the artistic temperament. He suggested that she should prepare the *Siegfried* Brunhild and finish with the *Götterdämmerung* Brunhild. The suggestion shows that Tietjen perceived, even then, that here he had someone who would personify the Brunhilds of the future, and that he was already considering her for these parts at forthcoming festivals. The theater man also knew that when there was such untapped talent in a singer, the appetite for suitable roles would eventually be so great that it would break down all resistance.

After spending twenty-four hours in Bayreuth, Kirsten Flagstad left the city late in the evening. Whether she wanted to be or not, she was now seriously in thrall to Wagner's universe. His music filled her body and mind.

## A Door Is Opened

It was not long before she appeared again onstage as Isolde. The Norwegian Opera Singers' Association put on extra performances in August. Flagstad noticed that her voice had developed and now followed her command with greater ease. The coloring of her tone had deepened after the hard work of preparatory study. Her progress had also produced something else, something about which she was of two minds. Her back had broadened as her lung capacity increased, and all her dresses were now too tight. Her vanity did not appreciate this aspect quite so much!

The National Theatre had made a new discovery and secured the Ukrainian Jewish bass Alexander Kipnis to play King Marke. He would open doors for Flagstad to the most prestigious opera stages. Just as we associate tenors with Italy, we instinctively think of bass singers as Russian. The bass voice is often used to embody powerful, evil, and dramatic characters. Kipnis felt that tragedy, and especially darkness, was usually associated with Russia. The harsh climate, in common with so much of Russian history, has a pall hanging over it.

Kipnis's upbringing in a turf hut in a Jewish ghetto in Ukraine had also been dark and dramatic. When he was twelve years old, his father became bedridden with tuberculosis. He suffered a slow death; Kipnis wiped the blood and mucus from his face in between coughing fits. Not far from the ghetto, there was a large synagogue with a cantor and choir. This is where Kipnis received his initial, fairly primitive, musical education. One day a choirboy told him that a cantor from a larger synagogue in what is now Moldova was coming there to listen for boy sopranos suitable for his choir. After the auditions, it was Kipnis he wanted. He gave his mother ten rubles, and, since she badly needed the money, the transaction went smoothly.

Kipnis had known little freedom in his life and thought it miraculous that you could walk the streets of Oslo without worrying about how far you were

## Part 1: The Making of a Singer (1895–1935)

allowed to venture. When he was a teenager, his curiosity had once driven him out of the ghetto to a little park where a theater troupe was performing. When he went to slake his thirst at a fountain, he was knocked to the ground. His next memory was of seeing blood floating in the water and feeling that he was about to faint. A police officer had struck the back of his head with a club and now picked him up with an instruction to get lost. Kipnis knew where he belonged.

After a time, he was admitted to the music conservatoire in Warsaw, where he also studied instrumental music and sat the conductor's examination. In 1912, he traveled to Berlin to study singing, but when World War I broke out, he was interned because of his Russian heritage. He was under constant police surveillance, and when he was not performing, he was detained in a hospital. It was from here that he built up his repertoire.

By the time the war ended, he was famous throughout Germany, and the offers poured in from every corner of the world. He became a lead bass at the Berlin State Opera and a regular guest at the Bayreuth Festival. He sang in Salzburg and at Covent Garden every year. As a member of the Wagner Festival Tour, he traveled to America in 1922 and was hired by the Chicago Opera, playing all the leading bass roles over nine seasons. These engagements also brought with them the benefit of gaining American citizenship in 1931.

In Oslo, Kipnis could only listen in amazement to the unknown soprano. Her voice sounded so effortless that, even at peak forte, its timbre was almost lyrical. She sang entirely without exertion, without overemphasizing any of the notes. The weightlessness of her voice embraced and consumed him, no matter how far from her he was seated. The only limitation in Kirsten Flagstad's voice was a lack of warmth, and he put this down to her Nordic heritage.[18]

He sought her out in her dressing room to have a chat with her, but she was very shy and spoke poor German. They communicated through a German-speaking mezzo-soprano. Flagstad later recalled that she was far too embarrassed to make an attempt at German and even more bashful about speaking English with this man who had such an impressive and fiery bass voice. She must have felt all his goodwill toward her, and he, her insecurity and shyness. Kipnis asked if she had ever sung outside Scandinavia and was surprised when she answered no, though she added that she was due to sing at Bayreuth the next year. He was himself a personal friend of Winifred Wagner and contacted her to share his impression of Flagstad. He also wrote to the opera house in Brussels and spread word of this unknown Norwegian singing phenomenon to central Europe and to America. Later in a radio interview, Flagstad would speak about the role Kipnis had played in many of the things that had happened in her life. He had talked about the Norwegian Isolde wherever he went and had been very kind to her.[19]

There were several talent scouts in the auditorium during these performances in August, among them an American critic who wrote about Flagstad in *Musical America*. He felt that this Isolde alone was worth the journey across the Atlantic. He was surprised that German and American opera houses could have overlooked such a uniquely gifted singer. For twenty years she had sung exclusively in Norway and at the opera in Gothenburg.

This same journalist also wrote a brief note in the *New York Evening Post* about the event: "Kirsten Flagstad is a singer whose vocal and dramatic talents will impress the world's leading opera houses. Few in our times have come anywhere near this Irish princess with such beauty and vocal majesty. Here the part was sung entirely without exertion, perfectly true to the score, and expressive and convincing from the first note to the last. So it is curious that the German opera houses have overlooked a singer so awe-inspiringly gifted."[20]

Her voice had acquired new dimensions. During her performance in the concert version of *Tannhäuser* broadcast on Norwegian radio that year, Flagstad had to stand at the very back of the room to avoid drowning out the other singers. That had been quite an auditory experience, but her next stop was to be the festival at Bayreuth.

## Black Eagles

Kirsten's husband, Henry Johansen, was delighted by her success. On April 16, 1933, he had read the political manifesto of the recently formed National Samling Party (NS). Vidkun Quisling attempted to explain why a new political organization was needed, emphasizing the hard times Norway was experiencing. A catastrophe was approaching, and the old political parties were unable to do anything about it. Quisling further claimed that voters were anxious about the future, broken by high taxes and debt, resentful about unnecessary labor disputes, and opposed to the rabble-rousing Bolshevik spirit that was spreading through the country. The NS was the organization to put all this right.

For Johansen, the party's third point was important, calling for peace and stability in the labor market to ensure free and uninterrupted production. Quisling also proposed to do something about the revolutionary workers' organizations, which would lose the right to have what he called a monopoly

Part 1: The Making of a Singer (1895–1935)          41

on work. In addition, the Labor Party could expect to be banned. This hostile attitude toward the Labor Party garnered Quisling a degree of support from business owners and capitalists who feared the growth of the trade unions.

NS was undoubtedly inspired by political trends in Germany. In the election of March 5, 1933, Hitler's National Socialist Party won 44 percent of votes and, in coalition with the German National People's Party, an 8 percent majority in the Reichstag. Hitler promised to add jobs for the workers and tackle the Communists for the business community. According to him, the economic depression in the country was the fault not of the Germans but of the Jews. He swore revenge for the Treaty of Versailles, which had treated Germany shamefully in the aftermath of World War I. The Germanic people would triumph over Europe once again, as they had done in the past.

Henry Johansen joined the newly established party, NS, which used Håkon Håkonsson's great idea from Henrik Ibsen's *The Pretenders* as its motto: "Norway was a kingdom, it shall become a people." At that time, NS was a legal political party that regarded the Soviet Union and Communism as its greatest enemies. Johansen's motivation for membership was to secure his capital interests. How did he reconcile himself to the party's fascism and its elevating of one ethnic group at the expense of others? There are no known sources to shed light on this question.

## Winifred Wagner and Adolf Hitler

Johansen's wife, Kirsten Flagstad, was not involved in politics but was completely focused on traveling to Bayreuth to sing at the festival. We glimpse here the outlines of a tragic shadow over Flagstad's life. Her concentration on art displaced a normal awareness of developments in society. She failed to see the warning signals.

The role of Ortlinde in *Die Walküre*, the Third Norn from *Götterdämmerung* (The twilight of the gods), and a soprano solo in the vocal quartet of Beethoven's Ninth Symphony together formed a respectable program for a Bayreuth debut. The concert was to be held on August 4, the anniversary of Siegfried Wagner's death. Flagstad took the train to Germany, accompanied by her mother. Her husband intended to follow later to see the performances. Maja had immersed herself in Wagner's music during the past year, and Flagstad felt a degree of support from having her mother as her singing coach. Kirsten spoke some German, whereas Maja spoke only Norwegian and had scarcely ever been outside the country's borders. Flagstad was now

42 THE VOICE OF THE CENTURY

thirty-eight years old, and since she no longer needed to think about money, she had offered to sing for free. In any case, she regarded singing at the festival as an honor.

The political climate in Germany seemed to completely pass the naive Norwegian women by. They simply did not give any thought to such things. Winifred Wagner also claimed that she was not concerned with politics, only the festival. At the same time, she supported the National Socialist Party, which she felt showed a great deal of common sense. The Wagner family had a strong appreciation of all things German, and so they sought contact with individuals who wanted to rebuild a German empire. German patriots were searching for a leader who could guide Germany out of the misery and depression that had followed World War I. Hitler's inflammatory speeches envisioned a new society, and the people went along with him. Winifred herself became party member number one hundred thousand.

Fru Wagner was not expressly antisemitic, despite her close friendship with Hitler. They had met in 1923, when he gave a speech in Bayreuth. Hitler made a profound impression on her. His personality, and especially his expressive blue eyes, fascinated her. She invited him to Wahnfried since he wanted to visit the master's grave. Hitler had venerated and admired Wagner from his early youth. Standing in the Linz State Theatre and Vienna State Opera, he had empathized so intensely with several of the composer's characters that he almost came to identify with them. In Wagner's works, he saw everything that National Socialism wanted to achieve. Later, he refused to acknowledge any predecessor, with the exception of Richard Wagner. Hitler wanted to build his religion on *Parsifal*.[21]

It is important to stress that these were his interpretations of Wagner, not necessarily what the composer himself had in mind. When Hitler claimed that compassion, which is accentuated so strongly in *Parsifal,* involved eliminating everything that was diseased in society, it is far from certain that Wagner would have agreed with such an interpretation.

In any case, Hitler's respect and affection for Richard Wagner extended to the composer's successors and to the festival. The year after his first visit in 1924, Hitler was imprisoned in Landsberg and unable to go to Bayreuth. At his request, Winifred sent him some writing paper, which he used to write *Mein Kampf.* She later claimed, with some justice, that she could not be held responsible for what he committed to the paper. In 1925, Hitler was a guest at the festival, but his presence there attracted attention and was heavily criticized.

## Part 1: The Making of a Singer (1895–1935)

He later wrote to the Wagner family, saying that he wanted to spare them from that sort of thing. Hitler would not return to the festival until he was in a position to help rather than damage them. He kept his word and stayed away until 1933, when he returned as chancellor—Der Führer.[22]

In a short time, Germany was transformed into a totalitarian state, where both the administration and the judiciary were under the direct control of the party. All cultural activity was subject to censorship and political manipulation. On April 26, 1933, the Gestapo—a political secret security police force that would investigate and fight all tendencies that could be harmful to Hitler's state—was founded. The Gestapo undermined the German courts, and, right from the start, brutality was ingrained in the system.

### Overture to the 1933 Bayreuth Festival

This was the Germany to which Maja and Kirsten Flagstad came by train in the summer of 1933. They were naively ignorant and thoughtless with regard to the politicized Wagner festival. They were not the only ones: most people drifted effortlessly through the miasma from the witches' cauldron, with its heady mixture of Norse mythology, Pan-Germanism, and German National Socialism. Anyway, the phenomenal music was created by a genius. In 1933, all cultural activity in Germany was consolidated and controlled by the state party, but through her friendship with Hitler, Winifred managed to maintain a certain degree of autonomy for Bayreuth, and 1933 was a watershed year there in a number of ways. *Parsifal* had continued to be performed using Wagner's own old stage scenery, which was now in such poor condition that fru Wagner wanted to replace it: she was keen to have a fresh stage design. This attempt at modernization sparked an outcry and ended with a deputation being sent to Hitler in the Reich Chancellery. Wagner's relatives protested against Winifred removing the master's flats, but Hitler dismissed them and supported fru Wagner. To some extent, he agreed with a fresh look for Bayreuth, and from then on, he was one of fru Wagner's most powerful supporters. Their private lives would also become part of a cultural and intellectual narrative. When he furnished his country home, Berghof in Obersalzberg, she sent him linens and porcelain.[23]

In May 1933, fru Wagner had received a letter from Arturo Toscanini telling her that he proposed to resign from his work at Bayreuth because of the Nazis' antisemitic propaganda. On April 1 that same year, he had, with Otto Klemperer, Bruno Walter, and several other distinguished musicians, sent a telegram to Hitler in which they politely asked his government to stop its persecution of musicians in Nazi Germany. They assumed that it was not Hitler himself who had given the orders for such ill treatment. He could not possibly wish to damage the high cultural esteem enjoyed by Germany throughout the civilized world.[24]

Devastated by the loss of Toscanini, fru Wagner phoned Hitler's adjutant to inform him of the situation. At first, Hitler avoided answering. He was annoyed because she had gone against him by insisting on retaining Jewish artists. Fru Wagner drove to Garmisch in Bavaria to ask Richard Strauss if he would come to Bayreuth to conduct *Parsifal*. She was dreading this, as she was afraid Strauss would interpret it as being asked to fill in as a substitute. Strauss was one of the greatest composers and conductors of the time and not someone to employ as a backup. The last time he had conducted *Parsifal* at Bayreuth had been in 1894, but he took a positive attitude. Winifred received the answer she was looking for, both to *Parsifal* and to Beethoven's Ninth Symphony, in which Kirsten Flagstad would sing the soprano solo.

Frida Leider, then regarded as the world's leading Brunhild, was fearful of Hitler's takeover. She had written to Tietjen from the US, asking how the situation would unfold in Germany and at Bayreuth. Leider was due, as usual, to come to Bayreuth to sing the Brunhild roles. Married as she was to a Jewish husband and stepmother to a son who was classified as half-Jewish, she had every reason to be worried. Tietjen reassured her that Hermann Göring had given him absolute authority to ensure the maintenance of artistic standards both in Bayreuth and in Berlin. He insisted that, as long as he was certain of Göring's support, the Jewish artists and their families would be safe.

On June 1, all Jews at the State Opera in Berlin were sacked, with the exception of Leo Blech, Alexander Kipnis, and Emanuel List. Permitting them to stay was a concession from Göring to Tietjen, who needed these outstanding artists in Berlin and Bayreuth. There were press campaigns against them, mostly directed at "the Jewish synagogue singer and Ashkenazi Jew" who sang the role of Veit Pogner in *The Mastersingers of Nuremberg* so sloppily that it brought German ears to despair.[25] This was how Alexander Kipnis was described.

Kipnis recalls being asked to sing Hans Sachs in *The Mastersingers* at Bayreuth in 1933, but as this was an arch-Germanic role, at that time being boosted by Hitler's propaganda, he was brave enough to turn it down. Quite unexpectedly, Winifred came to his apartment one day, wondering whether

Part 1: The Making of a Singer (1895–1935)

he would like to be introduced to the Reich chancellor. She was giving a small private reception where Hitler would meet a few chosen singers. The very thought made Kipnis feel sick. He later said it was difficult to express his state of mind, but he managed to extricate himself tactfully from the situation. That afternoon, he met the well-known English music critic and Wagner biographer Ernest Newman with his wife out on the street. He quickly made an appointment with them so that he could have an excuse ready for fru Wagner.[26]

In 1933, *The Mastersingers* was broadcast on radio to Europe and Latin America, and in one of the intervals, a speech by Joseph Goebbels was transmitted. According to the *Kölnische Zeitung* newspaper on August 5, five million people listened to *The Mastersingers* in 1933. The term *the nation's hour* was widely used about the festival and the radio broadcasts. In a lecture aired in 1934, it was said that Wagner was the spirit of Germany. Through the creation of a national German musical drama, the master had given his people and country an expression of the deepest foundations of Germanic thought and philosophical beliefs. The festival reflected the best of the nation.[27]

## German Yearning for an Ancient History

Many of Wagner's operas contain reminiscences of ancient mystery dramas. These conveyed a transcendental wisdom from the mythology of various cultures. The composer was extremely preoccupied with this subject, as witnessed by the many titles on myths and mythology in his personal library. The source of *The Ring*'s symbolic action is the old *Edda* poems from the age of migration and the Viking period (400–1050). The action mainly takes place behind time and space in an ancient age when gods and supernatural beings can appear among humans, beyond the normal passage of time.

Carl G. Jung, and to some extent Sigmund Freud, in their analysis of dreams have pointed out that the various gods in mythology can be regarded as elements of the human psyche. Their entanglements and adventures with one another and other beings in a sense provide answers to the long, drawnout conflicts within the human personality. Mythological episodes describe factual processes in the unconscious mind, and this is why they exert a timeless fascination.

In Old Norse mythology's direct contact with subconscious images, there lay an explosive power that could be exploited and misused for the purposes of both nation building and political manipulation. To all appearances, Old Norse legends are not particularly distinctive, nor do they adhere to such a

46 THE VOICE OF THE CENTURY

strong philosophical background as Greek mythology. The leitmotifs could therefore be placed within baseless systems of ideas such as Norwegian nationalism, Pan-Germanism, and later the ideology of the Nazi movement.

The first renaissance of Old Norse mythology occurred in Iceland toward the end of the twelfth century. The Old Norse legacy of *Edda* poems was saved there for posterity. Further access to this material came from the Danish monk Saxo through his translations of Old Norse myths and stories into Latin in the major work *Gesta Danorum*, and in his textbook for skalds—*Snorre-Edda*—the Icelander Snorre Sturlason retells many of the Old Norse myths. A new upsurge came in the seventeenth century when the *Edda* poems began to be translated into Latin, sparking interest throughout Europe. The first selection to be published in German came in 1789, and the Brothers Grimm in particular became known for disseminating the Old Norse material. The Germans had few runic inscriptions to which they could refer, and they were familiar only with the poetry of the high medieval period, with the exception of *Hildebrandslied*.[28] In the Old Norse *Edda*, the German yearning for an ancient history came to fruition: they found a deep well in the Nordic countries and made it into their primeval home.

The German nation then in development needed historical foundations, and the gigantic monument Hermannsdenkmal, begun in 1838, commemorates the time when Arminius the Cherusci gathered a number of Germanic tribes and destroyed three Roman legions in the Teutoburg Forest in the year AD 9. Kaiser Vilhelm II's Drang nach Norden (Push to the North) is famed far and wide: for example, he donated a colossal statue of the fictional hero Frithiof the Bold, which was erected beside a fjord in western Norway in 1913. In 1933, German officers arrived there to lay a wreath in the shape of a swastika beside the statue.

For his part, Wagner had taught himself Old Norse to study the *Poetic Edda*, which he owned in two German translations. In his book collection, there were also German translations of the Saga of Fridtjof the Bold, Snorre's *Heimskringla* (Orb of the world), and a version of *Gesta Danorum* (Deeds of the Danes) by Saxo Grammaticus. At the same time, he also based the plot of *The Ring* on *Nibelungenlied* (The song of the Nibelungs), a German epic poem from the High Middle Ages. *Nibelungenlied* was a new narrative based on the ancient motifs from the *Poetic Edda*, a verse cycle that records the conflict between Frankish and Burgundian princes during the age of migration. The characters were eventually idolized as German national heroes.

Part 1: The Making of a Singer (1895–1935)        47

The National Socialists tried to give Nazism a historical foundation by spinning a quasi-mythical political ideology around the Old Norse and Germanic traditional material. It may not have been easy for the majority of their contemporaries to see through the project. The Nazis created an image that flattered and elevated their fatherland and its people at the expense of every foreigner. People from a different cultural group obviously found it easier to expose the deception. The Russian composer Igor Stravinsky visited Bayreuth in the years before World War II. After attending a production of *Parsifal*, he gave the opinion that the prevailing atmosphere there was gloomy. Stravinsky recognized the trappings of the totalitarian regime and expressed dismay at what he called "the comedy of Bayreuth." The place was filled with ridiculous formalities and had an uncritical audience who swallowed the sacred idea of the theater transformed into a national temple. Stravinsky was astonished by the spiritual confusion that held sway there.[29]

## *The Ring of the Nibelung*'s Metaphysical Dimension

Wagner used several sources and wrote several more when composing his epic. For this reason, the central problem and message of the narrative occasionally gets bogged down in complex intrigue and added color not entirely in keeping with the sources. Even so, the *Poetic Edda* texts are the springboard for his work.

In myths and religious literature, fighting a dragon is often a symbol for the cosmic drama. The dragon, also depicted as a winged serpent, can be regarded as an archaic symbol for the power and force of the Mother Goddess. Mother Earth has an ambiguous character and authority; the symbol can represent chaos and death but also rebirth and renewal. It is the unconscious power of disintegration and regeneration that we face and that the hero meets when he steps into the subconscious world. In the Nordic countries, there are ancient legends about a dragon slayer called Sigurd. His battle against the monster and dragon Fafnir is portrayed on a number of doorways in Norwegian stave churches, timber buildings from the twelfth and thirteenth centuries that feature on UNESCO's list of world heritage sites. That this motif adorns the entrance to a sacred building tells us that older generations considered the subject to be of great importance. The danger of defeat in the battle against the monster, the disintegration of the collective subconscious, is critical; it is experienced as threatening the final destruction of the personality after death.

If the expression *original sin* is interpreted as the personality's attachment to images and ideas, to imagination and intellect, then fighting the dragon can be seen as the confrontation with original sin. Our emotional attachment to external objects and illusions of them is an inborn tendency. This complex hampers any chance for us to attain self-realization and condemns us, sooner or later, to dissolve into the collective unconscious. We must, as stated in Ibsen's *Peer Gynt*, end up in the Button Moulder's ladle, in the garbage, to be merged into the mass. And so the fight with the dragon can be seen as both essential and existential: it is the entrance into that sacred space, the self.

After having conquered the monster, the hero finds a princess, or as in the *Poetic Edda* and *The Ring*, a sleeping Valkyrie whom he wakes. Valkyries are powerful handmaidens in Valhalla. They give food and drink to fallen heroes and can ride through the air. Odin sends the Valkyries into battle, where, at his command, they choose which ones are to die. In this way, the Valkyries have control over victory. The hero's discovery of a sleeping Valkyrie, or a Sleeping Beauty, symbolizes that he has come so far on his journey that he has become aware of his spiritual element and thus also has made contact with true wisdom, intuition.

In the *Edda*, the hero Sigurd rides on Grane up to Hindarfjell, where he has spotted a bright light. When he goes closer, it turns out to be a sea of fire, which gradually diminishes as he dares to ride closer. Sigurd has brought with him the gold he has stolen from the dragon Fafnir. Within the sea of fire, he finds a rampart of shields, and within this is a warrior whose helmet and coat of mail have become rooted to his body. Sigurd cuts the armor away and discovers that it is a woman lying there. She awakes and tells him that Odin, in ancient times, cast a spell of eternal slumber on her. In other words, the soul and wisdom were condemned to unconsciousness.

The woman says that her name is Sigerdriva, "the one who drives to victory," and she is a Valkyrie. Odin has cursed her because she defied his will and chose for herself which warrior should go to Valhalla. And so wisdom surpassed intellect, represented by the great god Odin. Only someone fearless enough to steal the dragon's gold could break through the ring of fire and wake her from her sleep—in other words, only someone who had freed himself from the bondage to imagination and intellect, from the inclination toward image and idea. The gold can be seen as liberated curiosity and the life force, which the dragon (the complex) previously held. Sigurd can now take this with him on his onward journey. He asks if the Valkyrie will give him

## Part 1: The Making of a Singer (1895–1935)    49

her wisdom, since she knows many levels of consciousness. Sigerdriva gives Sigurd a memory drink and teaches him to draw runes so that he can foretell the future. In short, she gives him intuitive insight.[30]

In the *Edda*, we learn of a cursed ring owned by the dragon. Here we are not talking about a circular symbol of integration and wholeness but rather a possibility of regression into original sin, a return to an emotional attachment to external objects, the Wheel of Samsara. The craving for earthly power can drive the ring's owner to destruction, but it can also lead cultures and, in the end, the entire world to annihilation.

Reinterpreting archaic wisdom and dragging it into nationalism, National Socialism, and the worship of German superiority at the expense of other nations is a derailment at the very least. And so exactly what the sagas predict and warn against comes to pass: the person who covets the ring of power is destroyed. The ring also leads families and cultures into disintegration and destruction. This is a principal point in J. R. R. Tolkien's novel *The Lord of the Rings*. Tolkien drew some of his material from the same sources as Wagner, and the film trilogy based on *The Lord of the Rings* (Peter Jackson, 2001–3) has been faithful to the central premise of the work. The survival of civilizations, gods, and humans depends on the ring being returned to the depths of Mother Earth, to the Creation. A constantly growing substantive desire leads to greater and greater disintegration, with annihilation as the extreme consequence.

The strong warning that lies within these texts is not a dominant theme in the work of Wagner. He, like so many others, has not understood the necessity of distinguishing the universal mythology from the national. Wagner drags the archaic images into German nationalism and the worship of the idea of German superiority. This deprives the myths of their original purity and clarity, and their essential message to humanity is weakened and concealed. This debasement also left his work open to Nazification at a later date, making it easy for the Hitler regime to incorporate *The Ring of the Nibelung* into their political project. And so, just as the myths predict, an earthly Ragnarok comes to pass.

The *Edda* prophecies Ragnarok—the most famous part being the great apocalyptic poem, Voluspå (the prophecy of the seer). Terrible discord will prevail throughout the world. Avarice will cause brothers to kill one another, and conflict will be widespread. A winter called Fimbulwinter will arrive, and snow will come swirling in from all directions, accompanied by bitter cold and ferocious winds, and the sun will not shine. The earth and rocks will shake, the mountains will topple, and all bonds will be broken. Loke will set the world aflame, the sea will wash over the land, and humans and gods will be destroyed.

After this depiction of Ragnarok, the seer's prophecy brings an exalted wisdom, indicating a new golden age. The world will rise again from the sea, always green; innocent children of the gods will meet again; a new world tree will be chosen; and the religious cult will be taken up again.

> Now do I see
> the earth anew
> Rise all green
> From the waves again.[31]

## Creation of a German National Hero

In the mythology of various cultural groups, we find the presentation of a superhuman, strong, and courageous male figure who subjects himself to great danger, killing dragons and other monsters. The hero's expedition is crowned with victory, and he finally emerges as a conqueror. In an archaic meaning, he can be interpreted as the libidinal energy in the human psyche. Since this has a subjective/active character, it usually appears to be masculine. A strong life force is a fundamental precondition for success in achieving inner liberation, whether a woman or a man is making the attempt.

It all becomes more problematic when this inner drama becomes extroverted: when the hero is turned into a national hero, when, at the expense of foreigners, he fights for a particular nation and, in the end, for world supremacy. This distortion of the symbol goes back to the Norwegian Viking era and into Pan-Germanism, which was a political and cultural idea that originated in the early nineteenth century and sought to gather together all nations or peoples who belong to the German tribe. Eventually, this would include not only the German peoples but also the population of the Nordic countries. In the end, the idea became a framework within National Socialist thinking and the basis for German imperialism and expansion. The symbol for this libido-carrying power was gradually perverted and diverted into conquest, war, and conflict instead of liberation. It was the notion of Aryan blood ties that underpinned the original requirement that only men from Norway, Sweden, Denmark, Iceland, the Netherlands, Switzerland, and Flanders could voluntarily enlist in the Waffen-SS.

The gigantic dragon Fafnir was killed by Sigurd the Dragon Slayer. The hero's life is outlined in the Poetic Edda, and his fight against the dragon is a recurring motif in artwork from the Middle Ages. This wood-carving is from the entrance to Hylestad stave church of circa 1175.

Hermannsdenkmal is a colossal monument, 53.46 meters high, constructed between 1838 and 1875. It is located in the Teutoburg Forest in Germany. The statue was built in memory of the Cherusci leader Arminius who, at the Battle of Teutoburg Forest in the year AD 9, wiped out three Roman legions and united Germanic tribes.

Kaiser Vilhelm II of Germany was enthralled by the saga of Frithiof the Bold, the fictional hero of Viking times. He asked the German art professor Max Unger to create an enormous statue of his hero. The kaiser had it erected at Vangsnes, a village situated beside a fjord in western Norway, the Sognefjord. From its base, the statue soars 22.5 meters into the air, and it was unveiled on July 31, 1913. Thousands of people poured into Vangsnes to see Kaiser Vilhelm II and the Norwegian king Haakon VII. The kaiser gave a speech about the Viking era and the blood ties between the Germanic nations.

On Saturday, May 27, 1933, German officers in Nazi uniforms arrived to lay a huge wreath, made of spruce branches in the form of a swastika, at the monument. These officers had come from Balestrand, where the German cruiser *Deutschland* lay at anchor. This was an imposing battleship with a crew of 623 men. In 1934, the cruiser returned to the Sognefjord with Hitler on board. On April 9, 1940, the cruiser was number two in the attack fleet that sailed in to invade Oslo, Norway's capital city.

## What Passed Unnoticed

The paradox is that Nazism ended up worshipping a mythology that prophesied its destruction. The golden jubilee festival of 1933, fifty years after

Part 1: The Making of a Singer (1895–1935)    53

Bayreuth 1933. Tietjen is lying with his head on Lorenz's lap, and fru Lorenz is seated beside them. Maja Flagstad is enthroned in the center of the photo, with Kirsten Flagstad two places to the left in the same row. *Source: Flagstad Museum.*

Wagner's death, was opened with great ceremony. The town was decorated with swastika banners, and the distinguished audience walked in a triumphal procession to the festival hall. To mark the anniversary of Siegfried Wagner's death, Beethoven's Ninth Symphony rang out through the streets of Bayreuth, with Flagstad as the soprano solo. The concert was broadcast on radio to several countries.[32]

Flagstad was disappointed that she had no opportunity to meet Richard Strauss, who was conducting the orchestra. Instead, the old, stooped vocal coach approached her after the concert. He told her he had been the tutor at more performances of Beethoven's Ninth than he could count but had had to wait until he was in his seventies to witness a soprano soloist such as fru Flagstad. She was touched by this. Maja, Henry, and Kirsten had a little private celebration in Bayreuth after this success. She had agreed to sing in slightly more substantial roles the following year, as Sieglinde in *Die Walküre* and Gutrune in *Götterdämmerung*.

They cannot have avoided noticing that the festival they had taken part in was extremely politicized. Flagstad had no difficulty understanding German, so she must have sensed the excitement and may have heard something of the problems encountered by both Leider and Kipnis. The information that it was now forbidden for Jews to perform as professional musicians in Germany must have reached them, or was this a subject no one dared to mention there? They could not have spent time in Bayreuth during these years without picking up any of the many Nazi propaganda speeches given on the radio, as well as seeing all the swastika banners and flags decorating the town.

None of them had any influence whatsoever on what was going on, but it is strange that they did not give any thought to it at all. In Germany in 1933, a number of Flagstad's colleagues were banned from working, and some of the musicians she shared a stage with were threatened because they either were Jews or were married to Jewish people. She never spoke of it, and no contemporary journalist ever asked her any questions of that nature, as far as we know.

## Sieglinde

In May 1934, Flagstad traveled to Berlin to meet Tietjen, who had promised to rehearse Sieglinde with her. A message had also arrived from the opera company in Brussels, at the Royal Theatre of La Monnaie, asking if she could sing the role of Sieglinde in a performance of *Die Walküre* they were planning to stage there on May 24. She was taken aback that the head of the opera in Brussels had heard of her and that he had referred in his letter to her renown as a Wagner singer. Flagstad did not know that her friend Alexander Kipnis had also been there and told them about her. The engagement would provide good practice before the next festival in Bayreuth, and so she accepted the offer.

The days in Berlin were frustrating. Tietjen was preoccupied with a Strauss festival and kept postponing his meeting with her. While she waited, she attended his magnificent productions at the State Opera. But she was unable to meet him. Flagstad was not the most persistent of people, and so she traveled home, leaving unfinished business behind her. She had not received any instruction for Sieglinde apart from what she and her mother had been able to work out for themselves. It was therefore an extremely nervous singer who arrived a few days later in Brussels, where she was asked to sing with a visiting German company. Flagstad had never sung the role of Sieglinde on a stage before.

Part 1: The Making of a Singer (1895–1935)

It went surprisingly well, despite the fact that she had never dreaded a premiere so much, and everything seemed to fall into place. When the curtain went down on the evening of May 24, 1934, she was sobbing with gratitude and exhaustion. Her misgivings had been a waste of energy if we are to believe the effusive reviews she received. It was reported that Flagstad's Sieglinde had been a portrait of compassion, pain, delicacy, and desolation. The great plaintive role seemed to have been written for her, since she gave it a form that set an ineradicable standard for the part. She had no idea that her interpretation would soon make her an overnight success in America.

## Bayreuth Festival 1934

By 1934, it had become too dangerous for Jewish singers, even at Bayreuth. The festival had acquired a new singer in the role of Hagen since Emanuel List was no longer allowed to sing there. Flagstad could not have avoided noticing the absence of both Kipnis and List. In Bayreuth, both before and during the war, there were no curtain calls for soloists. The applause in the festival hall should be for only the master. It was afterward, in the restaurant, that soloists, conductors, and musicians received their applause and could meet their public.[33] Was the ban on employing Jewish musicians and their victimization mentioned around the tables there, or was this also a taboo subject among their artist colleagues?

At Bayreuth, there had been a smear campaign against homosexual people just before Flagstad's arrival. As a result, the posts and lives of several festival employees were in jeopardy. Legal action was taken against star singer Max Lorenz, later Flagstad's partner every time she sang at the festivals in Zurich, Vienna, and Milan. His intimate relationship with a young man backstage was exposed, and Lorenz was arrested. This was an extremely awkward affair for his employer, fru Wagner. She managed to put a stop to the lawsuit and have the singer released with the help of Hitler. Lorenz was to sing both Stolzing in *The Mastersingers* and Siegfried in *The Ring*, and it would have hindered the festival if he had not appeared. Hitler was so captivated by the brilliance of his voice that he was also willing to overlook the fact that Lorenz was married to a Jewish woman.[34]

In a postcard to her mother, Flagstad relates that Hitler came to Bayreuth and the entire town was decked in flags. The rehearsals had gone well. She received a great deal of praise, and they were delighted with her appearance. However, she mostly spent time on her own, knitting and writing letters.

Flagstad in the role of Sieglinde on August 17, 1934. *Source: Flagstad Museum.*

Bayreuth 1934. Flagstad and Leider sit in the middle with Tietjen and Lorenz up on the right. *Source: Flagstad Museum.*

Part 1: The Making of a Singer (1895–1935)          57

She was to stay there for a month but was already longing to return home to Norway.

The critics wrote that Kirsten Flagstad had a voice with a fresh, youthful timbre and considerable potential for development. There was good reason to have the greatest of expectations of her as a singer. As Gutrune in *The Ring*, with her dazzlingly beautiful mezzo and its resounding forte, she surpassed all her predecessors.

The plan was to see if Flagstad could develop into a worthy alternating leading soprano. In Bayreuth, they were extremely conservative; the management had a very specific understanding of how Wagner should be played and sung. This was not a place where singers could become famous overnight.

### Promised Land

In St. Moritz in Switzerland, those in charge of the Metropolitan Opera in New York, general manager Giulio Gatti-Casazza and chief conductor Artur Bodanzky, were living at a comfortable distance from both Germany and Bayreuth in the summer of 1934. They were searching for an outstanding Wagner soprano for the Metropolitan. The German Frida Leider, who had held this position, wanted to be released from her contract. She had never liked New York and was also increasingly nervous about political developments in her own country.

Bodanzky was to become an important person for Flagstad's future progress. Born in Vienna in 1877, he was the son of a Jewish merchant, a background that demanded some distance from Nazi Germany. He had studied violin with Alexander Zemlinsky, the Austrian composer and conductor, and worked as assistant conductor to Gustav Mahler at the Vienna State Opera. In 1915, he immigrated to the US and obtained work at the Metropolitan, where he was given charge of the German repertoire.

The Italian opera tradition was taken care of by Gatti-Casazza. He had been the general manager of La Scala in Milan for a number of years before he took over at the Metropolitan. Gatti-Casazza led the institution from 1908 to 1935. During these years, he had managed to bring the world's foremost conductors and singers to the opera in New York and made it into a leading world stage. Now he had come to Switzerland to hear selected singers.

They sent a telegram to Kirsten Flagstad in Bayreuth: Could she come to St. Moritz to audition with a view to taking over as Isolde and Brunhild at the Metropolitan the next season? The telegram bound her to professional secrecy about the offer.[35] Frida Leider had not yet been released from her contract, and

58 THE VOICE OF THE CENTURY

they did not want her to know of this. The Metropolitan was keen to secure a new Wagner soprano before they let Leider go.

Flagstad was not at all enthusiastic about the approach. All she wished for was to be allowed to live a quiet and reclusive life in Norway as fru Johansen. And so she laid aside the telegram, but she did at least call her husband to tell him of it. Johansen was delighted by this offer from America and thought she should accept. Flagstad obeyed but was far from happy when she telegraphed back to the Metropolitan management. In the next letter from them, it emerged that she should be ready in a matter of six days to audition for the Brunhilds, Isolde, and Leonore. She did not have the sheet music with her, and she had to search at Bayreuth for the piano version of Isolde. Amazingly enough, it proved impossible to find since the festival was not presenting *Tristan and Isolde* that year. Her husband phoned every day, encouraging her, and she practiced assiduously. She also received invaluable assistance from Tietjen.

Once she had arrived in St. Moritz, she was reminded that she had neglected to reply to two previous inquiries from them and must not think that she could take time to rest at her hotel after her journey. She had to report immediately for practice with a pianist down in the hotel lounge. There, she learned that it had been Kipnis who had recommended her in glowing terms as the Metropolitan's new Brunhild and Isolde.

She told this story to her biographer, but as far as we know, she did not ask about Kipnis. Had she no interest in finding out what had happened to a persecuted colleague who had opened doors for her? The biographer, Biancolli, did not ask her such questions either.

## What Happened to Alexander Kipnis?

Kipnis accomplished the difficult balancing act of being a Jew in central Europe. He had two advantages: his American citizenship since 1931 and the fact that he was deeply admired for his interpretations, both at Bayreuth and at Berlin. He had participated in the Wagner festivals of 1927, 1930, and 1933, in major roles. In the course of 1934, he realized that it was vital for him to get out of his contract with the opera in Berlin, but Tietjen reminded him that Göring controlled all Prussian theaters and that he would not permit Kipnis to be released from his contract. It was a matter of life and death, however, and in 1935, Kipnis resorted to drastic action.

He was a heavy smoker because he suffered from nerves, and his doctor felt that this would affect his voice, so he began to sing the most demanding

Clockwise from top left: Emanuel List, Alexander Kipnis, artistic director Heinz Tietjen, and Max Lorenz. Bayreuth, 1933. *Source: Kirsten Flagstad's scrapbook, Flagstad Museum.*

60                    THE VOICE OF THE CENTURY

parts and rehearsed as energetically as possible, five or six times daily, while at the same time smoking around the clock. His vocal cords became red and inflamed, and in the end, he was unable even to whisper. He went to the doctor, who told him it would take a year for him to recover. The doctor wrote a certificate stating that he would have to remain silent for at least seven months, with both smoking and singing banned. If he did not, he would lose his voice completely. Kipnis took this documentation to Tietjen, who forwarded it to Göring, who then gave his permission for Kipnis to be released from his contract and to leave Berlin. Kipnis traveled to Vienna and sang at the opera there but made it a condition in his contract that he could depart if any dangerous situation arose. In 1938, when Austria was annexed by Germany, he was on tour in Australia, and he returned to Europe only briefly before settling in America with his family. There, he encountered Kirsten Flagstad again.[36]

## Silver Scorpion

So the connections that paved Flagstad's way to the Metropolitan were complex and tragic and were not based solely on her talent. She did not dwell on this—her reticence about herself prevented her from taking this into consideration. Frida Leider was being victimized to some extent, and Flagstad could not change this, but why did it not concern her? Did she not wonder why the Met management had told her not to say a word to Leider, who had been her colleague at the festival? We cannot know what thoughts she may have had about this.

Leider's Austrian Jewish husband, the conductor Rudolf Deman, escaped at the last minute from Austria to Switzerland at the Anschluss in 1938. Leider sang at Covent Garden until 1938, but the dreadful events in her homeland of Germany caused her great mental distress. She relates in her biography that she was also on the receiving end of intense hatred and harassment from colleagues close to the Nazi regime. The brutality led to a breakdown that removed her from the stage for several years. She gave some performances after the war, the last of these in 1948. Later she worked as a professor of singing in Berlin until 1958. Leider died in 1975 and was buried with full honors in an illustrious grave at the Heerstrasse cemetery in Berlin.[37]

As far as Flagstad was aware at the time, this was just an audition that was supposed to be kept secret. While she practiced in her hotel room in the mornings, she spotted a little gold coin on the floor at her feet. It was a French fifty-centime, embossed with a silver scorpion. Flagstad showed it to the pianist,

## Part 1: The Making of a Singer (1895–1935)      61

who said she should keep it safe, as it was a good luck charm. Ever since then, she always wore it on a bracelet. But did the scorpion only mean good fortune?

The lounge was crowded with people, and the accompanist was annoyed because Flagstad did not know anything by heart. Flagstad was also irritated. She was not the one who had asked to come here, and besides, the men were behaving in an arrogant and disrespectful manner. To make matters worse, the room she had to sing in had heavy curtains that muffled sound. When they asked her to sing the Valkyrie call, it brought out the obstinate Norwegian devil in her. "Now I'll let them have it," she thought. And she gave vent to what she knew her voice excelled at. The sense of mastery slipped into the pure joy of singing, and the pianist sat back, completely stunned. The next day, the audition with the Metropolitan management took place, and they were quickly convinced that they had found the voice they were searching for.

Before their departure, they gave her a list that included the three Brunhild roles, Isolde, Leonore, and the Marschallin. Could she travel to the famous Hungarian conductor Dr. George Szell in Prague to study these roles? Finally she was instructed to study up on everything and not to put on weight: from then on, she was an entertainer who belonged to them and the whole of America.

"My goodness, to think I'm going to experience this," Maja exclaimed to a journalist. At that time, America was the Promised Land in the minds of Norwegians.

### Notes

1. Biancolli (1952), p. 26.
2. Svendsen (2013), p. 75.
3. Stefi Tyrihjell (Karen-Marie Flagstad's daughter), in discussion with the author, 2014.
4. Biancolli (1952), p. 29.
5. Biancolli (1952), p. 34.
6. "Aida gjör sucés i Göteborg," *Sydsvenska Dagbladet*, March 7, 1929.
7. Newman (1949), pp. 125–54.
8. Biancolli (1952), p. 45.
9. *Göteborgs Handels- och Sjöfartstidning*, October 19, 1929.
10. Bernard Miles, lecture on Kirsten Flagstad, sound b/692, Norwegian National Library sound collection.
11. Newman (1949), p. 191.
12. Drüner (2016), pp. 463–65.

13. *Dagbladet*, June 30, 1932.

14. Hamann (2002), pp. 20–22.

15. Hamann (2002), pp. 9–12.

16. *Wilhelm Furtwängler* (1964).

17. Hamann (2002), p. 71.

18. Solbrekken (2003), pp. 185–87; Drake (1991).

19. Kirsten Flagstad, in discussion with Torstein Gunnarson, Radio Archive ID: 1994/22375.

20. Oscar Thompson, "Tristan at the National Theatre in Oslo," *New York Evening Post*, October 8, 1932 and in *Musical America*, October 25, 1932.

21. *The Confessions of Winifred Wagner, Parts I–II*, dir. Hans Jürgen Syberberg, 1977.

22. *Confessions of Winifred Wagner, Parts I–II*.

23. *Confessions of Winifred Wagner, Parts I–II*.

24. Rosenberg (2019), p. 120.

25. Hamann (2002), pp. 242, 234–35.

26. Drake (1991).

27. "Stunde der Nation," Rundfunksendung des Ring, and *Berliner Tageblatt*, August 13, 1934.

28. Gisvold and Harris (2020), p. 20.

29. Solbrekken (2003), p. 211.

30. Sigerdrivemål in Mortensson-Egnund (2017), pp. 177–84; "Sigrdrifumál in the *Poetic Edda*" (n.d.).

31. Voluspå.org (n.d.), stanza 59; Mortensson-Egnund (2017), p. 29.

32. Hamann (2002), pp. 231, 239–47.

33. *The Confessions of Winifred Wagner, Part I*, dir. Hans Jürgen Syberberg, 1977.

34. Hamann (2002), p. 282.

35. Biancolli (1952), p. 62.

36. Drake (1991); Kipnis (1991).

37. Frida Leider Society (n.d.).

# PART 2

# The Voice of the Century
## (1935–41)

### Right of the Strong White Man

On December 29, 1934, Flagstad and Johansen boarded a ship that would take them across the Atlantic. The vessel arrived in New York on January 8, 1935—a blanket of thick fog had descended on them, delaying the crossing by several days. The harbor approach took place in the evening and made a strong impression on Flagstad. The Statue of Liberty appeared out of the mist while Manhattan glittered with a million bright lights.

They had left behind a Europe where Nazism, fascism, antisemitism, and nationalism were in the ascendancy. America did not lack for problems either. More than 10 percent of the population were the descendants of slaves, and the Native population was almost completely wiped out culturally and existentially. The African American people were downtrodden and relegated to worse living conditions than white citizens. This was a racist, segregated society they had come to, and the civil rights movement and Martin Luther King Jr. would not be active until the 1950s. The Jim Crow laws that prescribed racial segregation were not gradually dismantled until the period from 1954 to 1965, long after the fall of Hitler's Germany. Kirsten Flagstad would now also come into contact with these dark realities.

Flagstad's contemporary African American colleague, the contralto Marian Anderson, in common with Flagstad, was awarded a star on the Hollywood Walk of Fame, but her path to fame was strewn with thorns. In England and Scandinavia, Anderson did not encounter racial hatred but instead was highly esteemed, including by the Finnish composer Jean Sibelius. In her own homeland, on the other hand, she experienced racism firsthand. When she

The contralto Marian Anderson experienced discrimination and racism in her homeland, the US, which was then segregated. Flagstad publicly stated that this was both undemocratic and un-American. *Source: Wikimedia Commons, CC BY 2.0.*

traveled on concert tours, it was not unusual for hotel receptionists to turn her away, saying that the hotel was full. If she was allocated a room, she had to take her food there, as they did not serve Black people in the restaurant. When she journeyed by train, her compartment was often cordoned off so that fellow white passengers did not have to face the embarrassment of traveling in company with a Black woman. If she was addressed by strangers, it was usually by her first name and not as miss. The African American population lived through these and far worse humiliations. Quite simply, they were regarded and treated as second-class people.

Washington, DC, was a segregated city. The largest and most prestigious auditorium there was Constitution Hall, but the concert hall did not have separate toilets for Black people, as the law decreed.[1] The building was owned by the Daughters of the American Revolution (DAR). To gain membership, one had to be white and have forebears who had fought in the American War of Independence (1775–83).

In June 1938, Anderson's assistant wrote to the hall's management. They wanted to book a date for a concert in April 1939, but it seemed that none of

## Part 2: The Voice of the Century (1935–41)

the dates they suggested were available. The lie behind this was exposed by the famous pianist and composer Ignacy Jan Paderewski, a man who is often rightly described as a polymath, the first prime minister of an independent Poland in 1919, and later a member of the Polish government-in-exile in France during World War II. Paderewski, who was upset by the treatment of Anderson, applied to book the hall on the dates she had been told were unavailable. He received a speedy response to the effect that all these dates were free. Later, the chair of the Howard University concert program revealed that the auditorium had a clause forbidding performances by "negro artists."

The story, splashed on front pages, was so serious that Eleanor Roosevelt protested against the exclusion of Anderson and even resigned from the DAR, along with many others. The renowned violinist Jascha Heifetz, who had already committed to playing there, said that he would be ashamed to appear at Constitution Hall. In 1938, Kirsten Flagstad had become a megastar in America. Together with the conductor Leopold Stokowski and the opera singers Lawrence Tibbett and Geraldine Farrar, she sent a telegram of protest to the DAR. They stated that the treatment of Anderson was undemocratic and un-American.

The Washington, DC, Board of Education was opposed to Anderson singing in the city's Central High School. Huge protests, as well as the involvement of Eleanor and Franklin D. Roosevelt, led to Anderson in the end being invited to sing on the steps of the Lincoln Memorial itself, on Palm Sunday, April 9, 1939. She sang there in front of seventy-five thousand spectators, people of all nationalities. The concert was described as a triumph for American democracy.[2]

In the 1940s, Anderson held a number of concerts at the Metropolitan, but the opera company had nothing to do with these, other than hiring out the hall to her manager. Not until 1955 did she become the first Black vocalist to sing in a main role at the Metropolitan. Anderson retired from the stage in 1965.[3] Flagstad was a great admirer of her deep contralto voice and delicate musicality.

The community of Norwegian extraction, with which Flagstad came into conflict, did not raise their voices against racism in America. They had created an identity for themselves in their new homeland, of which she never became part. Many Norwegians had crossed the Atlantic—even the Vikings, with their outstanding ships and their competence as seafarers and navigators, which meant they could sail over longer distances than other people of their day. Leif Erikson, the Icelander of Norwegian descent who arrived in North

The Leif Erikson statue in Minnesota.

America around the year 1000, was one of them. He and his crew are considered to be the first Europeans to step ashore in Newfoundland, almost five hundred years before Christopher Columbus reached the Bahamas in 1492.

Norwegian Americans made Leif Erikson into an object of hero worship and romanticism, but this should be balanced against the fact that many of the

## Part 2: The Voice of the Century (1935–41)

Viking voyages also involved downright looting and plundering in which the Indigenous people were violated and struck down without mercy. The famous Icelandic skald and chieftain Egil Skallagrimsson (910–90) says in a poem that Erikson's mother had foretold that he would buy a boat with fine oars and journey with the Vikings. Standing at the prow, he would guide costly vessels, remain at sea, and slay a few men. In many ways, the verse illustrates the mentality of the Viking period.

In 1825, the systematic emigration from Norway to America began. At that time, Norway was an impoverished country. Many of those who traveled across the Atlantic belonged to the subjugated class of cottars, casual laborers, and the unemployed poor. They needed to reinvent themselves and took a fancy to the heathen Viking, who was quickly turned into a forefather. And so a memorial cult was spun around Leif Erikson. From the end of the nineteenth century onward, he was depicted as a hardworking conqueror and successful businessman with a love of democracy, law, and order. The Viking was resurrected as a good Protestant, a true believer who had brought progress and commerce to America. This cult was created while the ethnic white elite established their power in opposition to the growing influence of Catholic and Latin American immigrants.

The cultural heritage, as fashioned by Nordic immigrants, was integrated into an important element in America's nation building, in the narrative of the strong white man's right to political and economic dominance. In 1964, Congress voted that the sitting president should proclaim October 10 each year as a national Leif Erikson Day. This was intended as a gesture toward Americans of Norwegian ancestry and toward the Nordic influence on the cultural evolution of the US.[4]

### International League of Norsemen

The great Norwegian man of letters and Pan-Germanist Bjørnstjerne Bjørnson took the initiative of establishing the International League of Norsemen. It was founded in 1907 as a worldwide organization for Norwegians in all countries, but the association was most active in America. The aim was to promote Norwegian culture and interests internationally. It was extremely male dominated and nationalistic. In the eyes of the people of that time, it is perhaps understandable that a country such as Norway—a small, poor, and still fledgling state—felt the need to present itself as "the hero's native land." The International League of Norsemen, like Nazism and the fascist Norwegian National Samling Party (NS), adopted many symbols from Old Norse

68 THE VOICE OF THE CENTURY

times, such as the World Tree, Yggdrasil. The archetype was reinterpreted and applied as a representation of Norwegian exploits and generosity that spanned the globe.

The league's membership magazine was published eight times a year, and in the first issue in 1911, tribute was paid to a Norwegian colonel who led troops against an uprising among the Indigenous population in India. The article did not take into account that this had involved a brutal massacre and represented a massive suppression of the Indigenous people. Their view of the population was what we would nowadays call racist. The superior white man's right was used to justify the demand that the Indigenous people had to submit to the ruling powers.[5] The league's magazine reflects the prevailing mentality among colonists. Career diplomat Wilhelm Thorleif von Munthe af Morgenstierne was appointed general secretary of the league in 1914. In 1916, he became editor of *Norwegians Worldwide* (previously *The Norseman*), following in the footsteps of a man who later became Speaker of the Norwegian Parliament, Carl Joachim Hambro. These two men would become powerful enemies of Kirsten Flagstad.

## Metropolitan

However, some time would elapse before the meeting between Flagstad and Morgenstierne. The Johansen couple were installed in a splendid hotel with two rooms and a bathroom at the center of Broadway. From there, they had only a five-minute walk to the Metropolitan. The opera company's season lasted until the beginning of May, and Flagstad did not have a contract with them beyond this.

The Metropolitan opened in 1883 and contained seating for forty-six hundred. Until 1939, the company was considered to be the world's leading Wagner opera house. The management picked out the best singers from German companies and also succeeded in attracting Scandinavian experts. The opera house had a direct line to the composer himself through their first conductor, the Hungarian Anton Seidl, who had been Wagner's protégé and copyist. Seidl had lived in the Villa Wahnfried from 1872 to 1878 as a friend of the family. He brought the master's works to Vienna and Berlin and was then sent out into the world to conduct *The Ring*, *Tristan and Isolde*, and *The Mastersingers*. Wagner thought that Seidl had acquired such a depth of knowledge of his operas that he would be able to do them justice. Seidl's conducting of Wagner was as close as possible to the composer's own understanding of his works. Seidl was also the leader of the New York Philharmonic from its inception

The young conductor Artur Bodanzky. *Source: Theater Museum, Vienna.*

and developed it into a first-class orchestra. In 1911, the Czech conductor Josef Stransky took over the orchestra: he, too, had lengthy experience of German operas and concert stages and was a great supporter of Wagner.

In 1908, Gustav Mahler became the Metropolitan's Wagner conductor. He was impressed by the quality of singing in the opera company and found inspiration for several of his own works while he was working there. In addition, the Italian maestro Arturo Toscanini was deeply fascinated by Wagner and conducted his operas at the Metropolitan until 1915. Toscanini's interpretations took on a certain lyrical Italian quality that distinguished him from the two previous conductors, and his tempi are controversial.

Toscanini suggested Artur Bodanzky as his successor at the Metropolitan and left behind an orchestra dominated by Italian musicians. Bodanzky had been a pupil of Mahler in Vienna, and so a direct line to the Wagner tradition was reestablished at the conductor's podium. Bodanzky was in charge of the German repertoire at the opera house from 1915 until his death in 1939. A view

70 THE VOICE OF THE CENTURY

prevails that the Metropolitan's golden age as far as Wagner was concerned ended with this conductor.[6] One of Bodanzky's many achievements was that he developed Kirsten Flagstad into a unique Wagner interpreter.

After the young couple had settled into the hotel, they went for a walk to communicate with the management at the Metropolitan. What happened next? Flagstad, shy as she was, did not dare speak any English, but Johansen did. He was a worldly-wise businessman who, in addition to timber production and hotel operations, now took on a new occupation as the manager of an opera singer's international career. The first thing he did was to have her released from singing the Marschallin in Strauss's opera *Der Rosenkavalier*. Learning a completely new major role in a short time, as well as finishing everything else she had to do, was simply impossible.

The music world had a decidedly commercial side: there were contracts to be negotiated, future projects to be planned, a whole series of phone calls to be made, and letters to be written. He took care of all this, taking it in his stride as an extension of his business interests. The couple also set up a contract between themselves, which stipulated that he would invest a certain sum to launch her career in America, while she for her part agreed to repay this with an added percentage from the profits.

Johansen had brokered a contract with the Metropolitan that committed her from January 28 until March 31. For this she would receive $400 for transport with a companion and $550 per week, a gigantic sum in the eyes of contemporary Norwegians. With a rate of exchange of 4.08 Norwegian kroner to the dollar in 1935, she therefore received almost 4,000 Norwegian kroner a week. For the purposes of comparison, the average annual wage in Norway at that time was 2,340 kroner.[7] The only drawback was that the management refused to sign the contract until they had heard her sing at rehearsals. This made her nervous.

### Singer Addicted to Playing Cards

Flagstad was faced with an extremely comprehensive program that was also extended during the course of her contract. Between February 2 and April 23, 1935, she was to sing Sieglinde in *Die Walküre*; four days later, Isolde; nine days after that, Brunhild in *Die Walküre*; then Brunhild in *Götterdämmerung*. In March, the company was headed to the opera's outpost in Brooklyn, where she would sing Elsa in *Lohengrin*, and then she would return to New York for Isolde in *Tristan and Isolde*. Thereafter, she would head to Baltimore for Brunhild in *Die Walküre*, then back to the Metropolitan for Elisabeth in

## Part 2: The Voice of the Century (1935–41)                71

*Tannhäuser*. Following that, she would sing a concert accompanied by orchestra at the Metropolitan, then Elsa in *Lohengrin*, another orchestral concert, then Sieglinde in *Die Walküre*, yet another concert with the orchestra, then Elisabeth in *Tannhäuser*, followed by Isolde in *Tristan and Isolde*. Then she would travel to Boston Opera House to sing Brunhild in *Die Walküre*, then Elsa in *Lohengrin*, before heading back to the Metropolitan for Isolde in *Tristan and Isolde*, then to the opera in Rochester for Elisabeth in *Tannhäuser*, and finally back to the Metropolitan for two performances of Kundry in *Parsifal*, as well as two concerts in New York.[8]

She was to undertake all this in the course of eleven weeks. Nowadays, no singer would have agreed to such an itinerary. It was inhumane, and most people would have been unable to accomplish it. Was it defensible to expect one soprano to perform all the leading roles in the Wagner repertoire at the world's greatest opera house? However, fully developed and highly dramatic sopranos do not grow on trees, and there were also powerful financial interests behind the decision. The Metropolitan was in an extremely difficult economic situation; they had to keep expenses to a minimum and maximize takings. Henry Johansen negotiated the highest rates of pay possible for Flagstad and at the same time became fascinated by how much his wife and the opera company might actually earn in the future.

In the midst of the enthusiasm for prosperous business interests, something was lost—concern for Kirsten Flagstad as a human being. She obeyed without question when the "duty" light flashed on. Also, her years in variety theater had taught her to extend herself far beyond her own limits. She didn't know how to set boundaries and was therefore easy to take advantage of, by herself and others. Primarily Flagstad was an artist, but from then on, she also became the opera house's great moneymaking machine. High wages brought with them considerable comforts but also an enormous amount of stress and strain. That the Metropolitan had become financially dependent on Flagstad also gave her a position of power, something of which she eventually became aware.

At this point she was still young and full of energy. In letters to her mother, she wrote that she was terribly nervous about what was expected of her. She had a grand piano brought up to her hotel room so that she could practice. There was something unfamiliar about living so high up, on the ninth floor, with a view on two sides. Neon signs, both impressive and overwhelming in their abundance, were a new experience for her. Her husband was often out and about to familiarize himself with this new world while she, as usual, preferred to eat in her room. The industrialist was in excellent spirits and was exhilarated by America, with an infectious enthusiasm that rubbed off a little on her.

To ease her nervousness about everything expected of her, Flagstad took out her packs of cards. She was a passionate player of solitaire. She had started at an early age, and as the years passed, the games of solitaire had become so advanced and numerous that she had been compelled to use two decks of cards. She set methodically to work and wrote down all the games in a book she always carried with her. Flagstad could become so obsessed with solving a complicated game that she brought the cards with her to performances, and during the intermissions, she sat engrossed, struggling to make it all work out, and if anyone disturbed her, she grew mightily annoyed. A few minutes later, she could walk out onto the stage and perform, absolutely unruffled.[9]

Throughout her career, solitaire followed her as an intimate, confined space for play, and from that point of view, she would have fitted in well to our iPhone age. The games of solitaire kept her consciously focused, and the activity involved no one other than herself. The development of new layouts also required creative brain activity. They were such an important part of her daily life that she wrote about them to her mother: "Do you know what? All my games of solitaire worked out today—Tens, Diplomat and Spider."[10]

## High C

The impressions were great and overwhelming, and at first, Flagstad walked around the Metropolitan feeling a bit like Alice in Wonderland. It was an insignificant building when seen from outside, but in the public areas, everything was beautiful and comfortable, though backstage was dreadful. The orchestra comprised around one hundred men. Here she picked up a lot of fresh nuances, and everything sounded magnificent. One evening, they attended a performance of *Der Rosenkavalier*, dressed appropriately in their best bib and tucker. She allowed herself to become impressed by the audience at the Metropolitan, with their glittering diamonds, rings, and necklaces. The gowns and furs were incredibly beautiful and elegant, and the men sat beside their trophies, dressed to the nines, exuding power. In between them were people who are there only for the sake of the music. However, she thought that the decorations were shabby compared to the ones in Bayreuth. Perhaps they reflected the financial pinch being felt by the opera company.

The management now has a leading soprano who comes from what they consider to be an obscure place in a provincial corner of the world. They are

Part 2: The Voice of the Century (1935–41)          73

uncertain of how things will go, and this nervous energy transfers itself to Flagstad, who says that she was totally beside herself with fear when the rehearsals began. She had stuck her head out of the cabin window to sing every day aboard the ship, but now she had not practiced for several days, and to make matters worse, she had a mental block due to anxiety. Bodanzky said it would be best to give her a few days to prepare. These were not easy parts they were going through—the *Götterdämmerung* Brunhild is, alongside Isolde, the greatest musical and physical challenge a singer can face.

She practiced twice a day with the stage director. All the scenic aspects had to be relearned, and she had to become accustomed to singing straight out into the auditorium. It was difficult since she is used to being free to twist and turn onstage. "Don't sing into the wings," was the constant cry. Gradually, as her nerves calmed down, her usual confidence returns. She was helped by the fact that everyone was so kind to her. Flagstad was not without vanity. She wrote to her mother that a tenor fell down from the clouds when she opened her mouth and sang a few notes. The entire theater was talking about her, and they listened at the doors when she sang. They all believed she was at least ten years younger than her years, and she thought that was delightful. Bodanzky had been immensely friendly and encouraging. And then it was time for the dress rehearsal with the orchestra. A live horse was to be brought onstage, and a real fire would be lit. The long high C went perfectly. Bodanzky called out, "Flagstad, excellent!" and the orchestra drummed on their instruments as people in the auditorium clapped. Then they went through several difficult scenes, all sung impeccably.[11]

After the orchestra rehearsal of the first act of *Götterdämmerung* was over, Bodanzky handed his baton to an assistant for another run-through. He was keen to hear what it sounded like out in the auditorium. The management had been unsure whether it was up to the mark, but when the conductor heard how splendid and beautiful Flagstad's voice sounded as it reached into all the nooks and crannies of the opera house, he realized they had created something really grand. Bodanzky had a subtle understanding of Wagner, and now it had brought forth a brilliant voice. When another high C rang out, applause erupted in the orchestra and lounge, and the stagehands yelled and screamed.

After this, Flagstad and Bodanzky were called to see Giulio Gatti-Casazza, the general manager, to fix the date for the premieres and sign their contracts. Bodanzky understood what was about to happen and warned Flagstad against agents. She had to take advice from him on every detail. "He pinched and patted me on the cheek, treating me as if I were a little girl," Flagstad tells us.[12]

## Curtain Up

On February 2, 1935, Kirsten Flagstad was to make her debut at the Metropolitan as Sieglinde in *Die Walküre*. She had slowly matured into the great Wagnerian roles, and in less than six months, she would be forty years old. She had complete control over her breathing, and her voice was pitched perfectly. Flagstad had experienced a physical development comparable to that of a weight lifter. Gradually she had built up the right muscles—and with them, her voice. She was nervous but at the same time strong and happy, confident that she knew her craft.

The management did not want her to debut in a principal role. They awaited the audience's reaction to this unknown singer. Gertrude Kappel would sing the role of Brunhild. She was far older and approaching the end of her career: this was her last year at the Metropolitan. The Austrian bass Emanuel List, with whom Flagstad had sung at Bayreuth, was also backstage. Because of his Jewish descent, he had been forced to flee to America in 1933. Now he was to sing the part of Hunding.

The performance would be broadcast and aired as a Saturday matinee. Flagstad was aware that around ten million people were going to hear her this evening. These radio transmissions were of great importance—people who, for reasons of distance and finance, could not go to the Metropolitan in person still had the opportunity to experience operatic arts of the highest standard. Jessye Norman has stated that one of the things that kindled her interest in opera was listening to these broadcasts as a child.

The audience at the Metropolitan, at least the old guard, had the great Swedish Norwegian soprano Olive Fremstad fresh in their minds. She had made her debut as Isolde in 1908, with Gustav Mahler at the conductor's podium that evening. For many years, she was the Met's great Wagner star. And so certain expectations were attached to a new Wagner singer from Scandinavia. In a tiny studio in the opera building sat another former Metropolitan star, one who used to provide the commentary for the Saturday radio matinees. Geraldine Farrar had garnered many triumphs there, including in a legendary duet with Enrico Caruso. Now she was introducing the evening's newcomer, Kirsten Flagstad.

En masse, Americans were depressed, experiencing the repercussions of the financial crash that had hit the country hard. There was talk of the Metropolitan Opera having to close because of lack of funds. Flagstad was walking out onto the stage to meet an audience desperate for fresh inspiration. It is said

Flagstad after her debut at the Metropolitan as Sieglinde.
*Source: Flagstad Museum archive.*

that during the first act, the audience was sparse, but when act three began, every single ticket, to the very last standing room space, had been grabbed at the ticket office. Farrar, who was overwhelmed by Flagstad's voice, concluded to millions of radio listeners: "Ladies and gentlemen, today we witness one of the greatest things that can happen at an opera performance—a singer totally unknown to us has brought the audience into raptures with her wonderful voice. A new star is born."[13]

Such a message, naturally enough, caused the New York public to rush to the opera house to hear for themselves. The recording of her debut performance has been preserved, and through all the crackling, a voice shines through, clear as a bell, with unmistakable vitality and strength. It flows like a river in spring flood. It is easy to understand that this seemed refreshing

76 THE VOICE OF THE CENTURY

and revitalizing to depressed souls. The line outside her dressing room afterward resembled a long procession of demonstrators, and she was drowning in flowers and camera flashes. Her debut at the Metropolitan in 1935 created music history. In recent years, no Toscanini or Nellie Melba had succeeded in attracting so many people that the Metropolitan was completely sold out. Flagstad managed to do this and conquered America with her great talent.

## Kirsten Flagstad and Lauritz Melchior

Flagstad's next debut was as Isolde, a role in which she continually tried to immerse herself. Remembering a Wagner part that lasts as long as five hours is a demanding task. She always began by playing the piano excerpt, since the music was the first thing to lodge in her memory. Then she set to work on the text, word for word and stanza by stanza. Wagner was not only a composer but also a poet for whom words and music were inextricably linked. When the text and singing were in place, Flagstad went to work on the characterization. What had Wagner meant by Isolde?

Not until the role had grown within her mind did great things begin to happen. Often she suddenly caught a glimpse of an entirely new revelation as she stood onstage singing. It could be something as simple as a word unexpectedly taking on new meaning. With each performance, she came closer to Isolde, but she never solved her mystery.[14]

She was to portray Isolde with the Danish tenor Lauritz Melchior as Tristan. Later, he said that nothing like the pairing of Flagstad and himself would ever be seen again on the opera stage. Their collaboration unleashed art of the highest quality and inspired him to bring Wagner's characters to life—not least in *Tristan and Isolde*, an opera they sang together a total of ninety-five times. They really *were* Tristan and Isolde.[15]

Melchior was unquestionably among the best Wagner tenors the world had ever heard. He made his debut at the Metropolitan as early as February 1926 as Tannhäuser. The critics said of his performance in the first act that the singing was of a quality the younger generation of operagoers had never heard before from the mouth of a Heldentenor. From that evening on, he was firmly attached to the Metropolitan until 1950. Alongside Kirsten Flagstad, he was the driving force of the opera house. These two constituted one of the most legendary Wagner duets in the history of music.

Onstage, Melchior was the personification of Siegfried the hero, standing as he did at six feet six in his stocking feet and weighing nineteen stones. He had a voracious appetite for life, as a big-game hunter, boxer, angler, and cook.

Melchior and Flagstad as Tristan and Isolde at the Metropolitan, 1935. Karin Branzell as Brangäne. *Source: Flagstad Museum.*

Even in physical proportions, the Flagstad-Melchior pairing was very much larger than life and well able to give a convincing representation of Norse gods and goddesses. Melchior appeared onstage in a corset of leather and steel, a huge suit of armor that Flagstad once saw him being helped into by his dresser. When they stepped onto the stage in their winged horn helmets, chain mail, and spears, they were a sight to behold.

Flagstad thanked her lucky stars that Melchior was there to take care of her in the beginning. Without him, everything would have gone badly. He led her as if in a dance. "Just come over to me now," he whispered in between the notes of the songs. "Go over there, go to the right, now forward, now to the left!" She made many mistakes.[16]

Later, their stage partnership would not turn out to be quite so easy. Melchior felt overshadowed by Flagstad's enormous popularity, and he reacted in a childish manner. For her part, she responded with attempts to push him away. The time would come when these two would be major rivals of the opera world, causing a headache for theater managers. But for now he was the illustrious teacher who took her under his wing. It must have meant a great deal to Flagstad to have a partner with whom she could speak her own language.

## Rescue and Renewal of Opera as Art Form in America

The duo reaped great success. Nine sold-out performances of *Tristan and Isolde* in 1935 brought the endangered opera company a profit of $150,000. After this, the program was set up with Flagstad as the focal point. After her Isolde, the press decided that a new golden age had dawned at the Metropolitan.

When Flagstad stepped into the American opera world, it was under threat on two sides—lack of money and lack of public interest. The Great Depression had led to a shorter season, cut by several weeks, and a reduction in the artists' wages. Opera as an art form had lost ground to new technologies such as cinema and radio. This turned around on February 2, 1935, when Flagstad's debut was broadcast on radio. Listeners across the whole of America heard the huge ovation given to her at the end of act three. Then as now, it was unusual for spontaneous applause to interrupt an act in Wagnerian opera.

December 23, 1935, Flagstad featured on the cover of *Time* magazine. All of a sudden, opera was big business again, reaching out to millions through radio, film, and stage. The founder of San Francisco Opera, Gaetano Merola, arranged a meeting with her backstage at the Metropolitan to give her an irresistible offer. He wanted to stage *The Ring* in its entirety in San Francisco if she would agree to be his Brunhild in future seasons. This became an enormous

Part 2: The Voice of the Century (1935–41) 79

success, both for Flagstad and for Melchior. Opera in the city also benefited from a huge upswing.

## Breakthrough for Wagner's Mythological Dramas

Kirsten Flagstad now attracted projections and expectations from America as a whole, the scope of which she scarcely appreciated. She was able to withstand them as an artist but not as a private individual. The concept of projection, frequently used in psychology, simply means that someone is ascribed qualities and capacities they often do not possess. In short, an illusion is created. As Brunhild in *Walküre*, Flagstad strode out on a rock, wearing a winged helmet and carrying a shield and spear in hand. From here, she sang a war cry that blazed with vitality and technical expertise. The audience broke into applause as soon as they saw her because they really believed they were seeing an Old Norse goddess.

The war cry was circulated throughout the American continent via radio broadcasts with accompanying commentary, and a newspaper concluded that this was not the ordinary American Indian war cry. Loud shouts and shrieks have been instinctively used in many cultures to prompt and display vitality and aggression. The phenomenon had a renaissance when primal therapy was introduced in the US and Europe in the 1970s. In the America of 1935, Flagstad became an idol overnight, and thousands of people became dedicated Wagner enthusiasts.

It is noticeable that the Americans' perception of Wagner differed from the Nazi distortion that the Hitler regime used as propaganda. They experienced the musical drama as a pure manifestation of images and scenes from Old Norse mythology, as a mystery clothed in spectacular musical costume. The opera *The Ring of the Nibelung* was not ruined by association with a fatal ideology. Since the content and music also had their roots in a universal plane, they outlived the composer's bias and misuse by the Nazis.

When Flagstad later looked back on her roles, the *Götterdämmerung* Brunhild always stood out for her as the ultimate one. This was her favorite part, the one that allowed her to express herself 100 percent. The climax comes in the final scene, when Brunhild throws the cursed ring into the fire, mounts the horse Grane, and rides into the flames to die with the man she loves. In this scene, Brunhild unleashes the entire cosmic drama. As a consequence of the action, Valhalla, the warrior's citadel, collapses, and the Rhine overflows its banks, while the Rhinemaidens arise to fetch the ring that belongs to them. The lust for power sinks back into the unconscious.

The *Götterdämmerung* Brunhild at the Metropolitan, 1935.
Source: Flagstad Museum.

This is also the final motif in the film trilogy *Lord of the Rings*. Frodo, the bearer of the ring, hurls the ring representing lust for power into the depths of the earth, and with that the evil realm shatters.

## Powerful Illusion

Kirsten Flagstad created a powerful illusion of an Old Norse goddess of liberation on the Metropolitan stage. The experience seemed exhilarating, and this applied just as much to the American audience as to those of England, Denmark, Hungary, Austria, France, Switzerland, and Norway. Overall, the press reported an ecstatic response from the public, who believed they had glimpsed a divine being. The suggestion shines through the words of a Norwegian journalist who visited the Metropolitan and saw *Siegfried*. It is evident that he was not seeing Kirsten Flagstad; it was the archetype, the Valkyrie, that had captivated the public.

## Part 2: The Voice of the Century (1935–41)

Flagstad is singing, Flagstad is singing, is a murmur that runs through the rows of seats. We are an amazing mixture of Jews, Negros, Chinese—a sprinkling of white, yellow and black. Melchior sang Siegfried with such power that the whole building shook and such high spirits that everyone was swept away. He killed Mime, slayed the dragon, broke Wotan's sword and strode towards the rock that was enveloped in flames.

What an effect! The flames licked across the entire stage, smoke poured out, thick and grey-white, curling up, billowing and disappearing into the sky.

Excitement mounts. We knew that Brunhild was behind the flames—the woman we had awaited for such a long time. The orchestra strikes up. All the violins, all the timpani, all the bassoons, they all join in to increase the tension. Then the smoke drifts aside and there lies Brunhild.

The audience does not move a muscle. The air shimmers and a solitary violin soars from the orchestra. And then, Brunhild stands up, looks around, lifting her arms to the light, to the sun, and sings: Heil dir Sonne (Sun, I hail thee). It streams out over our bowed heads. None of us looks up; we simply let the notes fill the air. They rise, they exult, they bless us!

Is this Flagstad? She releases an excitement in us, she softens us, makes us bow and lights the stars in our sky. All the everyday greyness is gone, all fatigue has dissipated: we are no longer here, not in New York. She has united us all, we are no longer yellow, black or white. We are human beings who are listening, who are filled with beauty, experiencing a moment so intense that it almost feels like pain.[17]

Here it is the universal, metaphysical dimension that is being experienced. Perhaps the phenomenon cannot be fully explained. It arises in a point between the conscious and unconscious mind, where magic, religion, and art meld. Such a projection from the audience to the stage can be generated by outstanding artists, but a problem arises when the audience and the rest of society fail to let the illusion go when the curtain falls—particularly when the opera and media profit by the creation of a celebrity, a godlike diva who never leaves the stage and who keeps ticket sales going and the press busy.

The projections and expectations were also now directed at Kirsten Flagstad the private individual. It was inevitable that these illusions would clash violently with reality. Her tumultuous elevation would at some point switch to similarly vehement denigration. In any case, both extremes were delusions, preconceptions attached to a single person.

On February 27, 1935, Johansen had to travel from New York to attend to his businesses at home in Norway, and this made Flagstad even more insecure. She was also extremely nervous because she was in danger of coming down with a severe cold. The day after the ship had sailed, Flagstad was to appear as Brunhild at the premiere of *Götterdämmerung*. Johansen had told her that he would not survive seeing *Götterdämmerung*; he felt sure something dreadful would occur that evening, with a horse and real fire on the stage.

Flagstad sang the part with such reduced hearing that she could hardly make out the orchestra and her own voice. She relied totally on her excellent ear for music, a tremendous accomplishment. It went surprisingly well, and immediately after the performance, Gatti-Casazza sent a telegram to her anxious husband aboard the ship *Stavangerfjord* to tell him that Flagstad was in excellent shape and had gone down a storm at that evening's performance. Johansen could go to bed and sleep easy while the presses of the New York newspapers started to roll. *Words and Music* wrote that Kirsten Flagstad's Brunhild in *Götterdämmerung* was the best that had ever been heard at the Metropolitan, or anywhere else, for that matter. The press described a miracle of illusion: the audience believed what they saw and heard. Kirsten Flagstad was the *Götterdämmerung* Brunhild, and Lauritz Melchior was Siegfried.[18] The Old Norse gods and goddesses were now to be found in America, where they walked around, large as life, on the opera stage.

## Parsifal—a Vision of the Cosmic Christ

At the Metropolitan, it was traditional to perform Wagner's opera *Parsifal* every Good Friday since it is a sacred drama, loosely based on a legend from the Middle Ages about the Holy Grail, the chalice that held the blood of the Savior. The composer called it "a festival work for the initiation of a stage" that he wanted to be performed only at Bayreuth. When the Metropolitan presented *Parsifal* for the first time, in 1903, Cosima Wagner objected but she did not win in the courts. In 1933, Hitler took up the subject again with Winifred Wagner. He was keen to ensure that *Parsifal* was returned to Bayreuth as Wagner had wished. She had a more pragmatic view of it: Hitler did not have the authority to ban other countries from performing the work, and in light of this, she did not think it a particularly good idea.[19]

The content of *Parsifal* seems far removed from everything Hitler stood for, but even so, he wanted to base his religion on the work. We may speculate that he simply interpreted the symbolism of blood through the prism of "Blut und

## Part 2: The Voice of the Century (1935–41)

Boden" (Blood and soil), where blood symbolized heredity and "race," linked to native ground and territory. Did he really believe that it was "Aryan blood" that was held in the Grail? Anyway, confining the opera to a provincial town in Germany conflicts with the intrinsic vision of the work.

The central symbol of the opera is the Grail, filled with the Savior's blood and stored in the Grail Castle. The old king, Amfortas, suffering and close to death, can no longer fulfill his main duty as protector of the Holy Sacrament, distributed on Good Friday to renew the whole world. The tradition is now under threat, as the protector is dying. Only a holy fool, Parsifal, shining with compassion, can take over the old king's duties. In the drama we also meet a woman, Kundry, who is portrayed as a cross between a primitive woman and a witch, degraded, abused, and cast out by the Grail Knights and by society.

As in all other works of art, *Parsifal* is open to a wealth of interpretations. A central theme is a renewal of spirituality, progress toward holism. Christianity's historic restraint, symbolized by the old king, entails a powerful spiritual disadvantage. What belongs to the past has no redeeming power in the present. As long as a redemptive God is bound to a specific era, all the symbolism surrounding him will eventually lose its power as the eternal archetypes are dressed in new historical guises, conditional on psychologically and materially changed living conditions.

Jesus is said to have had an extraordinary ability to empathize with other people. He is thought to have declared that what is done to others is also done to him. Many great religious founders have held up compassion as a central element of spiritual development, but none has taken this as far as Christ. By treating others as a manifestation of himself, he lives up to his role as the bearer of humanity's self, the solar son of man, the cosmic Christ. As such, he can be reborn in each individual human being. Within this lies the central message of Christianity and its regenerative power.[20]

This is the vision that Richard Wagner primarily touches on in his drama. In the opera, the undervalued and ostracized feminine element, the force of nature, is also restored to the spiritual. Wagner wrote the opera when he was approaching old age: the lion in him had lost its claws, and his wildness was almost tamed. The music is thoroughly melodious and sublime, and many experience it as a genuine church service. It is traditional the world over not to applaud at the end of the first act, as it ends on a scene of Holy Communion. The opera is usually performed just before or in the middle of the Easter season.

*Above,* Flagstad as the beguiling Kundry, Metropolitan, 1935. Her costume emphasizes that Kundry is a seductress. *Source: Flagstad Museum.*

*Right,* Leider as the servile Kundry, a deeper interpretation of the character, Bayreuth 1933. *Source: Flagstad Museum.*

Part 2: The Voice of the Century (1935–41)     85

At the Metropolitan, the 1935 performance was staged on Wednesday, April 17, the Wednesday before Maundy Thursday, the Christian celebration of Jesus Christ's Last Supper with his disciples. It reprised two days later, on Good Friday. Flagstad sang as Kundry at both performances.

Kundry the enchantress is not an easy role, and Flagstad had only eleven days to prepare. Melchior sang the title role, Parsifal, but received little attention in the newspapers, which were full of Kirsten Flagstad. They believed her Kundry had revived an old tradition and created something entirely new. She had given the audience the opportunity to feel the timeless spirit inherent in the pilgrim, forever homeless. She embodied the nameless tragedy, sorrow, and loneliness of Kundry, the woman who symbolizes nature and life itself. Many in the audience had waited in line for four and a half hours to attend the performance.

Flagstad tells us that she was quite exhausted after *Parsifal*, her last opera of that season. In the first act, Kundry has to prostrate herself on the stage, and to her horror, Flagstad woke all of a sudden on the stage floor, having nodded off for a moment or two. Quick as a flash, she was back in character. It was tragic, but she was happy. Something indescribably immense and inexplicable flowed through her.[21] Perhaps it was proximity to the sacred, the metaphysical dimension within the work, that she had experienced.

Flagstad was God's gift to Gatti-Casazza for his final season as general manager at the Metropolitan, but it was the audience that had discovered her.

### Diva Worship

After *Parsifal*, Flagstad traveled straight to NBC's radio studio in Detroit, where facing the four-thousand-strong audience came as quite a shock. The General Motors Choir and Symphony Orchestra sang and played, with her as soloist. After the transmission, NBC had arranged a meeting with the director of General Motors, who urged Flagstad to come home with him to meet his family.

The train for New York was leaving in an hour, so she protested loudly. Besides, she simply wanted to be left alone: she hated being approached before, during, and after performances and concerts. In her private life, she wanted only to spend time with her friends. She did not understand that anyone could have any interest in her beyond her public appearances.

She was quite naive in this respect. Flagstad, in the course of a few months, had become a major celebrity on a par with a rock star. She had attracted

86 THE VOICE OF THE CENTURY

hopeless misconceptions and was viewed almost as a goddess. The director insisted she accept his invitation, and so she relented. In quick time, she greeted his family, a group of more than two hundred people. No one spoke a word to her; she was merely expected to smile and shake hands.

What actually happens when famous people meet and greet their assembled devotees? The fans have projected an illusion of something godlike onto the individual they worship, and the meeting and handshake transmit the subject back to them. They become part of it, just as the director's family felt they had received a share of something divine through their encounter with the world's greatest singer. They could now say to their friends, "I've met and spoken to her," with the implication being that they have also become part of her. Powerful forces from the subconscious drive this phenomenon, and a touch of primitive magic hangs over it; it is repeated constantly in every cult and form of idol worship.

This transference also affects the person on the receiving end of the idolization, who can become trapped and slip into playing a role. In spiritual pupil-teacher traditions and psychoanalytic theory and practice, positive and negative transference are consciously used as tools to liberate students and patients. When the phenomenon plays out collectively, either positively as in cults and idol worship or negatively as in persecution, it most often happens blindly and unconsciously. And so the effect is far from liberating. It can tie people to delusions and lead to havoc and devastation.

Could Kirsten Flagstad have prevented such "lies" being invented about her? It would have demanded a level of self-awareness beyond her capabilities. She would have had to come far enough in her development to eliminate her ego, and she would have had to completely see through all the motives as well as the mechanisms of the market forces swirling around her. Consequently, she would have had to refuse the press all access to her private life or spend her time exclusively on refuting the myths. Maybe she would also have had to leave the stage, but even then her legend would have lingered. The question is whether it is possible to avoid this type of thing, whether positive and negative transference can ever be entirely eliminated.

In Detroit, the train heading to New York with hundreds of passengers aboard was delayed by forty minutes, merely because of Kirsten Flagstad's meet and greet session. A police escort, with motorbikes and sirens, conveyed her like a queen through the city to the railway station. In the midst of the commotion, Flagstad the private individual was quite alone. Her husband had left, and she was now surrounded by nothing but a host of admirers, colleagues, servants, and assistants. She found some support from maestro Bodanzky, who at an early stage became a father figure of sorts.

## An Accompanist

The American pianist Edwin McArthur had followed the ecstatic articles in the press about the Flagstad phenomenon and now saw the opportunity of his life. McArthur was undeniably a very good pianist, but there were many of them in America. Few could have any hope of a career as a soloist. After a great deal of effort, he managed to obtain a ticket to a performance of *Tristan and Isolde* and was just as impressed as all the others. His old friend Marks Levine was the manager of the concert division of NBC, the broadcasting company that arranged work for various artists. Flagstad was one of the singers under Levine's wing, and this opened up a channel of communication to her.

McArthur wrote a couple of letters to her in which he explained that a considerable amount of musical activity in America took place on the concert stage. Singers and musicians normally set out on tours across the entire continent to earn money and make themselves known. He outlined all of this to her in a didactic and detailed fashion. He also had a background as a bureaucrat, and the letters contained a number of pieces of practical advice, everything from the length of concert tours to programs and the way she should dress. The level of detail must have appealed to her, as did the fact that he was over six feet tall. She herself was more than five feet seven, and she was afraid that a pianist of small stature would make her look like a giant onstage.

After some nervous waiting, McArthur received an appointment to see the singer in her suite at the Astoria Hotel. Meeting Flagstad in person gave him a bit of a shock. He stood watching her for a while, struggling to convince himself that this was the fabled Flagstad.[22]

As an American, he had fixed ideas about what a prima donna should look like and how she should behave. He was astonished by the simple way she received him and by her room, which was not filled with all the kitsch he associated with a celebrity. After some small talk, she asked him nicely to play for her. The pianist had wisely chosen two Norwegian romances, one lyrical and one dramatic, thinking she would find this touching. McArthur was a feminine and sentimental character, good at interpreting romances, and he played his way into Flagstad's affections. She replied by smiling and inviting him to cocktails. This was her shy and indirect way of accepting him as

Flagstad and McArthur.
*Source: Flagstad Museum.*

her accompanist.[23] The meeting between them marked the start of a lifelong friendship and an endless series of concert tours.

### "My Nerves Are Shaking"

For the time being, concert tours belonged in the future. Flagstad had completed her first marathon run at the Metropolitan and most of all now wanted to go home to Norway to unwind. On April 24, she finally embarked on the ship that would carry her across the Atlantic. That summer she should have sung in South America, but she had canceled the engagement. Her nerves were shaking with overexertion, and the stress disorder that had afflicted her in the past now came to the fore; the summer was not a particularly happy one.

Did she learn from experience and set boundaries for herself and others? No, she simply continued along the same lines and took on even more work.

## Part 2: The Voice of the Century (1935–41)

Flagstad had entered into a circle from which she could not break out. This one-sided, manic activity did not end until ailments and age brought her stage career to a natural end. Standing onstage eventually became her only pleasure in life: the stage was where she felt at home.

When the ship from America with the famous singer on board glided in toward the coast outside Bergen on the evening of May 2, 1935, a dozen journalists and a sea of flowers were there to greet her. They were all headed for the same boat and luxury cabin that looked more and more like a rose garden. There, Kirsten Flagstad played her role again, and the newspapers played along.

They had never seen such a radiant face as Flagstad's that evening. *Aftenposten*, as the most prominent newspaper in the country, took precedence. She repeatedly told the journalist that the general manager, Gatti-Casazza, had told her that his first gift to the Metropolitan had been Caruso and his last gift had been Flagstad. At the ticket office, they informed her that they had not seen lines like this since Caruso's time. She sang at twenty-one performances, and nineteen of those were sold out.[24]

She said little about the reunion with her daughter, but the question of their life together must have preoccupied her. At any rate, she had decided that Else should come with her back to America. Kirsten Flagstad may have dreamed that they could make some kind of home for themselves there and live as mother and daughter. However, she was almost totally burned out when she returned to Norway and may not have had much energy left over for their relationship.

Else did not make many demands of her mother, and Flagstad's husband coped by himself. Henry Johansen was not the kind of man who had to have his wife by his side. For lengthy periods, they lived their own lives, each on a different continent. Johansen did not starve to death beside the fridge. A retinue of servants took care of him in his everyday life, and emotionally he was not demanding or dependent, at least not until illness and loneliness came along.

At the Metropolitan and NBC, hectic activity surrounded the organization of the phenomenon Flagstad had become that summer. They now had a singer who could attract huge crowds. This meant a great deal of money, something the commercial interests attempted to exploit to the maximum. NBC and the Metropolitan vied for Flagstad's time and the associated cash. In the meantime, the opera house had acquired a new general manager, Herbert

Witherspoon, who entered into tough negotiations with Marks Levine of NBC. After a short time, the manager died, and the legendary Edward Johnson took over both the opera house and Flagstad. The chair of the board at the Metropolitan traveled personally to Kristiansand that summer to discuss the next season and secure a contract with her. NBC and McArthur were working at the same time to organize the program for all the concerts.

The Metropolitan felt that the concert program was so extensive that Flagstad would be exhausted when she returned to them. Concern for her was scarcely the grounds for their worries. Edward Johnson was busy with wide-ranging plans for her that would also distinguish him as the opera's new manager. Not only was she to sing the main roles in the Wagner repertoire but he also wanted to put her on in *Norma, Der Rosenkavalier,* and *Fidelio. Norma* would of course be performed in Italian, a language of which she did not have sufficient command in song.[25]

Flagstad's stress disorder afflicted her for most of that summer, but she failed to connect it with the workload she had taken upon herself. She did not realize that her heavy schedule was creating the stress. She was unable to set boundaries, either for herself or for the market forces that were bearing down on her, and so she went along with the idea of singing this whole repertoire in the course of a single season.

King Haakon was also keen to have a say in the matter. He called her to the palace to present her with the decoration of the King's Gold Medal for Meritorious Services. For Flagstad and most other Norwegians, the king was close to God in rank and prestige. The meeting with His Majesty was overwhelming in itself, and the award was the greatest honor conferred on her till that point. She felt incredibly flattered. The king may well have emphasized to her the glory Flagstad had brought to the Kingdom of Norway in America and beyond. The meeting with the king cemented a connection between artist and state, the consequences of which Flagstad did not appreciate.

## Return to the Stage

In September 1935, Flagstad returned to America, but this time accompanied by her fifteen-year-old daughter. Flagstad had found a private school for Else in Tarrytown on the east bank of the Hudson River, about twenty-five miles north of New York City. Else thought it exciting to go to the US, but she also found that her time there did not offer any family life, and she missed it. She nursed a deep sense of grievance, especially against her mother, who had

## Part 2: The Voice of the Century (1935–41) 91

deprived her of the opportunity to be an ordinary child, in an ordinary house with ordinary parents. It almost certainly did not improve the situation that her school had its own box at the Metropolitan from which all her friends could ogle the great diva Kirsten Flagstad.

Her mother tried to make up for this by going out to the school to visit her daughter as often as she could, but with the tremendous work schedule Flagstad had from October 4 until Christmas, they cannot possibly have spent much time together. In October, Flagstad set out on a concert tour with McArthur, and they gave a total of twenty-nine concerts before Christmas, the last of these on December 23. A highlight was the concert in New York's Carnegie Hall, where the city's most distinguished audience met up. The hall, which seats around twenty-eight hundred people, was full. In addition, *The Ring* was performed at the opera in San Francisco in November, and Flagstad performed the three Brunhilds there. She sang another six grand concerts with a symphony orchestra and also made a recording before the turn of the year 1935–36.

Mother and daughter were to celebrate Christmas together in New York, but then Johansen also arrived. All the same, the holiday did not last long, as the season at the Metropolitan began on December 30, when Flagstad would once again stand onstage as Isolde.[26] The distance and lack of time together could have aroused longing for closeness between mother and daughter that neither was able to give. When this frustration built up, the possibility of conflict and breakup came to the surface.

McArthur had the role of Flagstad's fixer and spokesman in Johansen's absence. The industrialist had charm, humor, and a twinkle in his eye but was generally reserved. He displayed a surprising naivete, with his constant unrestrained praise of Flagstad's singing. He did not tolerate anyone finding fault with her, and she enjoyed this protective devotion as much as any other woman would have done. Those who had fault to find were in particular the more intellectually sophisticated. Everyone agreed that she had a glorious, beautiful voice and that she was hugely musical, but it was obvious that she was not in the least intellectually schooled. Questions were therefore raised about whether Flagstad understood the complex roles she interpreted onstage, and the people asking did not accept her as an actress. When exclusively analytical articles of this nature appeared, she rarely understood what they were about. She had a sure but intuitive understanding of how her voice should be used, both musically and dramatically. In this simple intuitive understanding lay her greatness but also the paradoxical in her personality, according to McArthur. Despite her claims to the contrary, she was a complex personality. She was highly sophisticated in her artistic genius but totally unsophisticated in her personality. In common with every prima donna, she enjoyed the adoration and responded to criticism with fury and incomprehension.

Flagstad's simplicity and unusual sensitivity were rooted in something universally human, and this is why she was so artistically attractive.[27] Alongside her highly developed intuition for opera roles, Flagstad displayed clairvoyant abilities. She knew when the trains were going to be delayed. When McArthur suggested that she ought to investigate such paranormal areas of her personality, she merely laughed and replied, "I feel what I feel." Her premonition that she was not going to like Morgenstierne, the Norwegian minister in Washington, proved correct. Since he almost destroyed Flagstad's artistic career from 1940 until her death in 1962, Morgenstierne deserves a more detailed introduction.

## The King Wishes to Meet the Queen

The aforementioned minister, Wilhelm Thorleif von Munthe af Morgenstierne, went to America in 1917, along with others, including the polar explorer Fridtjof Nansen and Prime Minister Gunnar Knudsen, to negotiate a trade agreement and aid to Norway from the US. This was of vital importance to Norway. Morgenstierne quickly became Nansen's friend and supporter through his work in the International League of Norsemen. The three men concluded their negotiations with the American authorities in the spring of 1918, and with that, valuable exports from America to Norway commenced.[28]

Morgenstierne remained in Washington as a trade attaché. He refurbished the legation's offices with Morgenstierne family funds since the Norwegian Ministry of Foreign Affairs did not feel they could afford it. Undoubtedly, this created a sense of personal ownership of the legation, and it ended up being just as much a Morgenstierne firm as a state institution.

Morgenstierne was granted a powerful position in the diplomatic service at an early stage, and his standing increased steadily because of his pedantic competence and ability to forge alliances with powerful men. He continued working with Nansen, who was the most important and famous Norwegian of that time, after King Haakon. Morgenstierne also managed to have his brother-in-law appointed as Nansen's secretary. Morgenstierne rose through the ranks, from principal officer in the Foreign Office to consul general in New

Part 2: The Voice of the Century (1935–41)          93

York and finally minister at the legation in Washington, where he pulled all the strings as far as connections between the US and Norway were concerned. His primary task was to refute any criticism of his homeland.[29]

As a high-ranking diplomat with a certain interest in music, he represented his country at major concerts in Washington. From time to time, he sat with his wife and other contacts in one of the boxes at the Metropolitan. He had followed the Norwegian singer's glowing success and increasing fame in America. No Norwegian had ever achieved such renown there, with the exception of himself.

Morgenstierne was driven by his need for validation and by his ambitions. In the Norwegian diplomatic service, he was already a towering, influential figure. It is possible that, like King Haakon, Morgenstierne was of the opinion that Flagstad should primarily serve her native country in America. He therefore considered that, to some degree, she should also come under his management and influence. During Flagstad's first season at the Metropolitan, they had not met, but now he took the initiative for a face-to-face meeting.

Morgenstierne came from a completely different background from Flagstad. His father, Bredo, was a law professor and for a spell had been the principal of Oslo University. His father's side also descended from an aristocratic family, which had occupied high office for generations. As a young man, his father had had few prospects at a time when civil servants were on the wane and merchant classes were in the ascendant. He compensated for this by marrying into new money. Bertha Schjelderup did not possess the same innate good breeding, but she had the advantage of wealth. They were a good match for each other: the Morgenstierne name gave luster to the Schjelderup family firm and secured for her all the connections she could dream of within the royal family and aristocratic circles. Her parents were also shareholders in the National Theatre, where Flagstad sang.

In contrast to Kirsten Flagstad, Minister Morgenstierne had a privileged, protected, and well-heeled background in a high official's home. He had never lacked for means, but his family expected their sons to fill important positions, internationally as well as at home. From the outset, Morgenstierne set himself apart with his self-assurance and authority.[30] The minister's role model as he grew up was his father's half brother, Captain Wilhelm Morgenstierne, after whom he was also named. His uncle lectured in military history and tactics at a senior level at the Military Academy, and in 1898–99, he was sent out as a spy and King Oscar II's personal eyewitness in the Greco-Turkish War. His

*From left*: Bredo Henrik von Munthe af Morgenstierne; Wilhelm Herman Ludvig von Munthe af Morgenstierne, who was King Oscar II's personal friend and adviser; and ambassador Wilhelm Thorleif von Munthe af Morgenstierne, portrayed in the gold brocade Swedish court dress. The painting hangs in the Norwegian Embassy in Washington.

uncle's reports taught the boy something of the games that take place between major powers and smaller nations, about foreign policy and the manipulation of power.

Through his distinguished lineage, with connections to Swedish, Russian, and Prussian nobility through marriage, Uncle Wilhelm and the rest of the family had enduring links to the Swedish royal family. His uncle was also a close adviser to King Oscar II in the final traumatic years before the dissolution of the union in 1905, when Norway was uncoupled from Sweden.[31] From an early age, Minister Morgenstierne had rubbed shoulders with royalty and nobility, perhaps so much so that he identified with them. The fact that many years later he allowed his portrait to be painted with him wearing the gold brocade of the Swedish court dress may suggest this. To this day, the painting hangs in the Norwegian Embassy in Washington.

The minister had attended the best school in the city, and he was seemingly the first commander of the school's order and had the reputation of being extremely elegant. At the age of sixteen, he declared himself to be a socialist, but his name gave him little credibility. After an explanation of the socialism of the time, the school magazine called him a "socialist in patent leather shoes"

Part 2: The Voice of the Century (1935–41)    95

since he often sported Walk-Over patent leather boots. Morgenstierne provoked several of his fellow students, and they haunted him for years afterward. It seems they bullied him a little for what they took to be his arrogant vanity.[32]

He studied political economy in Christiania and later international law at the distinguished Wadham College at Oxford. After his final exam in political economy, he was appointed to the diplomatic service.[33]

## Beginnings of a Battle for Position

When Flagstad returned to America in the autumn of 1935, she received a letter from the Norwegian minister. He welcomed her back and expressed his hope that she would come to the Norwegian Legation in Washington to sing there in December. She did not reply herself but asked McArthur to write a letter on her behalf, in which she apologized but said that her schedule was so inflexible that she could not take part in social events.

This response must have seemed both surprising and hurtful to Morgenstierne, and it was also quite alien to the etiquette in which he had been schooled. He later took up this refusal with McArthur, blaming him for wanting to protect Flagstad from him. At the outset, the minister assumed that it had not been Flagstad who had behaved in such an ill-mannered fashion. On her part, she was so overworked and afflicted by nerves that she was unable to appreciate that her behavior might seem offensive.

Morgenstierne had been trained in sophisticated tactical and strategic games, but these disciplines were completely foreign to Flagstad. She liked to call a spade a spade and have things over and done with: primitive but straightforward. Besides, her intuition had picked up a touch of autocracy in the air. It was Flagstad's credo that no one should demand anything of her apart from the purely artistic. Life beyond the stage was private, and her shy, reserved nature wanted to keep it for herself.

In this, Flagstad and Morgenstierne were very different. Morgenstierne was almost always on the stage, whereas she stood there only when performing. Once the curtain had fallen, she was happy to take the adulation, but beyond that she needed no affirmation. The roles played by Flagstad and Morgenstierne in America were also very different. Morgenstierne served in the US as a minister and official representative of Norway, whereas Flagstad was living there as a private individual and performance artist. Through his work, he was obliged to represent his country; she was not.

Not until Henry Johansen arrived in America to celebrate Christmas did he learn that she had turned down an invitation from a representative of the

96    THE VOICE OF THE CENTURY

Norwegian government. Through *his* activities, the industrialist was well versed in strategic power play, manipulation, and lobbying activities. He considered her refusal an unwise move. On Boxing Day, 1935, he sat down at the writing desk in the suite at the Astor Hotel in New York and penned a cordial letter to Morgenstierne in which he apologized for the incident. He ordered his wife to send the minister a photograph of herself with a friendly inscription on the back. At the same time, Wilhelm and his wife, Marjorie Morgenstierne, were invited to the Metropolitan on December 30, as Flagstad's guests.

On January 6, 1936, Morgenstierne replied to Johansen's letter, writing that unfortunately they had been unable to come to New York on December 30 and that later in the new year would suit better.[34] Johansen therefore organized an intimate dinner with important guests when the Morgenstiernes came to New York. On parting, Flagstad took the opportunity to invite them to the Metropolitan. At a later date, fru Morgenstierne and some friends were Flagstad's guests there, seated in a box at her expense.

So far, Flagstad had behaved diplomatically, in accordance with the instructions she had received from her husband, to avoid getting on the wrong side of Norwegian officialdom in America. The snag was that it had all been done under some duress, and she had been forced to curb her instincts. Besides, an underlying psychological mechanism had already come into play between her and Morgenstierne, with negative projections based on very different components of their respective personalities.

## Daunting Schedule

The schedule organized around Flagstad brought enormous financial return but can also be regarded as damaging from a human standpoint. Admittedly, her husband had managed to remove Norma and the Marschallin from her list of roles, but what remained was daunting in itself. From January to April 1936, she sang absolutely all the main roles in the Wagner repertoire as well as Leonore in *Fidelio* at the Metropolitan, twenty-nine performances in all. In addition, she sang in five major solo concerts with symphony orchestra. In April, Flagstad and McArthur set out on tour in the US and Canada, with ten concerts and one recording resulting from their activity in that spring month.[35]

On March 14, Flagstad gave a charity concert at a day care center where the children of working parents were looked after, something that seems fairly ironic, given the life led by her and her daughter.

Part 2: The Voice of the Century (1935–41)    97

When there is no opportunity for leisure, when a person with such an itinerary does not practice yoga, meditation, or sporting activities beyond the demands of the stage, a huge amount of mental and physical stress must inevitably build up. Flagstad resorted to solitaire and in all likelihood the consumption of alcohol. As an American, McArthur politely declined to take part in Scandinavian hard-drinking habits, but he showed indulgent respect, saying, "Well, that's your business." On tour, Flagstad always had with her a specially made European leather case that served as a private bar. The case contained four glasses and four bottles, and it was one of McArthur's tasks to ensure that these were never empty. Two of them held martini, the third bottle was cognac, and the fourth was neat whiskey. Champagne came too, to be drunk in the evenings.

Cocktail drinking on transcontinental trains eventually became a fixed ritual on their concert tours. Flagstad had soon drunk the skinny McArthur under the table, and he had to sleep it off for several hours to be sober again after one of her large measures. She, on the other hand, had a great capacity for alcohol, but she never drank before a concert or an opera. She did not enjoy being intoxicated, but alcohol became a habit-forming self-medication to combat stress and pain as well as being a soothing, sleep-inducing aid. The alcohol was a reward at the end of a hard day's work, with no thought for the potential damaging effects. McArthur relates that when they left Carnegie Hall after a concert, they stopped the car farther down the street while people were still clapping so that Flagstad could have her cognac.[36]

The newspapers reported wholesale Flagstad fever throughout America, and the press was always obsessed with the innermost details of her private life, as well as her diet, age, and weight. Her posters proclaimed that she was the greatest singer alive, and it was rumored that her fees had soared sky-high. Her idol was the Swedish film star Greta Garbo, and she decided that since Garbo could live a secluded life, she could do the same. Moreover, the enormous focus led to great privileges and extraordinary arrangements.

## Introduction to Covent Garden

After Flagstad's successes in New York, the long-established Covent Garden Opera in London had engaged her for four performances of *Tristan and Isolde* as well as for a *Ring* cycle with the three Brunhilds. England's opera mogul Sir Thomas Beecham had pulled this off. He was to conduct *The Ring*, while Fritz Reiner would wield the baton in *Tristan*. Beecham himself financed

98    THE VOICE OF THE CENTURY

some of the operations at Covent Garden, and he is also regarded as England's first internationally famous conductor, central to the founding of the London Philharmonic in 1932.

Beecham was looking forward to hearing Flagstad at Covent Garden. Her agency had additionally arranged a couple of concerts in London. In May 1936, Flagstad journeyed across the Atlantic with her husband. Melchior accompanied them as her singing partner, and Emanuel List, the Wagnerian bass, also appeared onstage with them. England was a safe haven for Jewish artists.

Covent Garden is one of the major landmarks in the metropolis of London; its name and traditions trace back to the Catholic monastery located there until the seventeenth century. In 1663, it was turned into a theater, and at the beginning of the eighteenth century, concerts began to be given there. The composer George Friedrich Handel was the conductor at Covent Garden from 1735 to 1737, as well as being in charge of the opera for a time. The list of visiting celebrities and musical triumphs was long; the crowded atmosphere was perceptible, permeating the very walls; and the royal box clearly conveyed the opera house's links with the monarchy. Every evening, the stalls were filled with distinguished members of the nobility and other prominent individuals, while music enthusiasts and new arrivals spread out across the galleries.

The English press had not paid Flagstad's visit much advance attention. Their reservations concerned the extent to which it was possible to rely on something the Americans had given such an enthusiastic buildup. Many of them were eager to see if the success at the Metropolitan would be repeated in London. The opera house was therefore packed with the most elegant audience of art lovers that London could muster, with not a ticket to be had for love or money at the premieres. The audience in the galleries apparently broke all records, some having sat outside on small stools for forty-eight hours to be sure of a seat, and there was great disappointment among the many unable to gain admission to the opening nights.

The audience's expectations were fulfilled. The spectators in the galleries went wild when the curtain came down. They shouted, "Isolde, Kirsten, Isolde, Kirsten!" and their feet stamped an accompaniment to clapping and enthusiastic yells. It was an unparalleled spectacle. The elegant audience in the stalls and boxes was almost as wild. Ladies in diamonds and pearls and breathtaking gowns, gentlemen in evening dress, decked in their finery and decorations, waved their programs and applauded loudly, according to a Norwegian journalist.[37] All the music enthusiasts London possessed and all the

Part 2: The Voice of the Century (1935–41)    99

elegance and exclusivity the rich aristocrats could marshal were represented at Covent Garden that evening.

Listening behind this stage was Elisabeth Schwarzkopf, the singer who would become one of the most significant sopranos of the postwar period, especially famed for the intelligence and beautiful tone of her interpretations of Strauss and Mozart. She had not made her debut when she experienced Flagstad's voice for the first time. It made a tremendous impression on her. She relates that the voice had a sound that no one could forget, like the sun at its full brilliance. Flagstad's voice was an instrument with no gaps in it. It was consistent from top to bottom, and she almost never used a one-sided chest voice since her vocal range was so uniformly placed. It was the most natural voice Schwarzkopf had ever heard. It never compensated with the use of technique. In the transition from the chest to middle voice, which for most singers becomes a bit dubious, Flagstad had a warm passage with every possible sound.

Later Flagstad and Schwarzkopf would meet and sing together on various stages. Schwarzkopf tells us there were no other professional singers in possession of such a voice. They were all smaller in scale, but Flagstad always tried to reduce her volume to avoid drowning them out. She could sing at any time; even in the middle of the night, she could think of a high C and hit the note perfectly at full volume.[38]

## Voice of the Century

Flagstad's interpretation of Isolde made a deep impression on the public. There had been ten curtain calls by the end of the first act, twelve after act two, and sixteen at the end of the performance.[39] This was a record for Covent Garden, as not even the opera's great soprano of the past, Nellie Melba, had experienced anything like it. Flagstad had felt inspired by the opera house audience, which had sat with unusual concentration, with not a single cough in the course of the four-hour-long opera. Afterward, a whole series of distinguished people came to congratulate her, so it was long past midnight by the time Flagstad was able to leave the building.

She had caught a cold, and her husband proudly told the press that he had been her nurse. Her eyes were streaming, and she coughed so badly that it sounded as if she had an attack of bronchitis. The industrialist therefore sent all the journalists and admirers out of her dressing room and managed to bring her back to the Savoy Hotel. Throughout the entire performance, she had been terrified of sneezing and coughing. One of the best throat specialists in the city was called to her dressing room at the intermission to spray her throat. Her head was still throbbing, after an incident in which a heavy, sharp-edged powder compact had dropped from the balcony during one of the rehearsals, necessitating a number of stitches in the wound. However, what did that matter when everything was going so well? Her husband was there, organizing all the business and practical side of things, and there were several days before the next performance.

To be brief, the English press concluded that Kirsten Flagstad was the greatest singer of our times. As Brunhild in *Götterdämmerung*, she was a revelation: Flagstad sang throughout the entire opera with passion and great assurance. The final scene had taken on an exceptional aura of nobility and had been sung effortlessly, with unrivaled fluency. Her voice was of the kind that only emerged once in a century. Beecham succeeded in engaging her for the next season, and her annual visits to London became a tradition. In the following season, in 1937, the coronation year in England was to be celebrated with musical events on a grand scale. Newly named as the "Voice of the Century," she embarked on a ship that would take her to Gothenburg.[40]

Flagstad and Johansen had made Swedes of themselves that summer, since Flagstad was in conflict with the Norwegian tax authorities, which also demanded their share of her enormous success. She had had to prove payment of a tax bill in the US before being able to leave the country, and now the Oslo tax office was also claiming tax on her gross earnings. Johansen's lawyers took care of the negotiations, which lasted all summer, and in the meantime Flagstad resided in Sweden.

## Crystalline Spirit and Stupendous Voice

Maja Flagstad lived for a few weeks at her daughter's house out on the Swedish coast and told the banished journalists that she could answer all their questions. A "race biologist" in Oslo had recently come up with the idea that Kirsten Flagstad's family was more musically gifted than those of Edvard Grieg and Siegfried Wagner. Of course, he encountered opposition, but Maja found it all quite flattering. She said that she had tested her daughter. With the radio in the house at full volume, she gave Kirsten the command: "Sing 'I fjor gjætt'e gjeittinn' in B minor!" and the girl had sung "I fjor gjætt'e gjeittinn" (Last year I herded the goats) in B minor despite the terrible racket from the radio. The folk song was originally played in the key of B major, and Maja wanted to check if her daughter could sing it impromptu in B minor. Maja could only insist that this was completely true. Now they were to travel to Copenhagen, Vienna, and Prague, and Maja was looking forward to it so enormously that she could hardly sleep.[41]

In Vienna, Flagstad was to sing a *Ring* cycle as well as Isolde. She was well prepared in advance of her debut with the Vienna State Opera, where she had to sing the complete Isolde. The experienced singing coach Herman Weigert from the Metropolitan had gone to Strömstad in Sweden to rehearse the parts with her. *Tristan and Isolde* was often presented with major cuts in the score, but the opera company in Vienna was conservative and keen to present it in its entirety.

Vienna was at that time the musical capital of Europe, with its own orchestra, chorus, opera house, music critics, and audiences. The magnificent opera house in Ringstrasse was the most important opera stage in Europe before World War II. The opera orchestra was of exquisite quality, and most of the musicians there belonged to the Vienna Philharmonic as well. The Austrian Swiss conductor and composer Felix von Weingartner, who was also in charge of the Vienna Philharmonic's concerts, stood at the conductor's podium. He had been a personal friend of Liszt, Brahms, and Tchaikovsky, and it almost goes without saying that he had vast knowledge of Wagner's musical dramas.

The Vienna State Opera, considered the leading opera stage in Europe before 1939. *Source: Theater Museum, Vienna.*

102                    THE VOICE OF THE CENTURY

The rehearsals had gone well; Weingartner was pleasantly surprised by Flagstad's absolute understanding of the music. She was the only Wagner interpreter he had conducted who sang absolutely impeccably. She did not hold the note any longer than the composer had decreed, and she respected the tempo and pauses. Most singers often draw attention to themselves by holding the note too long, but with Flagstad, he found a prompt respect for the score.[42]

> Isolde the king's daughter, Isolde the sovereign, Kirsten Flagstad epitomizes the part. The radiance of the music refracts within her crystalline spirit and stupendous voice. Shades of passion float around her but she remains resting in pure white love. Had anyone ever seen Isolde's love unfold in such clear light, in such Nordic air? This is the Isolde who now celebrates global triumphs. Her discovery has come late, but this makes her stardom shine even brighter. Not only is she a beautiful fair-haired woman, but also a strong personality in command of that voice. A voice that doesn't flatter the ear, but controls it. Clarity, distinctness, nothing here is unintelligible or imprecise.
>
> I don't even know if her voice is particularly beautiful: there is little warmth to be found in it, and you don't lean back comfortably in your chair to enjoy its tones, but the voice is unrivalled. You have to follow her—the voice is song itself, a Wagner song of dramatic inspiration, confident diction, with a transparent melodic line rarely heard.
>
> Kirsten Flagstad's soprano has a wonderfully dramatic intensity. The sound is compact and concentrated and seldom dissolves into the softly poetic. But when it does, the effect is even more powerful because of the contrasts. Rich nuances are not accessible to her sound, and neither are delicate dynamics. Quite the opposite—it is filled with a musicality of an extraordinary driving force.
>
> In the realm of night, Flagstad's Isolde becomes a transcendental consciousness. No violet or romantic ecstasy, but a cold, glittering, scintillating star in a black sky. A brilliant accomplishment, however that is now still understood.[43]

After such reviews, there were of course great expectations attached to Flagstad's Brunhilds, which she would sing beside Max Lorenz. Flagstad as Brunhild was characterized by the music press in Vienna as a singing strategist of masterly stature. She implemented her tactical operations with such prowess and brilliance that she always kept something in reserve. After the *Götterdämmerung* Brunhild, the press wrote that such a voice had scarcely ever been heard in Vienna.

Part 2: The Voice of the Century (1935–41)　　103

With that, they could drive on proudly to Prague, where Flagstad was to sing the same repertoire. There, the critics were left speechless by a singer who, with every note, in every register, hit the nail right on the head. The cheers of the audience concurred.

The radio company RCA was hounding her to do some recordings for them. The company discovered that they could pick her up somewhere in Europe to make a recording, and Stuttgart was chosen as the place to do it. She arrived only a few hours before RCA's plane was due to fly back, rehearsing first with a pianist before she delivered a fantastic concert that went straight on air to delighted listeners in New York—showing how accomplished she was.

## Alone

Flagstad said goodbye to her husband in France and embarked alone on the liner to New York. Else no longer wanted to go to school in America, preferring to stay in Norway. Mother and daughter had returned to their old pattern. Flagstad was finding their attempts at closeness over the years, culminating in distressing rifts and partings, more and more painful. When McArthur asked her why her daughter was not with her, she refused to respond to the question. She lacked the ability to reveal herself emotionally and may also have been suffering from symptoms of perimenopause. She reacted by burying herself in her heavy workload.

In October, they gave thirteen concerts in various American states and Canada. For the concert audience in a crowded Granada Theatre in Santa Barbara, Grieg was sung in Norwegian, an innovation introduced that autumn. The Americans were not smug in matters of taste: they were open and liked new things. They enjoyed Norwegian songs, so she included some on the program. The audience was reluctant to leave the theater. Countless encores ensued, the lights kept flashing, and the end was announced several times over. But the audience stood their ground, and Flagstad continued singing Norwegian romances. In St. Louis, the audience, even the members who had never heard it before, thought the Norwegian language was extremely beautiful, and in Los Angeles, they had rediscovered Grieg after Flagstad's concert there.

The pressure of work continued. In November, Flagstad sang two Isoldes and three Brunhilds at the opera house in San Francisco, in addition to six concerts with piano accompaniment and one with symphony orchestra. In December, she held eleven concerts accompanied by piano before returning to the Metropolitan stage as Brunhild in *Die Walküre* and Isolde two days later. In December, at a jam-packed Carnegie Hall, she also held her usual end-of-tour concert, this time as a charity event for the women's trade union in the Ministry of Education. Eleanor Roosevelt was an honorary member there and a special guest at the concert. Kirsten Flagstad had preferred Norwegian composers that evening.

## New Season Opens at the Metropolitan

The opening night of the new season at the Metropolitan was approaching, and Flagstad again stood on the Metropolitan stage as the *Walküre* Brunhild on December 21, 1936; as Isolde on December 23; and again as the *Walküre* Brunhild on December 29. *Words and Music* magazine described a grand premiere, and there was no sign of the alleged American Depression when the Metropolitan opened its doors for a new season.

Driving slowly toward the three entrances of the historic theater, three never-ending rows of exclusive General Motors vehicles approached in perfect unison with taxis of all hues and models. Each of these carried a quota of hats, minks, sables, and silver foxes. Experienced photographers picked up the scent and soon homed in on the hats and furs that hid the best subjects. The opening night of the opera season was still America's number one show, in bad times as well as good.

The times had changed, and so had musical tastes. Previously, the exclusive audience at the Metropolitan's premiere would have been invited to a feast of Italian or French operas, but now the public came to hear Wagner's *Die Walküre*. It was reputed to be a shallow production but had become the opera house's most potent box office success. Not for thirty-six years had a German opera been selected to open the season. People arrived in their boxes long before their traditional time, at some point in the second act. They now liked Wagner so much that they were reluctant to miss even the overture. The Metropolitan audience had not displayed such cultural sophistication before the arrival of the great Flagstad.[44]

The star herself dreaded most of all the people who were desperate to meet her after the performance. This was when she felt the need to shut herself in, drink champagne, and play game after game of solitaire. After every performance, her part sang in her head, over and over again—it haunted her. She required total silence, without a soul to disturb her: only then would the singing stop and allow her to calm down.[45] She was an instrument that needed time alone to digest the reverberations of the music.

Part 2: The Voice of the Century (1935–41)          105

## Prima Donna at the Metropolitan

McArthur writes that Kirsten Flagstad had enjoyed undivided adulation and effusive ovations in the media, but in the season of 1936–37, negative comments began to appear in the tabloid press about her position within the ranks of other employees at the Met. "Prima Donna at the Metropolitan" was the headline, and the topic quickly found an echo chamber in other newspapers. Eventually, there was a lot of tittle-tattle in the corridors at the opera house, where a number of singers felt it unfair that the limelight was shining on only one singer.

Overwork, the start of menopause, and an inadequate, turbulent family life had brought Flagstad to a state of emotional imbalance. Now conflicts were also making themselves felt in her professional life. This made her oversensitive, and, feeling hurt by the reports, she reacted in a familiar pattern of rejection and withdrawal. One evening while she sat playing cards with Melchior, she characterized the epithet of *prima donna* as a somewhat false accusation. She was angry because unwelcome photographs had been taken of her with other artists, and she said that from then on, she would stand alone in her career. Above all, she did not like being photographed at railway stations alongside her colleagues.

As it happened, she and Melchior had been snapped together at a railway station that same day. Melchior, who had lived for years with headlines about Flagstad in reports of performances in which he had played her partner, felt both offended and hurt. When she met him again at the opera house in Rochester, where they were to sing *Lohengrin*, he refused to talk to her. After the end of the performance, he would not let her go out onto the stage to receive solo applause, physically restraining her so that they had to go out together.[46] She conducted herself with great professionalism, but inside she must have been furious at being denied the opportunity to stand before her public as an independent solo artist.

Else arrived just before Christmas, but she stayed for only a couple of weeks, and they can scarcely have spent any hours together. Friends of Flagstad showed Else around in New York so she was spared having to sit in the hotel suite where her mother had left her in splendid isolation. The focus from the press as well as Flagstad's shyness prevented her from behaving like other mothers. She could not meet her daughter at the quayside or see her back to the ship, go out shopping in town, or eat out at restaurants. Else must have

106 THE VOICE OF THE CENTURY

sensed her mother's frustration, loneliness, feelings of loss, and longing, from which she, too, suffered.

Flagstad's itinerary for the first month of 1937 is worth examining separately. On January 2, Flagstad sang Isolde; on the seventh, she stood onstage as Senta; on the eighth, as Sieglinde; on the eleventh, as Elsa; and on the fourteenth, as Senta again, all before traveling to New Jersey with McArthur for a concert there. After that, she went to Rochester for a concert with orchestra, before heading back to the Metropolitan for Isolde, as well as another concert accompanied by orchestra. Then came the *Siegfried* Brunhild, a concert, another *Siegfried* Brunhild, a concert, then Sieglinde, followed by Senta, Elsa, yet another *Siegfried* Brunhild, and finally a concert in Rochester with orchestra on January 31. The following months were equally chaotic.

## Intermezzo Flagstad-Morgenstierne

Whenever Flagstad sang in Washington, it was almost always at the Constitution Hall, an auditorium with thirty-seven hundred seats, including fifty-two boxes. On February 16, 1937, she held a concert there, and Morgenstierne had sent her an invitation in advance to a gathering at the legation. This time, her husband was not around, so Flagstad did as she pleased. She sent Morgenstierne a card turning down the invitation. She excused herself by saying that she would arrive in Washington just before the concert and leave immediately after it had ended.[47]

The concert in Washington included several songs by the Norwegian composers Edvard Grieg and Sverre Jordan since she was keen to make Norwegian music known in America. Morgenstierne and his party sat in a box, and it both annoyed and pained him that she had refused to fraternize with the members of the diplomatic service afterward. He may have wished for Flagstad to mirror his importance. Instead, he sent a huge bouquet of roses but did not make contact with her backstage. It was not easy to understand someone like Flagstad. Onstage, she was willing to exhibit herself totally to the public and receive their acclaim, but in private, she wanted to be secluded, on her own. This type of personality was alien to the aristocratic minister, and it provoked a more deeply lying problem within him: his narcissistic needs.

## Management of Personality Clashes

After the end of the season at the Metropolitan, Flagstad traveled to England, where she was reunited with her husband and daughter. They were to enjoy a

## Part 2: The Voice of the Century (1935–41)

few quiet days in the South of the country, where Henry had hired a car with a chauffeur as the weather was fine and the summer evenings long and balmy. Perhaps they felt some sense of being a family for a fleeting spell. McArthur relates that the strife between mother and daughter never came up as a topic of conversation. The next time they met, they were just as cheerful as ever and acted as if nothing had happened.

However, the situation surrounding Flagstad's next season had to be discussed. If McArthur is to be believed, Melchior insisted that Flagstad should not be permitted to take solo curtain calls at Covent Garden either, and this rancor between Flagstad and Melchior caused the opera house a real headache. The pair must have been quite a sight behind the stage curtain, sizing each other up with nasty looks before stepping onstage to give an impersonation of a loving couple. They did this so convincingly that the audience could have had no idea what was actually going on between them. The theater, then as now, is the site of consummate illusions.

The friction was one of the reasons that Kirsten Flagstad's impresario, Marks Levine, went to London to discuss the forthcoming season in San Francisco with her. She insisted that this would be her last appearance there since the atmosphere between her and her partner had become so poisonous. On December 12, she would celebrate her twenty-fifth anniversary as a professional singer, and she made it clear that the tenor at the Metropolitan that evening would not be named Lauritz Melchior.

By the time Levine returned to the US, he had gray hairs, which he subsequently transplanted to the heads of the management at the Metropolitan. General manager Edvard Johnson assured Flagstad that she would still be allowed to take solo applause after the final curtain. He was also forced to agree that the tenor on the night of her silver jubilee would be someone other than Melchior. Flagstad was aware of her power, as the number one moneymaker at the opera house. The manager was used to being the one who set the agenda. Now he was faced with a demanding prima donna challenging his authority. The situation would continue to escalate between them.

A naive impression prevails that when someone shows greatness in one area, then that person will be equally outstanding in all other fields. This expectation has particularly applied to artists. Winifred Wagner tells us that one of the first things her husband warned her against when she began to manage the festival was great artists who behaved like small children. Later she became expert at tackling all kinds of moods and childish reactions, including from Toscanini and Wilhelm Furtwängler.

## Wilhelm Furtwängler—the Metaphysician of Music

In the spring and early summer of 1937, London was a center for music enthusiasts. This was an important year for Great Britain: on May 12, George VI had been crowned king, with Elizabeth as his queen. The planning for the coronation year's grand opera program had already begun in the summer of 1936, when Beecham had spent a lot of time in Bayreuth negotiating with Furtwängler.

Tietjen had committed to a series of German performances, including *The Flying Dutchman*, in which Kirsten Flagstad was to sing the role of Senta, and they would also play two versions of the *Ring* cycle with two different casts, and Furtwängler was to conduct both of these. *Tristan and Isolde* was arranged with Melchior, Flagstad, and Beecham. In the first cycle, a number of stars would sing, Frida Leider, Max Lorenz, Maria Müller, and Franz Völker among them, and in the second, Kirsten Flagstad, Lauritz Melchior, Herbert Janssen, and Kerstin Thorborg would perform. Not even at Bayreuth was it possible to boast of presenting two complete *Ring* cycles with such star-studded casts.[48]

In London, Flagstad sang for the first time under the baton of Furtwängler, who would come to be her absolute favorite. Furtwängler was a pianist with ambitions to become a composer, but he had ended up as the conductor most often described in music history as a genius. He had no formal education, but eminent experts had been his teachers. His lack of institutional learning and upbringing may explain his strong individualism. He preferred to spend time outdoors and traveled to Norway to learn to ski after hearing one of Fridtjof Nansen's lectures. He was one of the few individuals in the Bavarian Alps who could do cross-country skiing.

In 1922, he became principal conductor at the Berlin Philharmonic, a position he continued to hold until 1945 and later held from 1952 until his death in 1954. Under the direction of Furtwängler, the orchestra gained international renown, including through their tours in the 1920s. Furtwängler introduced a symphonic style that still exists—he was a musician's musician who raised them up to more than they were, and in this lay his magnetism. He bound the orchestra to himself through his amazing honesty in pursuit of reaching into the vision of a work. His chief enemy was the technical routines of musicians and orchestras, which he regarded as frost and ice on the essence of the work. He wanted to bring to life the vitality and power of the work's character by honestly and ruthlessly attacking everything that was mechanical, lifeless, and extraneous. Musicians who understood this became his faithful colleagues for

Wilhelm Furtwängler. *Source: Theater Museum, Vienna.*

the rest of their lives, and he gave them a taste of the metaphysical existence of music.

The Swiss conductor and composer Rafael Kubelik says that he heard Furtwängler in Prague at the age of fourteen and the concert haunted him for the rest of his life. It influenced his entire understanding of music and made him choose to become a conductor. He claims that Furtwängler's approach to music was such that if you understood, you were lifted and reborn.[49] In other words, he emphasizes the genius of the conductor and his role as the musical mystagogue of the century.

Furtwängler believed that musicians, in the main, merely reproduced the score. His viewpoint was that it was impossible to confine oneself to a single line, when the work's distinctive character lay in the vision of its accentuation. One had to continually return to the style of the work itself. There could only be one interpretation, which one could merely hope to attain.[50] Such an understanding led to what some musicians considered to be endless rehearsals, but Flagstad herself was pedantic and loved his style. Furtwängler strove to conjure the spirit of the work out of the bottle. His belief that it had an independent life beyond the score aligns with Plato's world of ideas and Jung's archetypes.

## Furtwängler and Flagstad

The meeting between Furtwängler and Flagstad was a fusion of musical geniuses with perfect pitch. Soloist and conductor melded together in a common understanding based on their mutual immediate and intuitive comprehension of the music. This meant that with the greatest assurance, they could join all the notes together, from first to last, and thus draw up a uniform line. All the details they performed were accomplished against the background of an understanding of the whole as well as of each individual line. Quite simply, they made themselves into a medium for the composition, into an instrument through which the work's vision could shine. Their *Ring* cycles of 1937 in London and 1950 in Milan bear witness to the validity of their claim.

In London in 1937, the reviewers highlighted Flagstad's Brunhild, Rudolf Bockelmann's Wotan, and Furtwängler's conducting. Flagstad's Brunhild had the nobility of a divine being, according to the *Morning Post*. The *Daily Telegraph* compared Flagstad's and Leider's interpretations of the character, with the critics saying that Leider's Brunhild was intense and intellectual, whereas Flagstad's was the noble child of nature, in all probability more instinctively like Brunhild.[51]

Flagstad's Isolde had become a real sensation in London. There were in all likelihood other singers who sang this part with distinction, but Kirsten Flagstad was the most outstanding of them all. The critics strongly doubted whether Wagner's music had ever been sung by a voice that combined such ideal beauty and power. She did not appear to exert herself in the slightest but all the same dominated the fantastic sound that poured out far and wide.[52]

It was written that Furtwängler was in awe-inspiring form for *Die Walküre*. He succeeded in eliciting an effect of unlimited volume from the orchestra, without ever drowning out the singers. His synchronization of voices and orchestra, a difficult feat at Covent Garden, was so perfect that no phrase was indistinct and no syllable was lost. Several critics began to feel sympathy for the German assertion that Furtwängler was the greatest conductor of the times. He gathered the whole orchestra into his arms and made them play, as it was said, better than their capabilities.[53]

A summary compiled by the *Observer* of that coronation year at Covent Garden stated that as far as personalities were concerned, there were many to

Part 2: The Voice of the Century (1935–41)          111

choose from. However, the cream of the crop in terms of power and personality was most certainly Kirsten Flagstad. She had not been there long enough to become legendary, but all the same, she had gained such great fame at this first London season that from then on, the opera house would be sold out on her name alone.

## Music and Politics

The genius of Flagstad and Furtwängler was confined to music. In a number of other areas of life, they were perhaps below average, particularly with respect to people, society, and politics. Hitler had offered to send a complete Bayreuth *Lohengrin* to London as a gift in connection with the coronation celebrations, but this was rejected as a matter of principle by the government. Of course, this was a political decision. The international political climate and the advance of Hitler's Germany had begun to make their mark on the musical world.

Furtwängler's relationship with the Third Reich began in 1932, when he resigned from his position as the artistic director at Bayreuth because Hitler had started to take an interest in the festival. When Hitler came to power the following year, Furtwängler was on tour with the Berlin Philharmonic. When they returned, pressure was put on him. The Nazi Party wanted all Jewish musicians out of the orchestra. When the German Jewish conductor Bruno Walter returned from abroad, he was immediately ordered to cancel his concert with the Leipzig Gewandhaus Orchestra, which he led. When Walter turned up for rehearsals, the door was shut. Later he traveled to Berlin to conduct a concert there, but Joseph Goebbels, Hitler's minister of propaganda and communication, informed him that the concert hall would be wrecked if he attempted to go ahead. Walter left Germany and subsequently moved to America, where he continued as a conductor, including for Kirsten Flagstad.

Furtwängler was upset by this treatment of his Jewish colleagues and wrote a letter of protest to Goebbels. In reply, a decree was issued that Furtwängler should not be mentioned in any newspapers.[54] Goebbels also confiscated his passport to prevent him from leaving and becoming a propagandist against the state. Furtwängler fled to the mountains but eventually returned, and in 1935, he negotiated an agreement with Goebbels in which Furtwängler would continue in his post on the condition of remaining neutral, avoiding political involvement, and refusing to perform in occupied countries. After further discussion with Alfred Rosenberg and Hitler, his post as conductor

Wilhelm Furtwängler with his orchestra. *Source: Theater Museum, Vienna.*

was restored, and he also became principal conductor at Bayreuth. Since he led the Third Reich's preeminent orchestra, he also committed himself to conduct a series of Nazi events.

This was almost certainly where his judgment seriously let him down in that he believed it was possible to distinguish the regime's politics from its practice in music. The Berlin Philharmonic was renamed the Reich Orchestra, a decision in which Furtwängler had been included. The change would allow the orchestra to survive, but at the same time, it became a propaganda outlet for the Third Reich. The Faustian agreement, the pact with the devil, meant that the musicians avoided having to serve as soldiers in the war, but they lost their moral and political freedom. Furtwängler felt the full force of this when he continued to present works by Jewish composers such as Mendelssohn and by Hindemith, whose wife was partly of Jewish ancestry.

In 1936, a window opened for Furtwängler to leave Germany. On the recommendation of Toscanini, he was offered the position of principal conductor

## Part 2: The Voice of the Century (1935–41) 113

at the New York Philharmonic. However, this led to protests since his appointment came at the same time as Hitler reoccupied the Rhineland. This was Hitler's reaction against the Treaty of Versailles. While the campaigns against him were at their loudest, Furtwängler telegraphed the management with the following message: "I detest political controversy. I am not a politician, but a representative of German music, which belongs to the whole of humanity. Postpone inviting me until people realize that music and politics have nothing in common."[55]

This statement may be regarded as a reaction based on wounded pride, but at the same time, it reveals his naive opinion that music and other cultural life can be separated from politics. Both Furtwängler and Flagstad lived predominantly in the world of music, and their surroundings paid homage to them precisely because of their musical achievements. The question is whether their view that music is something separate also betrays a remoteness and disengagement from this external reality. Each in their own way would painfully come to experience politics becoming forcefully mixed up with the development of their professional careers. In 1937, Flagstad still had no idea that her work would become politicized. Musicians in Norway also believed that their domain could exist in isolation, even after the occupation had become a fact. Then as now, this is not correct. Politics makes a power grab on cultural life through its financial management and manipulates it to serve the slogans of the times. Music cannot be elevated above and detached from this reality unless music goes underground. In 1937, musical life in America and Europe still operated mainly as a democratic, free form of culture. Germany, where the entirety of cultural life had to adapt to the Hitler regime, was an exception, but other countries would follow.

The controversy around Furtwängler's method of relating to the Nazi regime has often been polarized between apologists and the anti-Furtwängler camp. His colleague and friend of many years Jascha Horenstein has given a more nuanced comment. He emphasizes that Furtwängler was certainly not a Nazi. He had frequently witnessed Furtwängler's outbursts and arguments with the regime. Furtwängler rescued and fought for many Jewish musicians and composers, but at the same time, he was an elitist. His rebellion applied to the great and famous. Horenstein acknowledges Furtwängler as a prominent musician and conductor but defines him also as a naive, weak man.[56] Maybe Furtwängler could not bear the personal cost of a total break from Nazi Germany. In any case, he was exonerated at a denazification postwar trial, at

114 THE VOICE OF THE CENTURY

which Jewish and so-called degenerate music colleagues spoke on his behalf. He continued to work with Flagstad until 1952, two years before his death.

## Else Leaves

Flagstad traveled home from London for a summer holiday. Until then, she had avoided appearing in Norway during the summer, when she was on vacation. A written invitation came to her in London from the Oslo Journalists' Club, asking if she could hold a major outdoor concert in the Norwegian capital. Since the letter was signed by a large number of journalists, in the end she accepted. "If you're going to sing at the skating rink in Frogner, I think I'm going to die laughing," Else said in reaction. Now seventeen, she was at an age when we all feel embarrassed at our mothers making an exhibition of themselves.

Late in the afternoon of July 8, 1937, the movement of people to Frogner Stadium began in earnest, and all the adjacent streets were mobbed. The flood of patrons was so great that all the seats were quickly sold out. A total of around twelve thousand people attended the concert.[57] Maja Flagstad and singing coach Ellen Schytte-Jacobsen sat side by side. King Haakon and Queen Maud arrived with their English guests. All of Oslo was present: from the diplomatic corps, members of the government, council officials, and representatives of the world of art and literature to ordinary citizens.

The Norwegian populace was unprepared for the beauty of the voice they were about to hear. A lady present thought there was something quite magical, that a single voice was able to carry across the whole stadium and hover in the air so that all twelve thousand listeners could hear the words and melodies. After countless ecstatic ovations, flowers, and congratulations from the royal family and the national government, Flagstad slipped out through the back door for the twentieth time. From there, she was given a royal escort of mounted police all the way to the Grand Hotel. She and her brother Ole sat in an open car, and people cheered them as if it were a coronation parade.[58]

After the concert, Flagstad was called to the palace, and King Haakon bestowed on her the decoration Knight First Class of the Order of St. Olav for her meritorious work as a musical artist. She was now acclaimed by the whole world and her own nation, though little did she suspect that all this would soon change.

Nor was she prepared for her daughter's strong reaction. A great deal of fuss had surrounded Kirsten overseas, but until now Norway had been free of such ballyhoo. Now the peace and quiet was at an end here too. American

Part 2: The Voice of the Century (1935–41)

tourist coaches paid visits to their home at Tidemands gate, and people came in past the entrance to catch a glimpse of her mother. Else had had enough: the performance at the skating rink was the final straw. She packed her belongings and tore everything down from the walls. In anger and frustration at being overlooked, she wanted to remove every memory of herself from Tidemands gate. The industrialist's children had had a completely different childhood from hers. She did not feel at home with the sudden change to well-to-do bourgeois life, her mother had become too unconventional with her global fame, and Johansen was too unconventional with all his money.

She was not interested in music, so it had not been wise of her mother and grandmother to send Else to Flagstad's old singing teacher, creating expectations of her in that way. How could she distinguish herself in singing when she had such a mother to be compared with? Perhaps it was a healthy, but painful, teenage rebellion that was taking place. Else wanted to be seen for what she was, and so she moved from her mother to her father.

On July 14, 1937, Kristin Flagstad wrote in her diary, "Else's gone away!"

## Naked, Storm-Tossed Professionalism

The move led naturally enough to a great deal of soul-searching by Flagstad, about her years of inadequate mothering. As an artist, she had always been obsessed with her work, and there had not been much space left for her daughter. Her own upbringing had also been like that, as Maja had put music first. The estrangement triggered two things in her: depression and a growing resolution to scale down her artistic activity. When she returned alone to the US for a new season, she lacked enthusiasm and any inclination to work. "She entered into a naked, storm-tossed professionalism, but still sang like a god to fulfill her commitments," McArthur writes.

On Christmas Eve, 1938, Kirsten Flagstad sang for radio listeners in the US. She took over a ceremonial American festive ritual that had been Ernestine Schumann-Heink's domain. Schumann-Heink, known as "Mother America," had a great alto voice. She was also called the last titan of the vocal arts. NBC had never asked any other singer to perform this glorious task, but in the last minutes of Christmas Eve, passing through midnight into Christmas morning, they presented Kirsten Flagstad, who sang "Silent Night, Holy Night" and gave a Christmas greeting.

After the recording, she drove back to the Dorset Hotel with McArthur. Safely back in her room, she flung open the balcony doors and cried out into the night, "Where is my daughter? Where is my daughter?"

## Symbiotic Entanglement

Her daughter's resolute rejection had triggered Flagstad's anxiety, and her own separation trauma rose to the surface. Such patterns are created over generations. Her mother's own mother had lost three girls before Maja was born, and it seems highly probable that she did not dare to bond with her fourth daughter, out of fear that she might die too. At any rate, fear must have disturbed the symbiotic phase between them. Maja did not enjoy a symbiotic period with her own babies either; shortly after giving birth, she rushed back to work and was rarely at home.

This lack created an underlying insecurity in Flagstad, for which she compensated through a rigid personality, a pedantic sense of order, and an immediate response to every duty. Now these defenses began to crumble. Her inner self, which she had kept hidden, could no longer be subdued. At the same time, she was quite helpless in her close relationships, of which she understood little. The absence of an early attachment can be traced through her lifelong inability to reach out to others. She rarely asked for help and did not talk about herself. She did not like to listen to other people's problems, and she found physical and emotional closeness uncomfortable.

These symbiotic traumas can lead to what is called symbiotic entanglement, types of relationship where neither party receives the love, solicitude, closeness, and support they need. Even so, they cannot manage to separate, despite all the conflict that ensues. Such an entanglement leads to a continual battle within any relationship and relationship system. For Kirsten Flagstad and her daughter, this was the case from the very beginning. When they tried to get close to each other, it ended in painful rejections and splits. They were propelled toward each other by fear of loneliness and isolation, but the daughter still rejected the mother when intimacy became a possibility. It was too threatening and too demanding.

## New Flagstad-Morgenstierne Altercation

The loss of her daughter caused Flagstad to miss her family and her own mother. This resulted in Maja and her sister, Karen-Marie, being asked if they would come to visit Flagstad in America. Karen-Marie had been there several times already, but for Maja the country was virgin territory. When the ship for America, the *Stavangerfjord*, berthed at the quay in New York with her on board, many people thought a celebrity had arrived since

## Part 2: The Voice of the Century (1935–41)

such a large crowd of journalists had gathered. They had all come to meet Maja Flagstad.

McArthur describes Maja as a fantastic lady who epitomized everything he associated with being Norwegian. She was stout, direct, very self-centered, and extremely stubborn. She was also an exceptional pianist. Her daughter's fame had nourished her pride and ambitions, and she possessed not an iota of shyness. She would have gladly turned up in Times Square to shake hands with everyone, and her daughter's reticence was a constant torment to her.

Nevertheless, she managed occasionally to take her famous daughter out on the social scene. Maja played while her daughters sang duets. The Flagstad trio performed in several locations, and they were also broadcast on national radio. These occasions led to spontaneous advances being made to Flagstad, something that really provoked her. Oley Speaks, one of America's best composers, was sitting in one of the salons when, out of the blue, Flagstad sang one of his songs. This had the immediate effect of him jumping up to embrace and kiss her. On one occasion in San Francisco, the conductor Fritz Reiner impulsively hugged her and gave her a kiss on the cheek. She thought this so outrageous that she took it up with McArthur afterward.

Flagstad disliked all kinds of intimacy and could not stand being kissed on the cheek. When anyone did so, she stiffened and blushed. However, at the same time, she was far too shy to reject anyone point-blank or speak up to anybody who overstepped her boundaries. McArthur had long experience of preventing such incidents. Flagstad had insisted to him that no one should meet them at railway stations when they arrived in a new town—not even the press, as far as it was possible to forestall them. To protect her personal life, she was always served food in her own private railway carriage: she never ventured into the restaurant car. It was McArthur's task to guard her dressing room from all intrusions. She was undeviating in her principles, and even the Metropolitan's own manager was turned away from Flagstad's door.

This would come to a head. Maja and Karen-Marie were with her in Washington, where they attended her concert in Constitution Hall on March 21, 1938. Thousands of people had turned up despite the dreadful weather. Flagstad was struggling with a head cold and had contemplated canceling the concert, something that almost never happened in the course of her long career. She was out of sorts and had an intense desire to avoid Morgenstierne. As a result, the manager had been given strict instructions that no one, absolutely no one, should be allowed to come backstage to see her, whether

Visit by mother and sister in Flagstad's dressing room at the Metropolitan, 1938. *Source: Flagstad Museum.*

before the concert, at the intermission, or afterward. Her sister was charged with keeping guard outside her dressing room.

The concert had a Norwegian flavor since half of it comprised romances by Grieg, sung in their original language. The audience and critics were pleased. Their ears were filled with a sound that lifted their souls. Maja was the only one who was dissatisfied. She was unhappy about the shield her daughter had erected around herself, as she was keen to be introduced to all the important guests. Morgenstierne had sent Flagstad one hundred red roses and expressed

Part 2: The Voice of the Century (1935–41)                119

a wish to meet her in her quarters at the intermission. McArthur realized this would cause a major flare-up on several fronts, and so he had quite simply fled from Constitution Hall.

Flagstad was furious when she heard that Morgenstierne planned to visit her backstage. Maja tried again to persuade her, but her daughter would not budge. Morgenstierne would not be permitted to enter: she depended on being able to rest and certainly did not want to speak to anyone. It was her sister who had to bear the brunt. Karen-Marie relates that Morgenstierne reacted with wounded rage when she turned him away from Flagstad's door. Maja was alarmed by Kirsten's refusal to allow all these kind, adoring people to pay her a visit. The idea that the minister himself had been rebuffed was too much for her, and she scurried back to her seat in the hall.

When Flagstad returned to her hotel later that evening, Morgenstierne called her. McArthur, who had come back, was told to answer on her behalf. In broadly diplomatic phrases, he apologized that the minister had been unable to meet Flagstad and promised to convey Morgenstierne's congratulations on the brilliant concert.

## Who Will Come Out on Top?

This rejection would be avenged. In 1938–39, Morgenstierne had his hands full with planning for the visit to America by Crown Prince Olav and Crown Princess Märtha. The legation functioned as the center of administration for the event, and Morgenstierne was at the forefront of the smooth running of the seventy-day-long journey.

The royal couple arrived in New York on the newly built ocean liner *Oslofjord* on April 27, 1939, and their reception was overwhelming. Many thousands of individuals lined the street and cheered the cortege of cars as they passed. As many as twelve thousand police officers, on foot and on motorcycles, provided security and safe passage while heaps of confetti were tossed from skyscraper windows. The next day, the royal couple visited President Franklin D. Roosevelt and his wife, Eleanor, in their home, Springwood in Hyde Park, where they discussed Hitler's recent speeches and the situation in Europe.

In New York, the World's Fair opened on April 30. The Norwegian Pavilion, for which Morgenstierne had responsibility, portrayed famous Norwegians in America. Kirsten Flagstad, the most famous Norwegian in America at the time, was left out. She was not mentioned at all. That same evening, Morgenstierne was in charge of a grand gala at the Metropolitan to welcome the royal guests. The opera house was mobbed with Norwegian Americans, and Morgenstierne delivered an opening speech.[59] He did not invite Kirsten Flagstad to sing on the occasion. She was the world's foremost vocal artist, the leading singer at the Metropolitan, and the most celebrated Norwegian in America at that time, an obvious choice for such an event.

She triumphantly sang the *Walküre* Brunhild at the Metropolitan on May 8, 1939, and gave the last Isolde of the season there on May 23. She left the US at the end of the month to take part in the June festival in Zurich before traveling home to Norway. Like Morgenstierne, Flagstad had a servile attitude to the Norwegian royal family, and she would never have turned down the opportunity to sing on such an occasion, especially not when she was in the country at the time.

Morgenstierne proposed that a medal be inaugurated for "service abroad to the Norwegian identity and the promotion of solidarity between Norwegian emigrants and their homeland." He thought "the Leif Erikson Medal" would be a fitting name for it, symbolizing the Norwegian urge to travel from the very earliest times.[60] He was given approval for his idea but not for the name. On March 17, 1939, King Haakon instituted the St. Olav's Medal, intended as a reward for spreading knowledge of Norway and furthering the link between those who had left Norway and their home country. One of the first he placed on the list to receive the medal was Kirsten Flagstad. It was therefore with ill-concealed pride that she told her American biographer of her relationship with King Haakon, who called her "his" cultural ambassador to America.[61] This may well have been a disappointment for Morgenstierne. All the same, it was seen to that Flagstad received the honor not at the Norwegian Legation in Washington but from the consul general at the Royal Norwegian Consulate General in New York. Fru Flagstad had asked him to convey her most sincere thanks to His Majesty the King for the decoration.[62]

Flagstad met King Haakon for the last time in 1939, when she was home on summer vacation and had an audience at the palace to express her thanks. She gave a few concerts in Oslo that summer. On August 28, she sang in the National Theatre to benefit the Artists' Association Pension Fund. King Haakon, Crown Prince Olav, and Crown Princess Märtha were all present. Relations between Flagstad and the Norwegian royal family were perfectly harmonious, and the family members were still numbered among her admirers.

## A Maestro Breathes His Last

Flagstad returned to the US in October 1939, first of all for the opera season in San Francisco. That autumn presented a formidable schedule in which she

## Part 2: The Voice of the Century (1935–41)     121

would sing a total of five Isoldes, three *Walküre* Brunhilds, two Sieglindes, one Elisabeth, one Elsa, and one Leonore. In addition, she had two recordings and seven concerts. The customary grand concert at Carnegie Hall took place on December 5. She had little pause for breath as the Metropolitan opened as early as December 7 with *Parsifal*, in which Flagstad sang the role of Kundry. Before she could take time off on New Year's Eve 1939, she was to give another four concerts and sing two Sentas, two Isoldes, one *Walküre* Brunhild, and one Elisabeth.

Bodanzky's poor health was a fly in the ointment that autumn. On Thanksgiving Day, November 23, McArthur brought Flagstad the sad news that her maestro had died. Bodanzky was one of the few people for whom Flagstad showed real affection. He had fostered her development of the great Wagner roles, and together they had brought the Wagner repertoire to new heights at the Metropolitan. On a personal level, they had entertained mutual respect and admiration. He had also been like a father to her, and so his death came as a shock.[63]

In April 1938, Bodanzky wrote an article in the *Etude* music magazine about the Metropolitan's great financial success with Wagner in the previous three years. Wagner had come to be regarded as difficult and meant only for the elite, and audience numbers had dropped as a result before Flagstad came to the Metropolitan. Wagner had not changed, so the transformation must lie in accessibility to the audience, but how could this be explained?

Bodanzky felt that the answer lay in the Metropolitan's new soprano, Kirsten Flagstad. It was her fantastic voice, with its dramatic, authoritative expertise and sincerity, that had created fresh interest in Wagner. People flocked to hear Flagstad, and since she sang Wagner, they heard his music at the same time. Being spellbound by her voice led to them also being spellbound by Wagner, a change in the audience's earlier apprehension of the composer as difficult and elitist. They began to attend even when Flagstad was not singing. Bodanzky wished that other composers would also experience such a renaissance with the public. A second Caruso would accomplish the same thing for Italian opera. Kirsten Flagstad was the best possible example of how an interpreter could change the public's perception of a composer, Bodanzky claimed.[64]

With iron discipline, Flagstad made her appearance on the opera stage in Chicago as Isolde the day after his death. A flood of memories may have carried her through that evening, but she did not speak of it. In his article about the passion for Wagner in America, Bodanzky had omitted mention of his own significance. There is a widespread view that the golden age of Wagner's operas at the Metropolitan came to an end with the death of maestro Bodanzky.

## Clash of Conductors at the Metropolitan

For the Metropolitan, the death of their principal conductor only a week before the start of the season caused a crisis. Bodanzky's successor to the Wagner repertoire was the young Austrian conductor Erich Leinsdorf, who had been Bodanzky's assistant. He had also been Toscanini's assistant in Salzburg and was appointed on his recommendation. In any case, it had been the intention for him to take over after a few years' apprenticeship. Flagstad and a few other senior Wagner interpreters found it difficult to accept his authority. This went so far that both Flagstad and Melchior declined to sign their contracts. They had received an offer from the opera house in Chicago, and anyway, they planned to sing in Europe for most of the following season. In their experience, Leinsdorf was often unsure of the tempo and so forced the singers to hold high notes excessively long.[65]

These two giants protested publicly about the opera house's choice and requested a more mature conductor. Flagstad was quoted as saying that she refused to sing if he was not removed. Leinsdorf's unconventional conducting made her ill. The level of conflict between the singers and opera director Johnson, who would not depose Leinsdorf, emerges forcefully in his statement to the press that their hostility to the young conductor arose from jealousy, adding that Melchior was "an old ship." The same evening that his words were made public, *Götterdämmerung* was performed, with heightened nervous intensity.[66]

Leinsdorf had made his debut as early as January 21, 1938, as conductor of *Die Walküre*. His first night was forced by the fact that Bodanzky was overloaded with other commitments. At that time, the music critic Lawrence Gilman expressed sympathy for the twenty-five-year-old, slightly built conductor who was to wield the baton in Wagner's major opera with the best singers in the world before a discriminating audience. At the same time, there were highly trained critics checking his tempi and comparing him to Bodanzky. His nervousness showed in his repeatedly having to wipe perspiration from his baton. Gilman praised his considerable talent but simultaneously pointed out that his timings were sometimes so rushed that the singers were not given enough time for their phrases and breathing. Leinsdorf was young and had plenty of time for further development, Gilman concluded.

## Part 2: The Voice of the Century (1935–41)

Disagreements between Toscanini and Furtwängler on rhythm and tempi were expressed on several occasions. Purely cultural differences could also have played a part: it is not only practical reasons that underpin the decision by major opera houses to run two departments, one for the German and another for the Italian repertoire. A weighty argument in this dispute, in any case, is that Wagner was strongly embedded in German culture. It may be that Leinsdorf was struggling to find his own understanding of rhythm and timing because his training dragged him in both directions. All the same, Flagstad used her power to force McArthur onto the conductor's podium at the Metropolitan.

All of this created great tension in Flagstad's relationship with Johnson, who felt that she had stepped beyond her sphere of authority. Flagstad and her husband, Johansen, had set out to promote McArthur for a conducting career, also at the Metropolitan, but the management did not want him. Johnson's later opposition to taking Flagstad back was not only related to the war but also based on the bitter dispute about the conductorship that had arisen at the opera house in 1939–40.[67]

### Another Flagstad-Morgenstierne Drama Behind the Scenes

Bodanzky's death may have made Flagstad more insecure and withdrawn. McArthur was her right-hand man but also had status as the Flagstad-Johansen couple's adoptive son. The sense of paternal security once provided in her life by Bodanzky now rested solely with her husband, who was in Norway. The stage served as a safe place of refuge, and she still could not understand why anyone would insist on meeting her as a private citizen, offstage. Morgenstierne, despite her earlier rejections, had not given up hope.

The next time he and Flagstad met was at a concert in Washington, DC, on February 14, 1940. McArthur was conducting the National Symphony. She had curbed her instincts and reluctantly invited Morgenstierne to join her backstage at the intermission. She probably should not have done so, because the meeting would be a total fiasco. It had not escaped Flagstad's attention that Morgenstierne had hired the Metropolitan for concerts to welcome the crown prince and princess without inviting her to participate. Emotional dynamite lay beneath the surface on both sides when they met. McArthur recalls that Morgenstierne strode in with three or four other men, and the first thing they did when they entered the room was to light up cigarettes, a real faux pas in a singer's dressing room. This also made Flagstad flare up. She hated smoke, which was incompatible with her sensitive airways. McArthur quickly perceived the explosive situation and asked the men to stub out their cigarettes. The rebuke triggered a strong reaction in Morgenstierne, who immediately left the room. He may have felt rejected and insulted—certainly Flagstad felt violated and disrespected.

Why did he not keep his distance? From what we know of Morgenstierne's earlier experiences of Flagstad's rejections, his continual approaches appear almost self-destructive. Afterward, Flagstad came to hear that Morgenstierne thought her brusque. Why did he call on her? What did he really want? She had no intention of giving the Norwegian minister any kind of proprietary rights over her. McArthur writes that Flagstad, in her simple and terribly stubborn fashion, saw herself as the center of the universe, with the right to dismiss anyone she chose. She hated anybody trying to bask in her glory, an aversion undoubtedly fostered in her upbringing through her relationship with her narcissistic mother.

As an artist, Flagstad depended on concentrating fully on the demands made by the music, and her long career had only intensified this need. When she had to sing another act in an opera just after an intermission at a concert, it defies credulity that Morgenstierne and other dignitaries lit their cigarettes and felt they had the right to engage her in distracting small talk. We see here the deep contrast between two perfectionists, one a diplomat and the other an artist. It is no wonder that the relationship between Flagstad and Morgenstierne would later plunge into an abyss of hostility and suspicion.

## Norway Occupied and Vidkun Quisling Stages Coup d'État

Kirsten Flagstad's original plan had been to end all her engagements in America after the 1940 season. In 1939, Else had come back to her: it was said that Johansen had intervened to get their relationship back on the rails again. The daughter was now living with her mother once more. They went through a short period of reconciliation, but the closeness also created emotional stress. The intention was that they should move back to Norway together, but this was not how things would turn out.

Else stayed in Montana for a few months that summer while her mother was singing in Europe. Here she fell in love with an American boy, Arthur Dusenberry. One morning, McArthur received a message to come to Flagstad's hotel at once. He feared that something tragic had happened in Norway and rushed there. When he entered, she showed him a telegram that said, "Mum, I want to marry Arthur—you have to say yes!"

## Part 2: The Voice of the Century (1935–41)    125

At first, Flagstad did not like the idea, but she realized there was no point in protesting. In any case, Else would have to arrange her wedding day around her mother's itinerary. As usual, Flagstad was engrossed in work, and her main concern was for Else to manage to find a time to get married that would suit her mother.

In the spring of 1940, Flagstad had packed everything she owned and was ready to go home. She had a ticket on the *Bergensfjord*, which would sail from New York on April 20, heading for Norway. Because of the tense situation in Europe, several people had warned her against traveling home. However, Flagstad demonstrated her usual obstinacy and could not be swayed. She had had plans to travel as early as 1939, after Else had returned to her, but she had allowed herself to be persuaded to sign a contract with the Metropolitan for a further three and a half months, for the 1939–40 season. This was not particularly wise, taking the uneasy situation in Europe into account, but Flagstad lived in her own little bubble and did not follow what was going on in the outside world.

According to the schedule she ended up with that season, from December to July rather than only until April, she sang on average every other day and gave one hundred performances, with many days on the move in between. Flagstad said the management had made so much fuss. Flagstad was a moneymaking machine for the Metropolitan, and the management of the time required $1 million to buy back the opera house from shareholders and beneficiaries. Flagstad was used as a financial draw. She also made an appeal to radio listeners to attend the opera more often.

On the evening of April 8, she found herself on a train from New York to Cleveland. The Metropolitan company was to give a performance of *Tannhäuser* there. Melchior, sitting by her side, let her know that the Germans might occupy Norway and Denmark at any time. She was taken aback at this, as she had really not considered such a possibility. The next morning, Melchior knocked on her carriage door to tell her that Norway and Denmark had been invaded by German troops.

All shipping between America and Norway ceased. The *Bergensfjord* remained in dock, and Flagstad did not return home. She also had no idea that Quisling had effected a coup d'état in a radio broadcast on April 9, 1940. He saw his chance to seize power after the king and national government had fled from the capital. In his speech, Quisling declared himself Norway's new prime minister. He welcomed the Nazis and claimed that further opposition to them was useless. The rest of the world believed for a long time that it had been the occupying forces that had installed Quisling, but this was not the case. He had appointed himself, and the NS was now the only legal political party in the land. The armed struggle lasted only a few weeks in the South of Norway, and on June 7, 1940, the king and government ministers escaped to England to continue the fight for a free Norway from there. The surrender treaty between the German and Norwegian high commands was signed as early as June 10, 1940.

## Flagstad Reacts by Immersing Herself in Work

Flagstad was fairly disorientated by what was happening in Norway. On April 14, she received a brief telegram from her husband to tell her that she should stay where she was and that at home all was well. In the course of that month, she received two more telegrams. He wrote that she must not believe everything she read in the newspapers and that everyone was fine.

Flagstad was afraid that everyone in Norway would be deprived of all their possessions. For the first time in her life, she had begun to read American newspapers: they were speculating about all sorts of things. Her instinctive reaction was that she should continue to work and earn money so that the others would be able to cope. After thinking things over for a while, she asked her impresario to arrange a tour around all the American states that summer. This was a common pattern with her: heightened tension drove her to take on more work. A busy schedule was organized for the summer of 1940 through North and South Dakota as well as Minnesota, where many Norwegian Americans had settled. She had made up her mind that the program would consist only of Norwegian works. She also agreed to sing at the Metropolitan for yet another season, until April 17, 1941, and this was confirmed by contract.

On the music front, however, things were happening that took her by surprise. German music had come into disrepute among Scandinavians living in America, and performers risked being caught in the crosscurrent. For the first time in her life, Flagstad received threatening and insulting letters because she sang in the language of the enemy.

McArthur writes that at the same time as these letters arrived, the organizers demanded that the program should be German. This was the repertoire for which Flagstad was famous and which brought the most money into the coffers. This cross fire caused her to feel extremely ill at ease, a feeling that never left her afterward. McArthur and his wife, Blanche, observed her agonies, but they never succeeded in breaking through Flagstad's stoic reticence. She

Part 2: The Voice of the Century (1935–41)          127

still remained a withdrawn person and for that reason also someone who was difficult to comfort and help. She enclosed herself in anxiety and insomnia, preoccupied with painful thoughts but unable to talk about them. McArthur writes that she simply did not understand the political implications brought by war. Flagstad could not grasp the differences between monarchy, democracy, fascism, and communism. Her only standpoint was that Norway should not have been attacked.[68]

## Language of the Enemy

The perception of the German language as the language of the enemy was not new in America. It is said that when Ernestine Schumann-Heink was about to introduce a Swiss choir on board a transatlantic liner just after World War I, she said to the audience, "You're now about to hear a few songs, and the language they sing sounds like German, but it is not. Please, don't shoot them."[69]

An almost supernatural belief existed among nationalists that performing and listening to German music in wartime would make it more difficult to defeat Germany. German-language lieder and operas evoked strong negative emotions, and in this, vocalists were especially vulnerable. In the 1917–19 season, Wagner was removed from the Metropolitan's roster. Gatti-Casazza described the cancellation as his greatest challenge, but he had to submit to the board's decision. In 1919, *Parsifal* was again presented at the Metropolitan, but in an English version. This was also repeated in 1920. Not until the 1920–21 season were *Lohengrin* and *Die Walküre* welcomed back to the Chicago Opera, and only in an English-language rendition. The following year, Wagner was performed in German for the first time since the end of the war.[70]

When Schumann-Heink gave her first concert in New Jersey after World War I, she included Brahms in the program, bravely announcing to the four thousand spectators that the war was over and the time had come to sing German songs again. If there was anyone in the audience who did not wish to hear these, they could leave the auditorium. Quickly and without any kind of disruption, two hundred people left the building.[71] Richard Strauss's successful tour of America in 1921–22 signaled that the relationship with German music was on the verge of being normalized again. Otto Kahn stated that the genius of Strauss had brought joy and inspiration to millions of Americans. The *Musical Courier* noted that a Strauss lied did not come loaded with dynamite and that there was also no obvious connection between Wagner's operas and the navy. The Americans declared peace and tolerance toward compositions from German-speaking territories as well as toward German and Austrian musicians.[72] If Flagstad had been aware of the complexity she now faced as a singer, she could perhaps have copied Schumann-Heink's clarifying method and given the audience a choice.

The Americans' turbulent relationship with the German language was related not simply to war but also to internal rivalry. In metropolises such as New York and Chicago, a German cultural elite had established their power through money, language, and music. In 1910, New York closely followed Berlin as the city with the densest population of citizens of German ancestry. In 1917, German-speaking residents in America were the largest group of immigrants, a total of 2.5 million people.[73] In 1919, 90 percent of the musicians in the New York Philharmonic were Germans and Austrians. They had established themselves long before this as the best instrument makers and had countless music teachers in the country. It is estimated that as many as five thousand Americans had studied music in German-speaking countries between 1850 and 1900. The *New York Times* reported that American families had paid $14 million per year, mainly to Germany and Austria, for various forms of music tuition.[74]

In the middle of the nineteenth century, American musical life had a German character, and Germans occupied an outstanding position in that life. The greatest number of the most significant composers of all time had been nurtured in a German-speaking world, and classical music had had its origin and golden age in central Europe. Conductors and musicians were still German speaking to a large extent, and it followed that German was the language used at every orchestra rehearsal. With few exceptions, all the key figures in classical music had come from a German-speaking background.[75] The collective picture created a sense of being faced with a cultural behemoth and perhaps also of being exploited by it. European culture did not need America, only its dollars.

The public associated composers with their national identities. Flagstad therefore sang a purely Norwegian program for Norwegian Americans. She chose not to sing Beethoven or Brahms, now associated with the enemy, despite the impossibility of linking the composers' lives and works with Nazism. Instead, Flagstad chose songs by contemporary Norwegian composers, such as Christian Sinding and David Monrad-Johansen, without realizing that these in a different way would come to be regarded as flunkies of the Nazi occupiers in Norway. The Norwegian American public was as unwitting as

Flagstad and clapped enthusiastically because they were hearing Norwegian music.

## Singing for Norway

Just after the fall of Norway on April 9, 1940, the *Chicago Daily News* and another thirty or so major American newspapers published an article by the well-known American journalist Leland Stowe, an astounding story about circumstances in Oslo on April 9 that would become widely known. Stowe depicted the situation in a way that threatened the reputation of Norway in America. He wrote that the Norwegian capital had been easy to capture. The Nazis had only to come marching in with a brass band. The country's navy was abandoned in the harbor, the artillery in the forts was silent, and the invading fleet glided into the capital's docks without a single mine exploding.

The fact is that the Norwegian Armed Forces had been severely wound down and were poorly prepared for war: the mobilization of troops had failed to occur. However, Stowe's article was unjust to the Norwegian civilian population and those parts of the country's defense forces that fought valiantly in the valleys against a far superior military power. The person who had to work hardest to restore this view of Norway was Morgenstierne, who answered Stowe in all the newspapers and established a comprehensive information campaign.

Morgenstierne was standing in the midst of this storm when he met Flagstad again. She had agreed to sing at a charity concert for the Norwegian Hospital in Brooklyn on April 16, 1940; the concert took place at the Academy of Music. It was a novelty for Flagstad to have to revise her program in the light of political events. At the same time, the aim was to bring in money, and German composers still earned more at the box office than Scandinavian music that was relatively unknown in America. In advance of this concert, she had again received threatening letters. She decided to solve the dilemma by deleting all the German music from the program and introducing new songs from the stage. During the concert, she announced that the program had been changed and that she was only going to sing works by Norwegian and English composers.

The evening was extremely emotional, and after the concert, Morgenstierne stood up in his box and gave a stirring speech in which he proclaimed Flagstad to be a wonderful artist and a great Norwegian. Afterward, they all went to the Norwegian Association, where Flagstad was made an honorary member of the hospital committee.[76]

## From Great Norwegian to Nazi Propagandist?

Kirsten Flagstad had no difficulty bringing in the public. She was known in America as a Wagner exponent, and audiences expected this of her. This was why the composer's works were always the main element at major concerts with symphony orchestras. On August 1, 1940, the *Washington Post* writes that 17,500 of the city's inhabitants defied the rain and traveled by car, bus, and boat to Water Gate to hear Kirsten Flagstad give a Wagner concert accompanied by a symphony orchestra led by McArthur. The Norwegian ambassador, Morgenstierne, and his wife were also present. They feature in newspaper reports with disapproving faces: Wagner and the German language made them feel ill.

In Grant Park, Chicago, Flagstad's Wagner concert did not lack for spectators either—the newspaper estimated the crowds at as many as two hundred thousand people. This was the largest audience ever gathered for a concert there in the city, according to the newspapers. Many diverse businesses—everyone from ice cream and hot dog sellers to parking wardens—sent Flagstad good wishes that day. The magnificent voice towered over the 110-strong orchestra and the noise from an aircraft that had lost its way above the park.[77]

On August 10, it suited Flagstad to attend her daughter's wedding. McArthur took her father's place and accompanied Else to the altar before he and Flagstad departed for a concert tour to Dakota, Minnesota, Illinois, and Michigan to sing especially for the many Norwegians and Norwegian Americans who resided there. Flagstad was keen to show her solidarity with her compatriots.

At the same time, she continued to receive anonymous letters from Norwegians in the US upbraiding her because she sang Wagner and other German-language composers. Flagstad showed all these letters to McArthur and gave him terse summaries of the contents. McArthur did not understand Norwegian and so was not in a position to detect the emotional quality behind words such as *forræder* (traitor), *svin* (pig), and suchlike. McArthur's rational explanations, that the letter writers were disturbed and cowardly individuals, did not prevent the words from affecting her.

In November 1940, Flagstad was engaged to hold a series of Wagner concerts in Washington. The last of these took place in Constitution Hall on November 27. The National Symphony Orchestra had arranged it with McArthur as conductor. Morgenstierne and his wife were invited by the chair of the orchestra association to sit in their box. They were not invited by Flagstad.

## Part 2: The Voice of the Century (1935–41)  131

The minister was the obvious choice, as everyone involved in the cultural and political life of Washington was present.

In a letter to the Ministry of Foreign Affairs on February 16, 1948, Morgenstierne interprets the invitation as a tribute *to him* because of Flagstad's Norwegian heritage. This was also the reason that the Norwegian colony in Washington turned up in numbers. They, and Morgenstierne in particular, had great expectations that the concert would also include a tribute to Norway.

The concert program, which included only German music, was advertised in advance. That all the encores also did so came as a shock to Morgenstierne and all the Norwegians who had anticipated a nod to Norway.

Since then, in several letters to the Ministry of Foreign Affairs, Morgenstierne has interpreted Flagstad's concert on November 27, 1940, as a hostile act and a betrayal of her country. Seen from his perspective, this was collaboration with the enemy, an unpatriotic performance in America that ended in German triumph. He claimed that it was Flagstad who had invited the ambassadors from various countries and that she had made sure that the German representative, Hans Thomsen, was placed directly opposite the box where Morgenstierne was seated.[78] He writes in a letter to the ministry in London on August 5, 1942, that the concert was a humiliation he would never forget: "This was a triumph for our German executioners."[79]

The correspondence raises Morgenstierne's emotionally freighted experience and associated misunderstandings to a political level. His portrayal of Flagstad as an enemy became an official perception. The concert was later used in internal correspondence within the ministry and in the press as proof of Kirsten Flagstad's unpatriotic attitude in America.

### Telegrams from a Demanding Husband

Despite the war, Flagstad and her husband, Johansen, managed to reach each other in brief telegram messages. On April 24, 1940, Henry wrote that she must not believe everything the American press reported about Norway. On their wedding anniversary, May 31, the couple exchanged "love and kisses" via telegrams.

From August onward, the telegrams from Johansen took on a different character. On August 12, 1940, he wrote that he hoped she was doing everything she could to come home. He missed her.[80] McArthur claims that the telegram gave Flagstad a shock. After all, in April her husband had written that

132            THE VOICE OF THE CENTURY

she should stay where she was, so what was the meaning of this? She replied the same day to say that she also missed him. On August 26, Johansen wrote that he was disappointed about her lengthy work contracts, which made it difficult for her to come home to Norway before April 1941. She answered in a telegram on September 1 that his reaction was making her unhappy. She had used her judgment and signed her contracts from a conviction that it would be impossible for her to return home until the war was over. He sent a fairly arrogant response in a telegram the next day saying that all her contracts should have been approved by him.

On September 11, she replied, reminding him that in a telegram in March, he had agreed that she should sign a contract for a short season at the Metropolitan. It would not be right of her to break the contract, and so he must be kind enough to understand that otherwise she would have traveled home to him.[81]

One day in November 1940, they reached each other on the telephone. During their conversation, Henry Johansen repeated a question several times over: "Why don't you come home?" Flagstad answered that she would try to travel back in April of the following year, when she would be released from her contracts. He threatened her by saying that this might be too late.

Why did Johansen suddenly become so demanding and clinging? One explanation is that he felt lonely; his membership in Quisling's NS and his business dealings with the German occupying forces may have diminished his circle of friends. Another is that he did not feel well, that he may have had health problems. Flagstad decided to go home, but after being warned by her impresario against disengaging from her contracts to travel to an occupied country, she chose to remain until April 1941. She sent this decision to her husband by telegram.

## Morgenstierne Warns Crown Princess Märtha against Flagstad

Several members of the Norwegian royal family lived in America during the war. On August 28, 1940, Crown Princess Märtha, the two princesses Ragnhild (ten) and Astrid (eight), little Prince Harald (three), Master of the King's Household Wedel Jarlsberg, adjutants, and ladies-in-waiting all arrived in New York. There were a total of eleven individuals in the royal retinue on board an American ship from Petsamo, in the North of Finland, at that time. They came as refugees via Sweden from occupied Norway. The crown princess later lived in Pooks Hill outside Washington, a property Morgenstierne had assisted the Norwegian authorities to purchase in all secrecy. The minister's

# Part 2: The Voice of the Century (1935–41)    133

tight bonds with both the crown prince and King Haakon were due in some measure to their gratitude for him placing a protective hand on the crown princess and her children while they stayed in America during the war.

Morgenstierne was the experienced, highest-ranking Norwegian official in the US. The royal family had placed their affectionate trust in him. On October 12, 1940, King Haakon sent him a letter from London in which he thanked the minister for his help in arranging safe passage to America for the crown princess. He expressed his concern and at the same time asked Morgenstierne to give her his help and support.[82] After this, Morgenstierne took over the administration of the crown princess's official life, in cooperation with Master of the King's Household, Wedel Jarlsberg. This information emerges from a circular Morgenstierne issued on October 14, 1940, in which he requested that all inquiries regarding the crown princess, as well as all her communications with the legation, should go through him.[83] It is probable that the crown princess, who was in exile and new to America, would comply completely with the Norwegian minister's advice and recommendations, without a moment's thought.

At the beginning of December 1940, Morgenstierne received a number of approaches from representatives of the Norwegian Relief Committee in Chicago. They were planning a major concert starring Kirsten Flagstad on Friday, January 17, 1941. The program consisted exclusively of Norwegian and English works, with the exception of two German encores. The Civic Opera House had been hired for the occasion. The management wrote several letters to Morgenstierne in which they urged the crown princess to participate in the event. They had also learned that Crown Prince Olav had arrived in the US and wondered whether it would be possible for him to attend. This was a grand concert to raise money for occupied Norway, most likely one of the largest to be held, and so the organizers emphasized the importance it would have if the royals attended to add prestige to the concert.

Morgenstierne had informed the Ministry of Foreign Affairs on a number of occasions of his negative view of Flagstad and her alleged unpatriotic behavior. He conveyed this to Wedel Jarlsberg and to the royal couple, and this had the desired effect. It is clear from a letter dated December 30, 1940, from Wedel Jarlsberg to Morgenstierne that a verbal confidential exchange on this matter had taken place with the crown princess.[84]

Morgenstierne replied to the committee on January 3, 1941. He had proposed the event to the crown princess, who thanked them for the invitation. Unfortunately, she was unable to go to Chicago to be present at the concert.

Flagstad's benefit concert for Norway. The crown princess, after advice from Morgenstierne, did not attend. *Source: Flagstad Museum.*

The same applied to Crown Prince Olav. Morgenstierne was also invited by the organizers, but he said that he was extremely busy. The organizers expressed their great disappointment that the royal couple had turned down the invitation.[85]

On January 17, 1941, Kirsten Flagstad performed at a sold-out concert in aid of Norwegian Relief in Chicago. It brought the organization considerable funds and was one of the most generous gestures witnessed at the Civic Opera House in many seasons. Norwegian and American flags waved from the stage, and Flagstad opened with the American and Norwegian national anthems.[86]

## An Apolitical Journey Home

Kirsten Flagstad tried to call her husband a few times over Christmas 1940 but did not succeed in getting through. McArthur writes that she spoke to him once from Chicago in January and once from New York on March 1, 1941. He noticed that she became rather upset by her husband's constant complaints that she was not returning home. As mentioned earlier, Flagstad had an old-fashioned view of marriage. She thought that her husband should be

## Part 2: The Voice of the Century (1935–41)                    135

in charge, as far as he was able. The wife should obey, and it was her primary task to please her husband. Probably this attitude reflects her uncertainty and lack of ability to function well in society. A husband should compensate for that deficiency.

She was preoccupied with his health. Back in February 1938, Johansen had become acutely ill and had to undergo an operation. A couple of days later, she received a message by telegram telling her to return home, as the doctor had given up all hope for him. She had immediately asked her manager to cancel all her concert tours and opera performances, as she had to go home to her husband, and made preparations for a speedy departure. Before she got that far, she received a message to say he was on the road to recovery and she had no need to come after all.

On March 4, 1941, she went on tour to the West Coast, determined to travel home to Norway as soon as her contract ran out on April 17 that year. Early arrangements were made for her to travel back to Norway. Steven Spiegel, an expert on emigration to America, was given her Norwegian passport and the assignment of organizing her journey to Norway. A representative of Spiegel's office went to Washington to obtain a transit visa through the countries she would have to cross: Bermuda, Portugal, Spain, occupied France, and Germany. This turned out to be problematic, especially as far as Portugal was concerned. The Portuguese Embassy in Washington was afraid to issue a transit visa without permission from Lisbon. The Norwegian Legation in Washington could, however, request such a visa for her.

A representative of Spiegel was sent to the Norwegian Legation to request their help. The legation asked the Norwegian government, then located in London, and the instruction from there was not to assist her with a Portuguese visa. Kirsten Flagstad could, however, be helped if she did not cross German occupied territory. This was the impression gained by Spiegel's representative.[87]

Her American channels did not have contacts that could transport her on the long sea route across the Atlantic. Since she had chosen to cross Europe, she received no help from Norwegian officialdom. Her impresario, Marks Levine, has written in an article from 1950 that everyone of importance within NBC contributed to help Flagstad obtain a transit visa through Germany so that she could get home to her family. America at that time was not at war with anyone. All of the country's diplomatic and business connections with countries at war were maintained through neutral countries such as Portugal,

# 136 THE VOICE OF THE CENTURY

Turkey, Switzerland, and Sweden. Diplomats and businessmen traveled continually back and forth through German-occupied countries to look after their affairs.

Flagstad was of the persuasion that the war would soon end. The evening before her departure for Portugal, Levine spent a couple of hours at her apartment in New York. In the course of the conversation, he asked her what she would do if the Germans asked her to sing in Germany or Norway or some other place for the purposes of propaganda. She answered that she could always lose her voice, take ill, or somehow make it impossible to open her mouth. It pleased Levine in retrospect that she really never did sing in Germany or any German-occupied country. He says, "I am Jewish. It would be impossible for me knowingly to seek a connection with anything or anyone directly or indirectly linked with or cooperating with the Nazi and fascist nightmare between 1939–1945."[88]

## Notes

1. Britannica (n.d.).
2. *Black History Magazine* (n.d.).
3. Metropolitan Opera (n.d.).
4. Guttormsen (2018), pp. 79–115.
5. "From Private to Colonel and Leader of the Colonial Forces in Natal," in *Nordmandsforbundet* (1911).
6. Horowitz (2014).
7. Statistics Norway (n.d.).
8. Kirsten Flagstad's performances, Flagstad Museum archive, https://dms-cf-02.dimu.org/file/022wazLzTnja.
9. McArthur (1965), p. 30.
10. Kirsten Flagstad to Maja Flagstad, January 15, 1935, Flagstad Museum archive.
11. Flagstad to Flagstad.
12. Flagstad to Flagstad.
13. *Die Walküre*, live recording with radio commentary, February 2, 1935, Archipel.
14. Kirsten Flagstad, in conversation with Torstein Gunnarson, Radio Archive 1994/22375:P, NRK Norway.
15. Lauritz Melchior, Kirsten Flagstad in memoriam, December 30, 1962, Radio Archive, NRK Norway.
16. *Berlingske Tidende*, July 21, 1936; Flagstad, in conversation with Gunnarson.

## Part 2: The Voice of the Century (1935–41) 137

17. *Dagbladet*, April 6, 1937.

18. *Words and Music*; in *New York Evening Post*, March 19, 1935; *New York Times*, March 28, 1935.

19. *The Confessions of Winifred Wagner, Part I*, dir. Hans Jürgen Syberberg, 1977.

20. Wasiutynski (1996), pp. 569–70.

21. Flagstad, in conversation with Gunnarson.

22. McArthur (1965), pp. ix–x.

23. McArthur (1965), pp. vii–ix.

24. *Aftenposten* May 5, 1935.

25. McArthur (1965), p. 10.

26. Kirsten Flagstad's performances, Flagstad Museum archive, https://dms -cf-02.dimu.org/file/022wazLzTnja.

27. McArthur (1965), pp. 8–9.

28. Ringdal (2008), p. 182.

29. Ringdal (2008), pp. 208, 378.

30. Ringdal (2008), pp. 1–9, 33, 37.

31. Ringdal (2008), pp. 42–43.

32. Ringdal (2008), pp. 81–82.

33. Ringdal (2008), pp. 70, 82.

34. W. Morgenstierne to Henry Johansen, industrialist, January 6, 1936, Archive code 38.8.15, vols. 1–2, re: Kirsten Flagstad, Ministry of Foreign Affairs archive, National Archives, Norway.

35. Kirsten Flagstad's performances, Flagstad Museum archive, https://dms -cf-02.dimu.org/file/022wazLzTnja.

36. McArthur (1965), pp. 40–43.

37. *Morgenposten*, May 30, 1936.

38. Elisabeth Schwarzkopf, in a memorial program about Flagstad broadcast by the BBC.

39. "Kirsten Flagstad Took Thirty-Eight Curtain Calls at Covent Garden," *Berlinske Tidende*, May 19, 1936.

40. *Star*, May 19, 1936; *Star* June 10, 1936; *Daily Telegraph* May 26, 1936; *Times* June 10, 1936.

41. *Aftenposten*, July 20, 1936; *Aftenposten*, July 3, 1936.

42. *Oslo Illustrerte*, September 24, 1936; *Neues Freie Presse* (Vienna), September 4, 1936.

43. W.R., *Neueste Nachrichten* (Vienna), September 4, 1936; *Neues Wiener Tagblatt*, September 8, 1936.

44. "Season at Metropolitan Opera," *Words and Music*, January 30, 1937.

45. Kirsten Flagstad, interview, *Stavanger Aftenblad*, January 16, 1937.

46. McArthur (1965), p. 48.

138      THE VOICE OF THE CENTURY

47. Kirsten Flagstad, postcard to Minister Morgenstierne, February 16, 1937, Archive code 38.8.15, vols. 1–2, file: Kirsten Flagstad, Ministry of Foreign Affairs, National Archives, Norway.

48. Solbrekken (2003), pp. 254–55.

49. *Wilhelm Furtwängler* (1964).

50. *Wilhelm Furtwängler* (1964).

51. *Morning Post*, June 23, 1937; *Morning Post*, May 27, 1937.

52. *Daily Telegraph*, June 28, 1937; *Daily Telegraph*, July 2, 1937.

53. *Morning Post*, June 23, 1937; *Morning Post*, May 27, 1937.

54. Ardoin (1994), pp. 44–46.

55. Ardoin (1994), p. 53.

56. Horenstein, interview (1969).

57. *Journalisten*, July 1937.

58. *Journalisten*; *Nidaros*, July 17, 1937; *Aftenposten*, July 9, 1937.

59. Schive and Olav (1939), pp. 47, 52.

60. W. Morgenstierne to Ministry of Foreign Affairs, November 17, 1938. The Ministry of Foreign Affairs archive, the National Archives, Oslo.

61. Biancolli (1952), pp. 18–19.

62. R. Christensen to the Legation in Washington, May 16, 1939, St. Olav's Medal, Embassy in Washington, box 374, Ministry of Foreign Affairs archive, National Archives, Norway.

63. McArthur (1965), p. 105.

64. Arthur Bodanzky, "Wagner and the Box Office: A Study of Musical Trends," *Etude*, April 1938.

65. "Lauritz Melchior Leaves Metropolitan," *Berlingske Tidende*, March 11, 1940.

66. "Who Will Conduct the Metropolitan Broadcast This Evening?," *Berlingske Tidende*, January 27, 1940.

67. Robert Tuggle, in discussion with the author, 2014–15.

68. McArthur (1965), pp. 115–20.

69. Tunbridge (2018), p. 43.

70. Rosenberg (2019), pp. 40, 98, 109, 118.

71. Tunbridge (2018), p. 44.

72. Rosenberg (2019), p. 116.

73. Rosenberg (2019), p. 24.

74. Tunbridge (2018), p. 50.

75. Rosenberg (2019), p. 26.

76. McArthur (1965), pp. 116–20.

77. Solbrekken (2003), p. 298.

78. Biancolli (1952), p. 116.

Part 2: The Voice of the Century (1935–41)      139

79. Morgenstierne to the Ministry of Foreign Affairs in London, August 5, 1942, Archive code 38.8.15, vols. 1–2, file: Kirsten Flagstad, Ministry of Foreign Affairs archive, National Archives, Norway.

80. Henry Johansen and Kirsten Flagstad, telegrams, 1940–41, Oslo Police Station: Misc, anr. 3194—Henry Thomas Ingvald Johansen, National Archives, Norway.

81. Johansen and Flagstad.

82. Haakon R to Minister Morgenstierne, October 12, 1940, in Morgenstierne, Wilhelm Thorleif von Munthe af. 1910–1949 RA/PA 1274, National Archives, Norway.

83. Circular, October 15, 1940, Archive code 38.8.15, vols. 1–2, file: Kirsten Flagstad, Ministry of Foreign Affairs archive, National Archives, Norway.

84. Master of the King's Household P. A. Wedel Jarlsberg to Morgenstierne, December 30, 1940, Ministry of Foreign Affairs archive, National Archives, Norway.

85. Norwegian Relief Committee to Morgenstierne, December 30, 1940, and January 6, 1941; Morgenstierne to Pastor Ingvoldstad, January 3, 1941, and January 11, 1941, Ministry of Foreign Affairs archive, National Archives, Norway.

86. McArthur (1965), p. 143.

87. McArthur (1965), p. 140.

88. Marks Levine, "New Aspects of Conflict around Flagstad," 1950, published in *Nordisk Tidende*, March 9, 1950, and elsewhere.

# PART 3

# The Years of Struggle
## (1941–51)

### Journey Home Interpreted as National Betrayal

Fleeing from Norway during the war was described as dramatic, and refugees went to Sweden or to Britain and the US. Escape was associated with the death penalty and the imprisonment of one's closest relatives. The ones who traveled voluntarily into occupied Norway were resistance fighters and saboteurs who were either dropped from airplanes or smuggled in by other illegal means. They all came to fight the enemy. In the narrative of the war in Norway, these journeys back are described as heroic. Flagstad's entry, to a husband who was a member of the National Samling (NS) Party and who also did business with the occupying forces, was of a very different kind. From her perspective, it had nothing to do with politics, but later many Norwegians interpreted it as a political act. They believed that by traveling home Flagstad had betrayed Norway: the journey made her into an antiheroine in the country's war history.

There were serious personal reasons for her leaving the US, and the decision was her own. Many individuals tried to dissuade her from going, from celebrities, friends, and colleagues to the ordinary man in the street. This was to no avail, as Flagstad had no intention of changing her mind. She was as stubborn as a mule. Once she was convinced of something, she found it impossible to reconsider. The public wished her bon voyage home and welcome back. McArthur drove her to the seaplane base on Long Island, and from there, a Boeing 314, an American four-engine long-distance aircraft, would take her to Lisbon. At the airport, the Norwegian consul general in New York, Rolf Christensen, had also turned up to wish her a good trip home. At 10:00 a.m. on

# Part 3: The Years of Struggle (1941–51)

April 19, 1941, the plane took off with a woman on board who had previously expressed a fear of flying.

In the bar at her hotel in Lisbon, she met three Norwegians who had escaped from Norway. They warned her that Henry Johansen was keeping bad company. He was a member of the NS, a party that supported the Nazi occupation forces. She reacted with surprise but instinctively felt that something did not add up. Her question about why it was wrong to be affiliated with the NS amazed the men. At the time, Flagstad was possibly one of very few Norwegians who did not realize that the situation had come to a head in Norway between the NS and the Norwegian authorities in exile and among the majority of the populace.

Was she really so naive and confused? Probably, combined with an underlying state of denial. She has said that she pushed it all to the back of her mind.[1] Her dependency, in addition to the accompanying simplistic view of her husband, blinded her to his political and economic treachery. This dislocation would come to cost her dearly.

## Start of an Organized Witch Hunt

Kirsten Flagstad made a few such personal misjudgments, but she never lived up to the picture of an enemy that Morgenstierne and the Norwegian Foreign Ministry created of her. After she left America, Morgenstierne initiated an organized witch hunt through the channels of the Foreign Ministry. At this point, she knew nothing about his actions. From Lisbon, she moved on to Madrid, encountering great difficulties along the way. From Madrid, she flew to Barcelona, making a stop in France before finally reaching Berlin. The plan was for her to travel from Berlin to Stockholm since the situation in Norway was unknown. This would be clarified at the Swedish Legation in Berlin.

When she arrived there, she was told that they did not have a transit visa for her to travel to Stockholm. Flagstad was taken aback, as she had been told that everything had been arranged. Instead, she was offered a transit visa through Sweden to Norway. She would have to obtain an entry permit to Norway from the German authorities. She received this, as well as a German transit visa for travel through Sweden.

What was the reason for these difficulties? Why was she not allowed to disembark from the train in Stockholm? Three days after she had left the US, on April 22, 1941, Morgenstierne had sent a telegram to the Norwegian Legation in Stockholm to notify them of Flagstad's journey to Norway via

Portugal and Sweden. He wrote that her trip home was in direct contravention of instructions given by the Norwegian Foreign Ministry in London and added: "At a grand concert here on 27 November 1940, at which the German chargé d'affaires and the Norwegian Minister were present, she sang not a single word or note of Norwegian, but exclusively German music. This caused great disappointment to Norwegians and drew a great deal of attention in Washington. Sent for your information."[2]

The legation in Stockholm made contact with the Swedish intelligence services, and it is likely that the Swedish authorities immediately gave the Swedish Legation in Berlin instructions that Flagstad should not be granted an entry visa for Sweden but only a transit visa. On April 21, Morgenstierne sent a letter to the Foreign Office in London to say that he had been in touch with the legation in Stockholm about the journey. Yet again, he did not fail to mention the concert in Washington on November 27, at which Flagstad had sung nothing but German music. He repeated that it was excruciating for them to be seated in a box with the chair of the Orchestra Association. The German chargé d'affaires, Dr. Hans Thomsen, had looked very pleased, Morgenstierne said.[3]

He also sent an identical letter to the Norwegian Legation in Lisbon, who then wrote a separate letter about Flagstad's stay there to the Ministry of Foreign Affairs in London the next day, April 22, 1941. The letters definitely leave an impression that Flagstad was a German sympathizer who used her art to spread propaganda and who should therefore be kept under surveillance.

Feeling extremely relieved, an unsuspecting Flagstad left Berlin by train. In Trelleborg, she changed to the night train for Oslo. When she arrived in the capital of Norway the next day, her husband met her at the station. She found it difficult to describe their reunion. They had not seen each other for nineteen months. As soon as she got home, she phoned Maja, who could not believe her ears.[4]

## Isolation at Home

Just after she arrived home, she was visited by a number of journalists, including from the NS newspaper, *Fritt Folk* (Free people). A press conference was held, and Flagstad told them she had come home for a vacation, not to perform. All the same, the Norwegian Broadcasting Corporation, or NRK, rang her at Tidemands gate and asked her to participate in a shortwave transmission for an overseas audience. In the course of the broadcast, Norwegian

## Part 3: The Years of Struggle (1941–51)        143

seamen would be encouraged to return home. She would have received a large fee for this, but she turned it down, on the basis that she was not for sale, and added that she had not come home to make propaganda for anyone. She did not want to mix art with politics: she had had more than enough of that in America.

Flagstad went on living as she had always done, in isolation. The couple moved to their house in the small town of Kristiansand on the south coast, where there was less focus on her. For Flagstad, seclusion was second nature. Her husband was a more social character, and isolation at home had made him lonely and clinging. The local residents did not like Johansen and called him Big Shot, with some considering him to be a corrupt capitalist who was willing to do almost anything for money. Others believed that his NS membership was motivated not by politics but purely by business interests.[5] However, Quislings and staunch Norwegians were divided into irreconcilable opposing camps that no longer had any truck with each other.

Two of Johansen's children were deeply involved in the Norwegian resistance movement. His daughter Kate gave Flagstad a crash course in why it was wrong to be a member of the NS and asked her for help to get her father out. They put pressure on him, and on July 17, 1941, he resigned from the party. Some believed that he had been forced to buy his way out, and in later interviews, he claimed that they wanted to give him a ministerial post and that this had been his main reason for pulling out. It was most likely the post of trade minister that Quisling had thought of for Henry Johansen. His resignation had little or no significance, either legally or for his reputation. Johansen had been marked in a way that was not easy to change, and anyway, his business continued its deliveries to the occupying forces. Production maintained Norwegian jobs but at the same time involved dealings with the enemy.

The local population had a different view of Flagstad. They regarded her as a homely, naive, and guileless artist. She was well liked in the village, and a young man later related that he had taken her replies to the post office in which she turned down offers from the Nazis to perform.[6] She was the world's greatest interpreter of Wagner, so it was not so strange that the German high command applied pressure to make her appear on formal occasions. When it became too uncomfortable, she traveled to Sigridnes, a smallholding situated in an uninhabited area in a forest. Only her closest family went there. Vienna and Budapest tried to persuade her to go to the opera houses there, but she was unwilling to sing in countries occupied by Nazi Germany.

## Norway—Cradle of the Ancient Germans?

She returned home to a country that had undergone a radical change. The elected government and the royal family had fled, and the Reich's Commissariat had moved in to take over the administration of Norway. The German occupying forces quickly set up a propaganda headquarters for the dissemination of public information and cultural material. This was led by Joseph Goebbels's former press secretary SS-Oberführer Georg Wilhelm Müller, who was given the task of developing a "bond of friendship between Germany and Norway." Goebbels entertained the hope that Norwegians could be won over, and his methods included sending Germany's foremost musicians, singers, orchestras, and ensembles to the country.[7] The German headquarters had received clearly earmarked resources to present the very best of German art and culture to Norwegians. Hitler had personally decided that three million reichsmarks should be set aside for the purpose of cultural propaganda in Norway.

The Nazi ideology, and Heinrich Himmler in particular, had fantastical ideas about Norwegians and Norwegian culture. Himmler was one of the most powerful men in the Third Reich, Adolf Hitler's right-hand man, and one of the architects behind the Holocaust. He regarded Norway as the "cradle of the Ancient Germans" and believed that the country's population showed splendid examples of the Germanic race. Blond, blue-eyed Norwegians, direct descendants of the Vikings, were not a diluted nation. With such convictions, he embarked on several "race safaris" in the country, to study the "racially pure" Norwegians who lived in remote valleys. He believed that this was where the soul of the race was still unsullied by foreign cultures. He also believed he could hear the German race's primitive voice in Nordic folk music. Himmler's interest left a pernicious taint on Norwegian folk music, and national symbols were misguidedly linked to Nazism and racism.

The Nazi ideology's fascination with Norway and the Nordic countries meant the occupiers initially went easy on the civilian population in Norway. They were to be won over rather than conquered before being integrated into Germany's advanced civilization.

## Culture Oils the Wheels of War

The working classes were to be raised up to new heights of culture. Art, previously reserved for the bourgeoisie, was now to be made available to those of

Part 3: The Years of Struggle (1941–51)

lesser means. The leisure organization Kraft durch Freude (Strength through Joy) was established when Hitler came to power in 1933. This organization bought up huge quantities of opera and theater tickets. They also arranged classical music concerts, conducted by experts such as Furtwängler, at lunch breaks in factories. Culture became an important part of Nazi political propaganda, with censorship following in its wake.

In 1939, Hitler had asked Winifred Wagner what they would do about the festival. She felt they ought to shut it down, as they had done when World War I broke out. Hitler responded that he did not want Bayreuth to fall into decay, neither its traditions nor its fabric. Winifred thought it would be impossible to run it, since the staff would be called up to active duty. In September 1939, Hitler decided that all workers at Bayreuth should be exempt from military service from May to August. Winifred asked where they would find their audience, since people working in war industries and other kinds of service had no time or money to come to Bayreuth. Hitler said he wanted to bring together injured and decorated soldiers, officers, medics, and war wounded. Kraft durch Freude would organize transport to Bayreuth for them as well as for workers in the munitions factories. The festival would be a reward for their war efforts and would boost morale for the continuation of the war. Every evening, fifteen hundred people would experience Wagner's operas with full board provided, all paid for by the Third Reich. The master himself had felt that culture should belong to the people and be freely accessible. Trenches were dug for audiences to escape into in case of aerial bombing. Hitler took up residence in Bayreuth during the festival and made plans to build a festival hall with seating for thousands.[8]

## A Valkyrie in Holy War

The fact that Wagner's works were now oiling the wheels of the war industry did not make circumstances any easier for Flagstad. Norwegian audiences were introduced to the link between Richard Wagner's operas and Nazism. The dramas were to support the idea that the Germanic peoples belonged to a divinely inspired "race," chosen to reign over the world. This would be achieved through a "holy war," where the end justified the means. Soldiers and terrorists were indoctrinated to believe they were fighting against evil and that their actions were therefore commendable. The concept of heavenly reward (Valhalla, Paradise, etc.) characterizes this kind of violation of fundamental respect for human life.

146 THE VOICE OF THE CENTURY

The Hamburg State Opera and Philharmonic Orchestra came to Oslo to take part in a celebration of German culture from October 3 to 10, 1940, with 160 singers, dancers, musicians, and technicians mounting a production of *Die Walküre* at the National Theatre. Many singers who would later find international fame took to the stage, including Joachim Sattler, Hans Hotter, and Ferdinand Frantz. Flagstad performed with both Frantz and Hotter several times after the war, both in Europe and in the US. It is evident from the review in the *Deutche Zeitung in Norwegen* newspaper published on October 10, 1940, that the opera's content reflected the unyielding strength of the German spirit. The triumphant intent of German culture was revealed through the work of art.[9]

Propaganda transformed the opera's lead character, Brunhild the Valkyrie, into a Joan of Arc figure for Hitler's Germany. The blazing female Mercury was presented as a demonic black figure who led the Nazi forces to death and destruction. "The Ride of the Valkyries" was deliberately used as background music in a film showing the Luftwaffe's attack on Crete. In modern times, the Nazi reinterpretation of the Valkyrie continues to be used—for example, in the film *Apocalypse Now*, in a scene that shows American helicopters invading and destroying Vietnam and its people. Hitler misused the figure of the Valkyrie as inspiration for his gory war, and later German officers had the idea of turning the archetype against him. This resulted in Operation Valkyrie, the attempted assassination of Hitler that took place on July 20, 1944.

Flagstad's interpretations, as well as films made by Paramount Pictures and Big Broadcast in 1938, in which Flagstad sings Brunhild's battle cry, "Ho jo to ho," had immortalized her in the role and identified her with the character. The battle cry had appeared on a whole series of her concert programs in the US and Europe. Audiences in Norway had also heard her "Ho jo to ho" a number of times. This now led to unfortunate associations.

In Old Norse mythology, it was the role of the Valkyries to choose who should fall in battle. They brought dead warriors to Odin in Valhalla, though Freyja also had her own kingdom of the dead. The most bloodthirsty among them remained with Odin, while ordinary warriors could look forward to Freyja's embrace. The expired warriors found life after death with Odin and Freyja until judgment day, Ragnarok, when they would fight side by side with the gods.

Mythical concepts such as these became destructive in the hands of Nazism. The idea that the Nazi movement was legitimate and "good," and sent to fight "evil," led to a culture of persecution, war, violence, and mass murder.

## Part 3: The Years of Struggle (1941–51)

Soldiers were presented with a code of honor that promised eternal glory in return for killing and maiming the enemy for the cause. These collective delusions became a powerful underlying force in the war machinery. We recognize the mechanism from more recent history, in radicalized terrorists, "martyrs" who, through their belief in eternal life and honor, blow themselves up, taking others with them.

### Old Colleagues in Performance

Although Flagstad did not sing in public, she maintained a practice regime to maintain the condition of her voice. Her husband extended the house to provide her with a separate room with good acoustics to sing in. It was said that when she opened the doors, her voice carried out across the sea and boats stopped with people sitting quietly on deck, listening. Certainly, she must have missed being surrounded by a musical life and colleagues with whom she could play and sing. Flagstad could not put in an appearance at any of Oslo's many concerts, where old colleagues now performed under swastika banners.

Cultural life in the Norwegian capital was flourishing when the Germans invaded the country on April 9, 1940. The National Theatre had made a binding agreement with Kirsten Flagstad that she should be the guest star in the spring of 1940, both as Leonore in several productions of *Fidelio* and as Brunhild in *Die Walküre*. The occupation, and the fact that she was still in the US, made this impossible.

While fighting in the North of Norway was still going on, life in Oslo quickly returned to its old ways. Painters, sculptors, actors, musicians, and singers all feared for their grants and paychecks. The huge numbers of German soldiers, workers, and businessmen who arrived all wanted greater opportunities for culture and entertainment, and the National Theatre had enormous success with several opera performances. Both the audience and concert institutions believed at first that musical life could continue as a neutral, nonpolitical sanctuary. The Flagstad family—Maja, Karen-Marie, and Kirsten Flagstad's two brothers, Lasse and Ole—had formed a quartet, the Flagstad Quartet, which performed at the National Theatre. They held concerts that were broadcast on radio, including on December 1, 1940.

Radio was quickly Nazified and censored, with the management replaced by either NS adherents or German occupiers. The censorship caused a number of radio programs to be dropped. At the same time, it was important for the Nazis not to give the impression that they were suppressing Norwegian

148                THE VOICE OF THE CENTURY

national culture. For this reason, the recording of concerts in Oslo was important, and music was given a major place in the radio transmissions. Impoverished Norwegian musicians and singers performed willingly in this initial phase. At the beginning of 1941, the concert agencies announced that the spring season would have an abundance of concerts equal to the previous autumn. Since these concerts had been regarded as a refuge from politics, still no distinction was made between artists who were Nazi sympathizers and those who were opponents, but that situation would soon change. This was the position in the world of music when Flagstad arrived in Norway in April 1941.

Isolation from the capital city protected Flagstad from close contact with her old colleagues. She clearly wanted no close relationship with musical life in Norway, though various festivities celebrating great musicians from abroad took place at her husband's hotels. In the spring of 1941, the Berlin Philharmonic came on tour to the Nordic countries. They gave concerts in Oslo on May 22 and 23, with Hans Knappertsbusch as conductor. As mentioned previously, Furtwängler had refused to conduct the orchestra in occupied countries, and Knappertsbusch was considered to be the best conductor in Germany after Furtwängler. Himmler was back in Oslo to inaugurate the first cohort of Norwegian SS soldiers and to attend one of these concerts arranged by the NS. On May 24, a reception was held for the orchestra and conductor at Johansen's Bristol Hotel. Knappertsbusch visited Oslo again in 1944.[10] After the war, Flagstad would sing several times under his baton. In vain, Furtwängler tried to persuade Flagstad to be the soloist at the Berlin Philharmonic's concert in Stockholm; she must have realized that it would not look good for her to sing with an orchestra financed by the Third Reich, even though it took place in a neutral country.

The Czech German soprano Maria Müller, famed for her interpretations of Wagner, was the guest star at two concerts in Oslo. Müller made her debut as Sieglinde in *Die Walküre* at the Metropolitan in 1925. On the occasion of her visit to Norway, she gave an interview to the country's leading newspaper, *Aftenposten*, in which she said that between 1925 and 1935, she had taken part in two hundred performances at the opera house and had sung with Kirsten Flagstad three times. Müller was reputed to be a favorite of Hitler, and she lived in Bayreuth until her death in 1958 and was buried there between Franz Liszt and the Wagner family.[11] When Flagstad made her debut as Brunhild in *Die Walküre* at the Metropolitan on February 15, 1935, Müller had sung the part of Sieglinde. At Müller's first concert at the Aula Hall in Oslo, the entire

# Part 3: The Years of Struggle (1941–51)    149

occupying German top brass sat with Vidkun Quisling in the front row. Josef Terboven, now in charge of the country, presented her with flowers. The following day, Müller laid the bouquet at the memorial for fallen German soldiers.

She performed again in Norway in December 1941. The concerts were advertised in *Aftenposten*, and Kirsten Flagstad probably read the reviews the next day. Her intonation was occasionally slightly uneven, according to the reviewer, Reidar Mjøen. He had been *Aftenposten*'s music critic since 1925, but because of his condemnation of the NS and the German occupation, he was fired from the strongly Nazified newspaper in the summer of 1942.[12] The Oslo press was eventually left with only music critics sympathetic to the regime.

Flagstad probably also learned that the coloratura soprano Erna Berger came to give a concert in Oslo on September 17, 1941. With Rita Streich and Elisabeth Schwarzkopf, Berger was one of Germany's greatest coloratura sopranos and made guest appearances on the major European opera stages. She was happy to sing for the soldiers and allowed herself to be pictured with them. She also gave concerts on Hitler's birthday and other important state occasions. Berger returned to Norway to give concerts in Oslo on March 5 and 20, 1942. The Reich's Commissariat engaged her to give a series of performances for German soldiers throughout Norway during the autumn of 1943.

In 1947, Berger resumed her international career without any difficulty. She sang at Covent Garden and received a contract at the Metropolitan in 1949, remaining there until the spring of 1951. Edward Johnson had no problem allowing her to debut in the role of Sophie in *Der Rosenkavalier* on November 21, 1949, more than a year before Flagstad was welcomed back there. A critic notes that Berger had sung the role in Switzerland with Strauss conducting. On February 7, 1951, Flagstad was to stand side by side with Berger on the Met stage, singing the *Siegfried* Brunhild with Berger singing Waldvogel. Presumably, through articles and reviews in *Aftenposten*, Flagstad had learned of Berger's activities in Norway during the occupation, but she expressed no opinion on what she knew.

Flagstad loved Beethoven but chose not to attend a concert at the Aula Hall in Oslo on October 30, 1941, where the eminent German pianist Wilhelm Backhaus gave a concert with the Philharmonic. The hall was packed, and his interpretation of Beethoven's Piano Concerto no. 3 was greeted with rapturous applause. Backhaus was one of the Nazi propaganda unit's most prominent figures during the entirety of the war. In 1936, he said he thought all musicians should vote for Adolf Hitler. In thanks, Hitler appointed him professor of music and senator of state culture. Backhaus continued his career after 1945 without any real difficulties.[13]

Performing artists who did appear were worshipped by the Nazis. On January 19, 1942, the renowned Finnish soprano Aulikki Rautawaara came to Oslo to give a concert. She also sang at the hospital for German soldiers who had been injured on the western front and subsequently returned a few times to tour Norway. She was introduced with a great flurry of propaganda in the press and received a mink coat worth 30,000 Norwegian kroner from Terboven.[14]

On October 5, the world-famous German violinist Georg Kulenkampff came to give a concert at the Aula Hall under the auspices of the Norwegian-German Society. He told a Norwegian colleague that he felt ashamed but opted for this as his military service. He had the choice between playing at propaganda concerts or being sent out on active service. In 1943, he succeeded in moving to Switzerland.[15]

The musical life of Oslo during the war years was first rate, but the background to it was such that Flagstad and patriotic Norwegians discovered they could neither take part nor benefit from it.

## Music Front under Development

Throughout 1941, new expressions and classifications were introduced to Norwegian society. People were patriots, Quislings, or collaborators. The last two groups were regarded as traitors, since a large majority of the populace felt the invasion to be an aggressive attack on their land and people, their king and government.

Singers and choristers were among the first to notice that something was changing. The Nazi-controlled Culture and Public Education Department began to monitor and censor song lyrics in works that were to be performed in public. The Philharmonic Choir was subjected to such rigorous censorship of the texts of various works that it became ridiculous to go ahead. When the choir received a request to sing at a concert in memory of fallen frontline soldiers, their management replied that they had not been able to assemble their members in the spring of 1941. After this, they closed down their activities.[16] When it dawned on them that they were now pawns in the propaganda of the NS and the occupiers, most refused to perform. The soloists did not want their concerts to be broadcast, despite many of them having to endure pressure and threats. The musical life of Norway had most decidedly become political.

Part 3: The Years of Struggle (1941–51)

In the beginning of 1942, Quisling's minister of culture, Gulbrand Lunde, sent a telegram to Joseph Goebbels, reporting that the cultural exchange between Germany and Norway was in a state of continual growth and development. Goebbels replied, "I'm delighted that the feeling of intimate racial and cultural fellowship is gaining increasing acceptance from the Norwegian people."[17] In the course of 1942, censorship was introduced to music, and any performance of Jewish or Russian music was considered to be a political act. Around 2,200 Jews lived in Norway at the outbreak of war, and they were audited before mass arrests took place in October 1942. A total of 773 were deported from Norway to concentration camps, and only 34 of these survived. Around 1,000 Norwegian Jews succeeded in escaping from the country, most of them to Sweden.[18]

All word-based performances were subject to inspection and censorship. Singers had to sign a form committing to adherence to the regulations in order to perform on NRK, the state broadcaster. Patriotic vocalists responded by reducing their participation in public musical life to an absolute minimum. After this, vocal music moved into the private sphere and reorganized its activity there. The Philharmonic was in danger of being made into a state orchestra. Great effort went into retaining the orchestra's independence, but the price paid was that the orchestra was obligated to play for NRK, and as a radio orchestra, it had to play at NS events. For the remainder of the war years, the orchestra existed as a free Norwegian musical institution, but at the same time, it was a government-endorsed radio orchestra used in Nazi propaganda.[19]

In September 1942, all radios had to be handed in, and only NS members were permitted to keep theirs. A Music Front was created, linked to the Home Front's Coordination Committee, and this sent out written commands. In October 1942, they announced that a certain amount of participation in concert life could be accepted. Soloist performances could take place to some extent with the Philharmonic and orchestras from out of town. By the turn of the year 1942–43, Norwegian musicians and soloists had withdrawn increasingly from public life. Only NS musicians and German guest artists performed at the Aula Hall or other concert venues of the time.[20]

## Wartime Festival in Zurich, 1942

Because of these circumstances, Flagstad was virtually shut out from her career and unable to attend concerts at which her former colleagues were performing. But an invitation from the music festival in Zurich and another to sing in Stockholm proved too tempting. A sojourn abroad would also make contact with America possible: she would be able to call and telegraph her daughter and McArthur once she had left Norway. Like Furtwängler, Flagstad was naive enough to believe that performances in neutral countries would not damage her reputation.

The repertoire she was to sing in Zurich in May and June 1942 was extensive. Flagstad was the mainstay of the festival, and she felt the need to go through the major parts with a singing teacher and vocal coach. There were several to choose from. Through her family, she knew that an opera class had been established at the Norwegian Drama School, where Cally Monrad was in charge, and that Flagstad's old teacher Albert Westwang worked there. The school was run by the Quisling regime, and most of the teachers were therefore suspended after the war.[21] Flagstad was sufficiently politically aware not to approach them.

Instead, she asked the singing teacher Haldis Ingebjart. The elderly woman gave her quite an abrupt and forthright reply, saying that Flagstad would have to travel to her home: "As you know I can't come to yours." Patriotic Norwegians would not set foot in the houses of NS adherents, out of contempt and fear of being associated with them. There was also a widespread perception that interaction with NS members increased the danger of whistleblowing. Ingebjart's response gave Flagstad a shock. She misinterpreted it all, thinking she herself was under suspicion, and with that, she ended their long-standing friendship.

Ingebjart did not suspect Flagstad: if she had done so, she would never have invited her into her home. It was Henry Johansen whose home she refused to visit. This admission, that the community around her regarded her husband as a traitor, was something Flagstad never managed to accept. It would have placed their marriage in peril, leaving her high and dry once more. She did not dare to go there. The connection to a man people regarded as a Quisling supporter made Flagstad increasingly isolated, suspect, and despised.

She had brought her sister with her to Switzerland, and they stayed at the Dolder Grand Hotel, an ornate, turreted castle that towers on a hill overlooking Zurich. They had brought Norwegian flags with them and celebrated Norway's National Day, May 17, with their hosts. The hotel remained open throughout the war, but often with only a handful of guests. Flagstad was given her usual corner room: they were familiar with her requirements. Dolder was famous for its flexibility and ability to take care of special guests. This was why it was a favorite resort of famous, eccentric artists, such as Wilhelm

## Part 3: The Years of Struggle (1941–51)

Furtwängler, for example. He had also booked a room there for the duration of the festival. The hotel had specially trained staff to look after him when he returned in a state of ecstasy after concerts and operas, when he continued his conducting and had to be discreetly ushered to his room so that he would not come to grief while continuing his arm movements during the night.[22]

Flagstad had turned down Furtwängler's invitation to go to Stockholm and sing with the Berlin Philharmonic. Now the management of the music festival in Zurich had invited them both. It is probable that Flagstad saw Furtwängler simply as a conductor and friend on this occasion, rather than a representative of Nazi Germany. Many people were critical of his complex relationship with the Third Reich, a relationship that had led him to conduct the Berlin Philharmonic at special events, including a celebration of Hitler's birthday on April 20 that same year.

Flagstad had a substantial program, including Rezia in *Oberon*, Brunhild in *Götterdämmerung*, and Leonore in *Fidelio*. Furtwängler wielded his baton through *Götterdämmerung*, the high point of the festival. The opera was also associated with the times and so was performed with particular intensity and gravity. The manager of the State Theatre wrote that they had never before had such an influx of the public and that at the same time it had never been so difficult to obtain performers. For the unusually high numbers attending the theater, this was an escape from the terrible events of the time and a retreat into a higher world in which a refined experience was not yet banned and human beings still had value.

The manager relates that a broader stratum of the population now visited the theater. The higher social classes, who had previously been in the majority, now appeared to be fewer and fewer in number. The younger generation were replacing their elders. They had made every effort to meet the enormous demand, and from October 1941, every performance was sold out.[23] Kirsten Flagstad was mentioned as the main attraction from the earlier music festival in June.

The newspapers took several column inches to describe the performances of both her and Furtwängler in *Götterdämmerung*: "It is impossible to give this music more vivid expression than Furtwängler does. For no greater devotion can be shown to it—no greater subtlety in the execution of detail and no greater intensity of sound. It is also impossible to surpass Kirsten Flagstad's Brunhild. This emotionally mature artist outshines everyone else with her interpretation and her voice. She remains triumphant to the very last note. Her exceptional, indescribable and enchanting singing is so heartfelt and

154 THE VOICE OF THE CENTURY

mellifluous that no one else can match it. Not even the exquisite voice of Max Lorenz."[24]

## A Type of Espionage

While the management of the State Theatre, music critics, and the public were all enjoying and praising Flagstad's artistic flair, the official Norwegian representative in Switzerland chose to keep his distance. The Norwegian Foreign Office instead sent a spy to keep track of her. Against the background of the rumors spread through the channels of the ministry, especially through Morgenstierne's letters, the Norwegian envoy Arnold Bakke, who was stationed at the legation in Bern, was assigned to make inquiries about Flagstad. He was to find out discreetly whether she was sympathetic to Quisling and whether Henry Johansen was connected to the NS. To Flagstad, the lunch invitation seemed to be a friendly gesture from the Norwegian diplomatic service. Naive as she was, she was easy prey. Flagstad did not discern the ulterior motive of the meeting.

After some correspondence, Bakke finally arranged an appointment with the Flagstad sisters at the Dolder Grand. His conclusion after their conversation was that they both had the right Norwegian attitude. Flagstad had also told him that her husband had resigned from the NS and that he longed to be rid of both the Germans and the Quislings. Bakke wrote back to his superiors that Flagstad, with her great name, was an illustrious representative of Norway in the rest of the world. Since scurrilous rumors of Kirsten Flagstad's Quisling sympathies were being spread, he also asked others to make sure that these were repudiated. It was not advantageous for Norwegians of international renown to be regarded as Quislings.[25]

The Norwegian representative in Switzerland, Finn Koren, had also written about the matter in a "confidential" letter to the Ministry of Foreign Affairs, which he enclosed. He found it gratifying that Kirsten Flagstad had the right Norwegian attitude and that Henry Johansen had resigned from the NS. As this had not been clarified in advance, he had thought it safest not to attend her performances in Zurich. As a Norwegian envoy in Switzerland, he would have been placed in an awkward position if he had attended a performance at which a Norwegian artist friendly to the Quisling regime made an appearance. Now that the matter was cleared up, he requested that the Foreign Office give all Norwegian consulates in the US clarification of this.[26]

Koren further requested that the government's information office and *Nordisk Tidende*, a Norwegian-language newspaper published in the US, receive

## Part 3: The Years of Struggle (1941–51)

a confidential duplicate of his letter and that the International League of Norsemen be advised of the situation. In an attachment to the Norwegian Foreign Office, based in London, he included three cuttings from newspapers in Zurich with pictures of Flagstad. He writes that she had been a great success and that as far as she was concerned, regardless of her husband's former connection to the NS, she was truly in all her conduct Norwegian through and through. The envoy was convinced that her actions had been of decidedly positive benefit to Norway's cause in Switzerland.

### Flagstad Declared a Nazi Lover by the Government

The Ministry of Foreign Affairs did not follow Koren's advice. Morgenstierne had already sent a number of letters via the ministry's communication channels, and naturally also to the government-in-exile in London, concerning Flagstad's "crazy outlook." His extremely personal picture of her as an enemy and his opinions on the matter had become fixed as the only correct assessment. This emerges from a "confidential" letter sent by the minister of foreign affairs, Trygve Lie, to the legation in Bern on July 13, 1942, in which Bakke is taken to task and corrected with reference to his perception of her. The foreign minister informs Bakke that he has received information to the contrary from Morgenstierne and that therefore he will not commit to taking any action on the matter.[27]

Trygve Lie was a man of influence and authority. He took over as minister of foreign affairs in November 1940 and was temporarily appointed as prime minister from April 16 until July 7, 1942. The letters from the Norwegian diplomat in Bern were sent by courier to London on June 23, and Lie replied on July 13, 1942. It is therefore possible that he dealt with the matter while he was still acting as prime minister. Soon, the Norwegian Legation in Bern would make far more serious approaches to Lie, warnings that he also chose to ignore. In August 1942, he received from them a confidential report that included this information: "The most horrendous accounts are coming from Poland about the treatment the unfortunate Jews are receiving, the intended end result of which, as far as we understand, is the 'liquidation' of this entire race."[28]

Around the same time as the transport ship *Donau* left Oslo harbor on November 26, 1942, with 532 deported Norwegian Jews bound for the extermination camp at Auschwitz, two secretaries in the British section of the World Jewish Congress wrote a report about what was happening to the Jews in the German-occupied areas of Europe. This landed on Foreign Minister Lie's desk in London. The report concluded with an appeal and a plea, also to the

156 THE VOICE OF THE CENTURY

Norwegian government-in-exile: "We therefore suggest that radio broadcasts in your country should include repeated appeals to the general population to resist the deportation of Jews sent to mass slaughter in the strongest terms, and to protect individual Jews, especially children, from being caught by the Nazi terrorists." On December 1, the World Jewish Congress received a reply from Trygve Lie, in which he expressed the opinion that it was not necessary to make such appeals to the Norwegian people about fulfilling their duty as human beings toward the Jews in Norway.[29]

Almost two years later, in September 1944, Ambassador Morgenstierne received a missive from the American Jewish Committee, which included a description of the conditions in the concentration camps in Poland. At the time, it was clear that 1.5 million Jews had been killed in the Majdanek camp. The American Jewish Committee asked the Allies to establish a special commission to investigate the "most dreadful crimes in human history." However, the Norwegian ambassador felt it unnecessary to do anything about this letter since the Jewish committee was not particularly influential or important. Trygve Lie followed the ambassador's recommendation and forwarded the letter to the Ministry of Justice on October 2, 1944, where the matter was shelved with no comment.[30]

On February 1, 1946, Lie was chosen as the first secretary-general of the United Nations, a post he held until November 10, 1952. Would he have been regarded as a worthy candidate if his lack of judgment in such grave circumstances during the war had been common knowledge?

Morgenstierne rose through the ranks. The legation in Washington was made into an embassy, and Morgenstierne went from being a minister to an ambassador, the first Norwegian ambassador. The same thing happened at the Norwegian Legation in London. This change was a gesture made to Norway by the American and British governments, partly because of the significance of the Norwegian merchant fleet and its contribution to the war effort. Before 1942, only the representatives of major powers to other major powers could call themselves ambassadors.

## Ambassador Morgenstierne's Fury

Trygve Lie sent a copy of this correspondence to Ambassador Morgenstierne in Washington, and Morgenstierne became indignant. On August 5, 1942, the ambassador sent the Ministry of Foreign Affairs a letter marked "confidential" regarding the matter. In this, he expressed his surprise at the trade envoy's judgment. He believed that the statements Flagstad had given

## Part 3: The Years of Struggle (1941–51)

to Arnold Bakke in Zurich merely confirmed the impression he had gained of the woman in America. He asks rhetorically about when Henry Johansen had left the NS. Johansen had certainly continued his membership after April 9 and so had betrayed the king and supported obvious traitors who only held their posts with the help of enemy troops. As far as Flagstad was concerned, Morgenstierne once again reminded the ministry of the concert in Washington on November 27, 1940, at which she had nothing but German music on the program. He writes that he cannot forget this humiliation and that the concert became a triumph for the German executioners. In a postscript, he wonders whether it had not been the case that the woman in question, after her return to Norway, had been interviewed by the NS newspaper, *Fritt Folk*, and had praised the conditions in Berlin, where she had spent time on her journey home.[31]

A trade representative and an envoy are subservient to the foreign minister and have to follow the instructions given by the ministry. It probably gave Bakke a shock that the foreign minister, Trygve Lie, had overruled his assessment of Flagstad. Morgenstierne's emotional missive may also have scared the trade envoy, who now wrote a different letter about Flagstad, in which the ministry and Morgenstierne heard what they wanted to hear. Bakke writes that he had had no idea about Flagstad's conduct in America, as explained in Morgenstierne's many letters. If he had known this, his interview with her would have taken a different tone, and he would have received her statements with a greater degree of skepticism. After he met her in Zurich, however, he had heard things about her that did not put fru Flagstad in a favorable light. Had he been in possession of the information given by Ambassador Morgenstierne, he would not have paid her a visit at all. Bakke concludes his new message thus: "After receiving Ambassador Morgenstierne's information, I agree that she cannot possess Norwegian patriotism or any sense of honour and even if she was telling me the truth in Zurich, it was only from a sense of expediency that she has allowed herself to change her mind."[32]

### Stink Bomb in Stockholm

It was certainly far from advisable to travel to Stockholm to give a concert with the permission of the occupying forces, especially given that those Norwegians who had succeeded in escaping over the border had done so in peril of their lives. There was already a large colony of Norwegians and members of the resistance who organized their activities from exile in their neighboring country. Flagstad obviously did not appreciate the effect it had on them for her to travel freely in and out of Norway to perform. The Norwegian Intelligence Service and the Home Front had offices in Stockholm, and they had probably received information that the government regarded Flagstad as a traitor. Rumors of this were spread into the community of Norwegian exiles in Sweden, and they, too, drew the erroneous conclusion that Flagstad, like her husband, was a Quisling supporter.

At the beginning of November, travel arrangements were made for her to go to Stockholm, with a return ticket. She was to hold a concert on November 5, 1942, in the city's concert hall, and the program had undergone censorship in Norway. She had deliberately chosen to include few songs from her German repertoire, but this did not change the image of her as an enemy in the minds of Norwegians. She knew there had been protests in the newspapers about her singing there. She received threatening letters sent to her hotel, and these included all sorts of accusations. Norwegians had waited outside the hall in an attempt to persuade the public to boycott the concert. The hatred became fairly aggressive, and she could smell the reek of a stink bomb thrown at her out in the artists' foyer.

A young Swedish singer, who would later become Flagstad's successor, was seated in the hall. Birgit Nilsson tells us there had been demonstrations against buying tickets for a concert featuring a singer who was a Nazi lover. The atmosphere was ice cold when Flagstad stepped onto the podium. Nilsson could clearly see how nervous and on edge she was. Despite the stony mood and absence of applause, she showed great inner strength by continuing, and by the time the concert was over, she had won the hearts of the audience.[33]

Flagstad took two lessons with her from Stockholm. One was that her voice had the power to turn an audience around, and the second was that she had become an object of hatred to which Norwegians had attached many negative ideas. She understood that untrue stories were being spun about her and that the air was thick with rumors.[34] The exaggerations and absurdity in these may have contributed to her inability to grasp her own input to all this, in that it had not been particularly wise to go to Stockholm in the first place. She was also probably unaware that this image of her as the enemy had reached America. In that year, a book was published in New York that described Flagstad as a *Nazi nightingale*. The book claimed she had attempted to trick Norwegians into Russian death camps. Flagstad was to have given a concert in Oslo to raise funds for soldiers on the front line. Her husband, a supporter of Quisling, had promised he would give jobs to all surviving soldiers who returned home from the eastern front.[35]

## Part 3: The Years of Struggle (1941–51)

Many people in America may have believed these wild rumors. The Norwegian diplomatic service, following everything Flagstad did and said very closely, found no reason to repudiate the allegations. The Norwegian Embassy in Washington allowed the flood of false rumors to spread unchallenged.

### Flagstad's Declaration of Solidarity with the Music Front in Norway

In 1940, around 140 members of the Oslo Musicians' Union were unemployed and destitute. The Musicians' Union had recommended they apply for work in the Deutsches Theater (German Theater) and had held benefit concerts for them on a number of occasions. After the war, some of them were fined for these activities, but others got off scot-free. What were they to live on? The most idealistic of them chose to starve, but the ones with the most pressing family responsibilities may have chosen to hold on to their jobs.

In the autumn of 1942, a 30 percent luxury tax was imposed on all independent musical activity, with the proceeds going to the Nazi state, meaning that from then on, artists would be giving direct financial support to the NS. It also became dangerous to perform in public as immediately afterward the artist could be invited and pressured into performing at political events. Pictures were taken of them and subsequently used against them to apply further pressure. Patriotic Norwegians had to be careful which concerts they attended. People with connections to the Music Front would stand at the entrance and make a note of who had turned up. "Everyone who holds concerts risks being regarded as a Nazi or collaborator" was how it was expressed.[36] The Music Front's ban on public concerts was common knowledge as early as August 27, 1942. In September, fresh orders were issued to the effect that no soloist should perform in public.

Flagstad received vivid reports from her family about the terrible circumstances of musicians and vocalists. Her whole family joined the Music Front and gave no public performances after this order came into effect in the autumn of 1942. As for Flagstad herself, she lived in fear of finally being forced to perform. It must have given her a shock to read *Aftenposten* on December 1, 1942, in which Arne van Erpekum Sem reviewed a Wagner concert and pointed out that Kirsten Flagstad, the most famous Brunhild in the world, was living in Norway: "Norwegians never had the pleasure of hearing Ellen Gulbranson, one of the most famous interpreters of Wagner in the world. Now her successor as the world's most renowned Isolde and Brunhild, Kirsten Flagstad, is at home in Norway. Are we not to be allowed to see and hear her either, in the Wagnerian musical drama and the roles in which she has aroused the greatest admiration and enthusiasm throughout the globe?"[37]

Flagstad sympathized with her patriotic colleagues in Norway who lacked the means to earn a living. On December 19, 1942, she set up a trust fund of as much as 200,000 Norwegian kroner to benefit young musicians, preferably the children of professional musicians. The endowment was established in gratitude to Flagstad's parents and bears their name. She most likely had their battle to survive economically as professional musicians fresh in her mind. Converted to today's money and taking inflation into account, the value of this would have been 4,740,000 kroner, the largest endowment ever administered by the Norwegian Musicians' Union. Initially, the wording was that it should assist the children of musicians who were training to be musicians themselves, but it was quickly changed to apply more widely. The war years substantially drained the original capital. The fund's purpose and modification may well have been tactical stipulations to prevent interference from the NS.[38]

This was unquestionably a political move, given that most unemployed musician families were in that position because they refused to perform in Nazified settings. Flagstad's considerable contribution supported the Music Front in Norway.

## Under Pressure

In 1943, Flagstad came under great pressure. This was the year in which Norway's greatest composer, Edvard Grieg, would have been one hundred. Nazi propaganda linked Grieg to the concept of a Greater Germanic Reich. His music, strongly influenced by Norwegian folk music, incited Goebbels's fantasy of the Proto-Germanic. The Nazi Ministry of Culture had therefore organized a grand celebration with guests from home and abroad. Centenary concerts were planned for the entire country: the occupying powers and the NS were keen to demonstrate to the populace that they valued Norway's culture.

For Norwegians who had seen through their motives, it all seemed to be a lamentable sacrilege. The nation's great tone poems were being misused for political purposes, and people reacted by turning away. The Ministry of Culture knew that a world-famous singer—one who had done a great deal to make Grieg known in America and throughout Europe—was now living in Norway. Flagstad must have been subjected to great pressure to perform. She must have expected this and had made other plans. She would give a polite refusal, explaining that she would be leaving Norway for several months.

## Part 3: The Years of Struggle (1941–51)

In March, she gave two charity concerts in Malmö, Sweden. In May, she returned to Switzerland, and at the music festival in Zurich, she sang three major roles: Alcestis, Isolde, and the *Walküre* Brunhild. The festival organizers could not have arranged such a program without her cooperation. *Alceste* had not been presented in any theater for seventeen years, and the concert stayed long in the memories of both audience and critics.

Kirsten Flagstad emerged as the supreme interpreter of the title role. Her noble, majestic bearing as Alcestis, the grandeur of her diction, and her spiritual rapture constituted a vocal and scenic perfection impossible to surpass. With a magnificently fluent, exquisite display of singing, the highly dramatic arch of the aria "Divinités du Styx" (The deities of the Styx) was cool and smooth as marble. The applause grew into ovations, and the audience gave thanks not only for the splendid performance but also for her interpretation of Alcestis. Kirsten Flagstad revealed to the public the musical euphoria that lies within the work.[39] *Tristan and Isolde* became almost a sacred experience. The drama and tragedy of contemporary events must have strongly affected the experience. "We have never, ever had such an elevated festive mood in our theater," concluded the theater manager.

The letters from the Norwegian trade envoy Bakke to the Ministry of Foreign Affairs stand in stark contrast to these ovations. He had again insisted on meeting Flagstad for lunch, and four years later, he wrote a letter to the Foreign Ministry about the encounter, claiming he had given her the third degree. It was certain that she had refused to sing in Germany despite great pressure to do so. After all, she would have had to travel through Germany to arrive in Switzerland. During both of her visits to Zurich, she lived in total isolation at her hotel outside the city. Bakke asserts that she was told of everything he had heard about her from New York. He writes that Flagstad denied the truth of this. She said of Morgenstierne that he bore a grudge against her after an episode that had taken place at an intermission at the opera house. Bakke concludes his letter by saying that there can be no doubt that Flagstad had offended greatly against her duty as a Norwegian citizen.[40] This was how Bakke presented the case to his superiors in 1947.

### Did Flagstad Flee from *The Flying Dutchman*?

In November 1943, Flagstad set out alone on a journey to an outlying Norwegian farm sixty kilometers from the Swedish border. Her mother had vacationed there and was friends with the owners. It was exceptional for Flagstad to venture out on such a trip, as she really preferred to be on her own. Flagstad was a shy person, and it was no easy task to have her leave her home and settle into someone else's private quarters, even though they belonged to old friends of the family. Moreover, it was winter and cold. The great, mysterious question is why she "decamped" from her home to seek refuge on the farm at exactly this point in time. Was she fleeing from the henchmen of the occupying forces and needing to lie low in an unfamiliar location? The farm she came to was a meeting place for a resistance group that transported refugees across to Sweden.

The answer to this hitherto unsolved mystery is most likely to be found in Oslo's cultural calendar. The country had no opera house, and the occupying forces compensated for this by establishing a German opera house in Stortingsgate, where Flagstad's old workplace the Casino had been. Norway was the only occupied country in World War II in which the Nazis built an opera house. Goebbels supported the project because he felt certain that opera would have a strong impact on cultural propaganda. The Casino was transformed from a cinema to an opera house, and a number of unemployed musicians came from outside the city to work there.

In June 1941, the new German opera house in Oslo, the Deutsches Theater, opened. German publications boasted of the cooperation with the scenic country, the homeland of blond people, with lineage from the Germanic Vikings to Peer Gynt. The redevelopment continued throughout the autumn of 1941, with the construction of a fourteen-meter-deep stage and installation of advanced new technical equipment. The opera house existed for three and a half years and put on performances of high artistic and technical quality. Guest appearances were made by the very best talents from Germany in various fields, such as the tenor Martin Kremer from Berlin. He stated in a newspaper interview that he had stood onstage with Flagstad in Bayreuth. Hans Hopf was occasionally employed at the opera house in Oslo; he later became world famous and made his debut at the Metropolitan in 1952. Many Norwegian singers took part in the chorus at light opera performances there.

No Norwegian solo vocalist was ever engaged there, but Flagstad was primarily a world-renowned interpreter of Wagner. She may therefore have received a strongly worded request to sing the role of Senta in the Deutsches Theater's greatest production to date, *The Flying Dutchman*, which premiered on December 20, 1943. The opera was being presented to mark the centenary of the original production in Dresden. Senta was the only role the German opera house presented during the war that would have been suitable for Flagstad. The action takes place in Sandvik ("Sandwigen"), near Tvedestrand on

Kirsten Flagstad as Senta in *The Flying Dutchman* at the Metropolitan in 1947. She had been involved in the making of the costume, which resembles a traditional Norwegian regional dress. The customary silver filigree brooch may have belonged to her. Senta is a Norwegian girl, the daughter of a sea captain from the south coast of Norway. *Source: Flagstad Museum.*

164 THE VOICE OF THE CENTURY

the south coast of Norway. Senta is the daughter of a Norwegian sea captain, so Flagstad would have been an ideal choice. She was known for the role, having sung it at Covent Garden as well as at the Metropolitan, most recently in March 1940. "Senta's Ballad" often featured on her concert program. Flagstad knew the part so well that she could have gone straight into the dress rehearsal, and the management of the opera house probably knew that. She may well have received a demand to appear, behind which lay a certain threat. It could also have been suggested that they would seek her out in Kristiansand, and this may be why she had chosen to go into hiding.

Wagner once described *The Dutchman* as representing the universal longing for rest amid the storms of life. Flagstad, on the other hand, was afraid that "Nazism's Dutchman" would take hold of her and cast an eternal shadow over her life, and so she fled from the coast in Kristiansand to the forests of inland Norway. At the Irstad farm in Romedal, she held her only concert in wartime Norway, for twenty-plus people from the resistance movement. In the living room, there was a piano, on which she accompanied herself. The songs were mainly Norwegian and made a strong impression on the somber gathering. Some time later, the escape route was bombed by the Gestapo, the farm was raided, and several people were arrested and tortured.

It was not only the occupying forces that were looking for Flagstad but also the Norwegian Intelligence Service. She had no inkling of this. The Home Front and intelligence service had offices in Stockholm, London, and Washington during the war. Information regarding Flagstad was exchanged and sent to the exiled government in London. This emerges from a "confidential" telegram sent from the embassy in Washington to the minister of foreign affairs, Trygve Lie, in London on November 29, 1943, for example: "Police Superintendent Iversen requests the intelligence service to send him via courier the information they must have on Kirsten Flagstad and Henry Johansen senior and junior, without delay."[41] On November 30, the foreign minister forwarded the telegram to the intelligence service office at the Ministry of Defense. They were well aware of Johansen's circumstances and kept Flagstad under surveillance, suspected of being friendly to the Nazis. In more diplomatic language, it was a question of the degree to which she had "the right Norwegian attitude."

## Husband's Situation during the War

Flagstad kept her artistic path clean, but being married to an opportunistic capitalist and NS sympathizer left her vulnerable to suspicion that she had

## Part 3: The Years of Struggle (1941–51)          165

Nazi sympathies. Johansen owned several timber companies whose operations included the production of materials for barracks and landing strips for the occupying powers. One of his companies had also taken on the business of managing deliveries from many other Norwegian timber producers that also did business with the Germans. The findings made about his activities during the war bear witness to his appetite for profitable transactions but also to a lack of political involvement. Johansen did not socialize with his old friends in the NS, nor does he feature on the membership list of the NS club that power seekers in Norwegian business life frequented during the war.[42]

The absence of any ideological stance meant that he moved between both camps, dealing with the Nazis while also supporting the Home Front. Two of his children were heavily involved in the Norwegian resistance movement. His eldest daughter, Kate Gjerdrum, worked within an illegal group whose activities Johansen financed. Henry Johansen Jr. took part in the publication and distribution of the illegal newspaper 5 på 12 (Five to twelve). These activities took place in one of Henry Johansen Ltd.'s offices, and the newspaper was distributed through the firm. The industrialist knew of this and gave financial support to these activities. His firm was also involved in other illegal acts. Members of resistance groups who produced fake stamps, passports, and identity papers recall that some time before the German action against Norwegian Jews in October 1942, they received requests to make false stamps for use by refugees. The group continued with this work until Easter 1945, when one of them had to go into hiding. He says that one of his contacts during the war was the departmental manager Siegel at Henry Johansen Ltd.

Siegel was a timber agent in Henry Johansen's firm. During the war, he was contacted by Henry Johansen Jr., who asked for his help to produce false passports since Siegel had contact with employees in the passport office at Oslo Police Headquarters. Siegel wrote out the cards, and Johansen Jr. falsified the signatures. These fake identity papers were distributed by Johansen. "In particular there was a lot to do during the student campaign in 1943," Siegel states in a subsequent witness interview.[43] The passport office issued false ID cards and arranged for fake stamps from a number of police stations in both the cities and rural areas. People involved in this activity, assisting resistance workers, Jews, and students, may have produced around four hundred false passport papers. It was the task of Henry Johansen Jr. to deliver false ID papers and passports to people in the East Zone (the Home Front had divided the capital city into various zones). In the case of Johansen Jr., this may have amounted to several hundred papers and cards. On November 30, 1944, Siegel

166 THE VOICE OF THE CENTURY

had to produce a false passport for Johansen Jr. and his family because the Gestapo were breathing down his neck. Passport no. 34925/45 was issued for all countries, but Johansen contented himself with escaping to Sweden.[44]

One witness states that Johansen Sr. and his office manager Stake called on the Gestapo and reported Johansen Jr. the same day he fled. Apparently they emphasized that personal disagreements had been the cause of his escape. A political exit would have damaged Johansen Sr. and his firm.[45] According to the ordinance passed by the occupying force on October 12, 1942, escape from Norway incurred the death penalty, reduced to imprisonment in mitigating circumstances. The assets of escapees would be confiscated by the Treasury. Anyone who assisted others in their escape would be punished, and their family would be taken as hostages. A detective inspector in the Gestapo, Wilhelm Esser, explains that on this occasion he had refrained from taking the usual measures, such as arresting family members and confiscating assets. The Gestapo was satisfied with seizing Johansen Jr.'s house. Esser had done this out of consideration for Johansen's wife, who was a famous singer. At the time, he had come into personal contact with Henry Johansen Sr. and evidently thought he was a nice man.

### Gestapo Boss Cannot Be Fooled

The brutal head of the Gestapo in Norway, Albert Weiner, was not taken in by Johansen Sr.'s smoothness. He proposed to uncover the illegal activity in the industrialist's company and sent an agent there. The Gestapo agent, who pretended to be a member of the resistance, managed to get 2,000 kroner handed over, purportedly to be given to the Home Front. In December 1944, Weiner sent another agent to Stake's office. The agent said that he had just been released from Grini prison camp and asked if he could borrow some money to travel to Bergen, where he had business interests. Stake found all this very suspicious but gave him 200 kroner. In February 1945, the Gestapo arrived and arrested Stake. His office was sealed off. Three days later, he was brought in front of Weiner, who showed him the photograph of the man he had loaned 200 kroner. If he did not tell everything he knew about illegal activities, Weiner would send him to a concentration camp in Germany. Stake was released after being interrogated overnight and told that they would be keeping a close eye on him.[46]

In the summer of 1941, the German commander in chief, Terboven, introduced a law permitting him to declare a state of emergency and use courts-martial. He made use of this facility three times: in Oslo in September 1941,

## Part 3: The Years of Struggle (1941–51)

then in Trondheim in October 1942, and again in February 1945 after the Home Front's liquidation of police chief Karl Alfred Marthinsen. Flagstad's husband was brought before this last court-martial. Weiner ordered Henry Johansen's arrest on February 9, 1945. He was imprisoned and told that he would be condemned to death and shot. Johansen was imprisoned for a total of eight days. Weiner also dealt with the case of one of Johansen's relatives-in-law who was a member of the same resistance network as Johansen's two children. This relative was condemned to execution by firing squad. The German officer Wilhelm Esser put in a good word for Johansen with the SS principal judge in Oslo Police District, Hans Latza. Latza was the one who had the last word. Johansen Sr. escaped execution at the very last minute. Latza claimed he had told the German police chief Heinrich Fehlis that he did not want to subject the industrialist Henry Johansen to court-martial because he was over sixty years of age.

That Johansen's life had hung in the balance at this time is confirmed in a letter Quisling's informal foreign minister, Finn Støren, wrote to the police chief Heinrich Fehlis on February 9, 1945, concerning Johansen's reprieve. It emerges here that Fehlis had notified Støren that Henry Johansen had donated large sums over a period of several months for the support and development of illegal activity in Norway. Støren had passed this information on to Quisling. They were of the opinion that Johansen's case should be taken very seriously, as he was guilty of the most grievous offenses.[47]

Kirsten Flagstad told her American biographer that her husband, after coming home from his imprisonment in February 1945, had said that he would tell her everything that had happened once the war had ended. She obviously knew nothing of either the secret resistance work that was going on around him, some of which he had financed, or his extensive business dealings with the occupying forces.

### Diplomatic Service Spreads Untruths

On February 23, 1945, the Norwegian ambassador in Washington issued a press release exclusively to the *New York Times*. In this, he writes that Henry Johansen, husband of Kirsten Flagstad, the opera singer at the Metropolitan famous for her interpretations of Wagner roles, had engineered a face-saving setup with the Gestapo. They arrested him to reinforce his alibi. Johansen had earned large sums trading with the Germans, and a day of reckoning awaited him.[48] It also emerged that the embassy, through the Royal Norwegian Information Service in New York, had passed this on in a radio program

168 THE VOICE OF THE CENTURY

for American listeners. At peak broadcasting time, on February 28, this conspiracy theory was presented as truth. The embassy later issued transcribed copies on request.[49] In March, the embassy issued another press release about the case. It was repeated on March 2 in the publications *Her og der I Norge* (Here and there in Norway) and *News of Norway*.

Johansen was unknown to the American public. This type of "news" would probably not have appeared in the *New York Times* or been transmitted on the radio if it had not implicated a celebrity in the US, Kirsten Flagstad. The report links her to Johansen's business affairs, also suggesting a connection to her repertoire, since her fame rested on her interpretations of Wagner.

## Postwar Legal Purge in Norway

Germany surrendered unconditionally on May 7, 1945. On the very next day, May 8, legal action began against all those who had collaborated with the enemy in one way or another during the war. This began with the imprisonment and interning of suspected persons according to lists drawn up by the Home Front and the Norwegian authorities in Sweden and Britain, the so-called List no. 1. Mass arrests were carried out of the twenty-five to thirty thousand members of the NS and others who had collaborated with the Germans the length and breadth of the country. These arrests and the forthcoming treason trials had been planned over several years by the government-in-exile in London, working with representatives of the Home Front.

The death penalty, not used in Norway since 1876 and removed from civil criminal law in 1902, was reintroduced by the exiled government in London on October 3, 1941. Anyone who had been a member of the NS, or organizations linked to the party, after April 8, 1940, could be punished by loss of public trust, which could mean loss of the right to vote, military service, work in the public sector, access to public services, public positions that required authorization or endorsement, independent professional activity, management positions and honorary posts in organizations or associations, and permission to own and acquire real estate, ships, shares, and interest payments.

For the members of the NS, collective guilt and collective liability for damages were established so that they, one for all and all for one, had to answer for and repay what the NS regime had cost the Norwegian state, estimated at 281 million Norwegian kroner. A body of laws was introduced, comprising fifty-one paragraphs of rules about punishment, confiscation, and restitution, and a separate Reparations Office was set up to administer cases of confiscation and

## Part 3: The Years of Struggle (1941–51)          169

restitution. There was no limit to what could be demanded of individuals. Life insurance policies could be confiscated, and if anyone was unable to cover the sum of compensation required, it could be seized from the spouse even if that person had not been a member of the NS. This also applied even when a legal arrangement for separate marital property was in force. The deceased could be criminally prosecuted by having their estate impounded and heirs held responsible for the sum of compensation and forfeiture. This was later dropped.

The treason laws of 1944 led to the pursuit of all NS members, even those who had only been passively connected. This resulted in the most comprehensive postwar treason settlement in western Europe. Around 92,810 cases were investigated, and 46,085 of these led to convictions. It was unique in Norwegian history for so many people to be suddenly excluded from society.

In retrospect, fundamental objections to the legal purge have been made. The financial consequences of the treason trials did not affect only members of the NS. The major war profiteers went free, while around thirty thousand passive NS members were punished. During World War II, 130,000 slave workers came to Norway, a workforce that Hitler's Germany had forcibly recruited. They worked for the Norwegian State Railways, the Public Roads Administration, Norwegian Hydro, the Norwegian aluminum industry, and a number of other Norwegian companies through the Todt organization. A total of seventeen thousand slave workers died in Norway. The country was, relative to the size of population, the area of German occupation that accepted the highest number of slave workers. In the court settlement, none of the Norwegian employers were held to account for this use of slave workers.[50] No forced labor, as far as is known, worked in any of Johansen's companies.

In the press, Henry Johansen was portrayed in 1945 as Norway's greatest war profiteer. He most certainly was not. The far from honorable first place goes to the so-called Oslo Consortium, which in 1941 invested 7.9 million kroner (around 24.5 million kroner in 1971 values or 172 million in 2013) in Norwegian Hydro's heavy-water and light-metal production. The investment meant that Norwegian Hydro could start up new production vital to the war effort and become a prospective producer for the Luftwaffe, which was fighting for world dominance. This investment occurred at the same time as the German occupation of Norway moved into a more brutal phase.

The investors comprised pragmatic Norwegian businessmen and companies that, like Johansen, passed no judgment on the moral aspect of cooperating with the Nazi regime. None of them belonged to the NS, and they were

170  THE VOICE OF THE CENTURY

not prosecuted in the postwar legal purge. The authorities also let them retain their profits, thus making them into the war's greatest profiteers.[51] Several prominent bankers could be added to the list. Norwegian banks gave willing assistance to Nazi Germany, providing, for example, a loan of millions to IG Farben, a major German chemicals company, with a view to establishing the industry in Norway.

## Demand for Astronomical Sums in Reparation

Henry Johansen was arrested on Friday, May 11, 1945, and sent to Ilebu treason camp. On June 26, 1945, the Reparations Office lodged a claim for compensation from Henry Johansen for as much as 750 million kroner (15 billion in present-day value). The demand came in the form of a telegram to Kristiansand Police Station. No individual in Norway in 1945 came close to owning such a vast sum of money. Johansen's estimated assets after the war were 2 million kroner and an income of 140,000 kroner. How out of proportion this demand for compensation was is best illustrated by the fact that between the original demand and the final judgment in 1950, there is a difference of almost 748 million kroner. The total amount collected by the Reparations Office for all treason cases in Norway came to 288 million kroner, and what the NS had cost the Norwegian state was calculated at 281 million kroner.

The judgment in Johansen's case in 1950 was appealed. On October 9, 1951, the Reparations Office wrote to the Supreme Court that the appeals from all parties in the case were waived because an agreement had been reached. The office's archive card states that the sum to be paid for the case to be concluded was 1,850,000 kroner.[52] This was the final compensation sum in the case.

## Total Sequestration of Kirsten Flagstad's Assets

The Reparations Office therefore originally demanded 750 million kroner from Johansen. Naturally, he was unable to cover this cost, and so Kirsten Flagstad's independent assets could also be seized. On June 29, 1945, an inspector from the police visited her at home and instructed her to compile an exact inventory of all her household effects, which were later subject to valuation. In the National Archives of Norway, her lengthy lists of household furnishings and other personal effects, from attic to cellar, are on file. Pedantic as she was, everything is included, right down to each and every pot holder. After this, she had to live on small monthly payments from the Reparations Office. In a letter from February 10, 1946, she writes that she has to be very

Part 3: The Years of Struggle (1941–51) 171

careful with her money. The number of telegrams she could send to the US was extremely limited because they were expensive.[53]

Flagstad had personal assets worth around three million Norwegian kroner in the values of that time, divided into different bank accounts in Norway and the US. She had been the highest-paid singer in the world for several years, with an extensive workload in both America and Europe. Her annual gross profits may have been as much as three million kroner. Flagstad's independent wealth consisted of savings, money she had earned before the war. She owned no shipyards, shares, or any other equity stake in her husband's business activities.

Johansen and his companies absolutely qualified for financial settlement through the Reparations Office. Even so, if the original demand had been fairly reasonably proportionate to the final compensation sum, Johansen would have been able to cover it himself by some margin. There were large sums of money in his companies, and his personal wealth alone had been sufficient. It was the absurdity of the sum, 750 million kroner, that meant involving Flagstad and her private wealth in the case. Most likely she understood none of this herself: her lawyer sent objections, but these were ineffectual.

This obvious absurdity reinforced her perception that they both were victims of a wicked, unfair process. Flagstad lacked both the ability and will to regard her husband's business activities with an occupying power as unpatriotic. As far as she was concerned, he was the best husband in the world, and it was impossible for him to do any wrong. This unqualified solidarity and naivete also linked her to his adversity. She wrote to friends in the US: "He has kept his business interests going without German control and, like so many others, was forced to deliver what they asked for. It is easy for people living in England, Sweden and America rather than here, to pass judgment on such things."[54]

This was how she saw it, and this was probably also the way he presented the situation to her. Occupation involves an element of compulsion, but in Johansen there was also a considerable willingness to cooperate. Her husband would probably, like many other Norwegian businessmen, have got off more lightly if he had not been a member of the NS until 1941.

## Caught in Hitler's Shadow

A glaring and almost inexplicable example of naive solidarity to a husband is shown by Winifred Wagner in Syberberg's lengthy documentary film about

172 THE VOICE OF THE CENTURY

her from 1977. Here she speaks openly and honestly about her relationship with Adolf Hitler. Like Flagstad, she declares herself to be a completely apolitical person. Her relationship with Hitler was personal and emotional, and they never spoke of politics. She experienced only one aspect of him, qualities that very few people would associate with him. As far as she was concerned, Hitler was not Der Führer but a fascinating, warmhearted man who never disappointed her throughout the twenty-two years she knew him. What went on outside of Bayreuth had nothing to do with her and did not affect her. She did not connect Hitler with politics: their association was private and personal, rooted in a mutual love of Richard Wagner. Hitler was a good uncle to her children and a support to her son Wieland during the war as well as to her. When she attached herself to someone in this way, she remained loyal through thick and thin.

She would never deny her friendship with him. If someone close to her were to kill someone, it would not change her relationship with that person. She understood that this may well be baffling to most people, but she could entirely disassociate the Hitler she knew from everything of which he stood accused. For her, only personal experience mattered. This might well be difficult to fathom, but Winifred Wagner left it to the psychologists to explain: "All the shady side, I know it existed, but it did not exist for me. I don't know that side of him."[55]

There is little reason to doubt that she may have experienced Hitler like that. She may have seen and appreciated a human element that history, from its knowledge of Hitler's incomprehensible atrocities and insanities, is unable to ascribe to him. Winifred Wagner left it to psychologists to explain the separation and contradiction between the collective experience of Hitler and her individual knowledge of him. It is no easy matter to get to the bottom of this question. Emotional relationships in which dependency plays a part often make us blind. The emotional aspect is divided from the intellectual. Our intelligence is clouded by an unconscious psychologically qualified denial, and we are unable to comprehend that those we are emotionally attached to can have major flaws.

If Winifred Wagner had taken Hitler's atrocities seriously, she would as a consequence have had to repudiate him. Was she able to do that? A woman with a traumatic upbringing in a children's home, the leader of a major German cultural institution in Nazi Germany, the mother of four children, where did her requirements lie? From an absolute, idealistic perspective, she should of course have cut all contact and resisted everything he represented. This

Part 3: The Years of Struggle (1941–51)     173

could have led her to a concentration camp and death, as happened to many others. The Danish philosopher Søren Kierkegaard claims in his work *Practice in Christianity* that no one can call oneself Christian without first placing oneself in the times of Christ. The control question is this: If you had been living at that time, would you have stood by his side, even if it had resulted in persecution and cost you your life?

Flagstad's husband was no war criminal, but he was a capitalist and an opportunistic profiteer long before the outbreak of war. This side of him did not exist for her. Flagstad's emotional relationship and dependency refused to accept that this was also an aspect of her husband. This blind spot led her into confrontation with the official belief.

## Kirsten Flagstad Declared Dead in Norway

Flagstad as an individual had attracted from the public an unrealistic adulation as a deified celebrity. This was about to turn to the exact opposite, and she became an object of hatred. The Norwegian Embassy in Washington bore responsibility in the run-up to this change of opinion.

On May 14, 1945, the *New York Times* printed an article stating that Flagstad was keen to return to America as quickly as possible to see her daughter. Flagstad had received a visit from an Associated Press journalist who penned an article claiming that Flagstad felt finished with Norway and wanted to become an American citizen.

The Norwegian Embassy in Washington issued an official telegram about her on June 14, 1945, and extracts were published in the *New York Times* the next day. This telegram is a key document as the Ministry of Foreign Affairs later always referred to this statement when they received any questions about Flagstad. The embassy later refused, on instructions from the ministry, to give any "official" declaration about her until March 16, 1947. The telegram from Washington, dated June 14, 1945, included the following:

> The situation and status of Kirsten Flagstad, former Metropolitan soprano, was explained today by the Norwegian Embassy: She was in this country when Norway was invaded. Her husband, Henry Johansen, was in Norway. Very soon after the German invasion, he joined the Nazi party. He is a big business man in Norway, in the lumber business, and he made sixty million crowns in dealing with the Germans. That is an awful lot of money—probably no other person profited more.
>
> Kirsten Flagstad decided to leave the United States of America and join her husband in Norway. She was aware of the fact that her husband was a

174           THE VOICE OF THE CENTURY

Nazi. Norwegians both inside and out of the country feel that her place was not at home—it was in this country, where she could do a job for Norway. She went to Portugal and from there to Berlin and was flown from Berlin to Norway....

There is nothing to prove that she was an active Nazi or even a passive Nazi. But I can quote C.J. Hambro, the president of the Norwegian Parliament, as having said at a meeting at Town Hall in New York that as far as the Norwegians are concerned, Kirsten Flagstad was dead.

Kirsten Flagstad has not been arrested. She probably will not be. Her husband, of course, is in prison. The fact that she wants to leave Norway now might very well indicate how the Norwegian people feel towards her. But the question of refusing her an exit permit might very well be under consideration.[56]

This statement continued to stand as the single definitive official Norwegian document about Kirsten Flagstad's situation until 1947. Everyone in America who approached the Norwegian Embassy regarding Flagstad in the period 1945–47 was referred to this press release, written by Tor Myklebost, the press attaché at the embassy in Washington. It had huge consequences for Flagstad and inflamed opinion in the US against her. An avalanche of negative comments was unleashed about her in the American press. The media industry realized they had free rein since the embassy would not protest no matter what they wrote about her.

On June 15, the day after this statement was released, the first attack on Flagstad came in the *New York Times*. A journalist called Irving Spiegel had called the manager of the Metropolitan, Edward Johnson, and confronted him with the embassy's declaration. Johnson replied that it was up to the American authorities to decide whether Flagstad could return to the US. It was not possible for the Metropolitan to consider a new contract for her before she was in the country. He also said that the Wagner repertoire had been very successful in Flagstad's absence.[57] The journalist then went on to quote from parts of the Norwegian Embassy statement.

Immediately afterward, an article appeared in a music journal, the *Musician*. The publication had devoted one and a half pages to slander and false accusations. The article rounded off by saying that Flagstad would never sing again. No amount of whitewashing could ever remove the stigma of "traitor" that the Norwegian people had placed on her. After this, the gossip columns were filled with negative reports.[58]

Part 3: The Years of Struggle (1941–51)            175

## Kirsten Flagstad Denied Passport and Exit Visa

The embassy statement started the bitterest controversy that any artist had ever faced in the postwar US. The music critic Oscar Thompson used his entire column in the *New York Sun* three Sundays in a row to discuss the story. The Metropolitan had not made any comment until Johnson was confronted with the Norwegian Embassy's pronouncement, which was repeated in a number of newspapers and used as an argument to deny her entry to the US.[59]

From what Flagstad read in the Norwegian press and their reiteration of reports in US newspapers, she gained the impression that no one wanted to hear her voice anymore and that Americans did not want her back. "Is that so?" she asks in a letter to McArthur.[60]

On July 12, 1945, she turned fifty and received a visit from her closest family. Norwegians had regained their freedom, but she was facing an uncertain future. Since her assets had been seized, she had a pressing need to start earning money again. Stake, the office manager, began to draw up a plan of work based on the requests that were pouring in. There was a great demand for artistic events after the war, and Flagstad did not lack for offers. To travel, she had to renew her passport, and she made an application through a lawyer.

On June 20, 1945, six days after the embassy had issued its statement, Morgenstierne wrote a letter marked "confidential" to the Ministry of Foreign Affairs. It bears the heading "Kirsten Flagstad's Political Views." In it, he refers to something Flagstad was alleged to have said to a journalist, that she was not a friend of Norway. Morgenstierne again reminded the ministry of the bitterness and disappointment felt in Norwegian circles when she had had exclusively German music on the program at her concert on November 27, 1940. He also reminded them of his previous letter to the ministry about the matter and referred again to her statements to Bakke, the trade envoy. He writes:

> Isolde could have made an enormous effort for Norway during the war years, with her preeminent position in the USA. Instead she travelled to Norway, with German assistance, not to take part in the fight by the Home Front, but to join her husband who was a notorious member of the NS, a fact of which she was aware. Norwegian seamen did not go home to their families. Thousands of Norwegians travelled out of Norway, in mortal danger, to take part in the war effort abroad.
>
> In her present state of mind, Kirsten Flagstad could do great damage if she were to come to the USA now, where she most assuredly has many

The voice of the century was kept as a political prisoner in Norway until December 1946. *Source: Flagstad Museum.*

admirers and connections. It would be easy for her to confuse people's ideas with respect to the difference between Norwegians and Quislings, and about the situation in Norway. The ambassador strongly urges that if possible, she should be prevented from travelling to the USA.[61]

Part 3: The Years of Struggle (1941–51)     177

He also sent a similar telegram to Foreign Minister Trygve Lie. The Ministry of Foreign Affairs and the foreign minister applied to the Ministry of Justice for their assistance in preventing Flagstad from leaving Norway. This is clear from official stamps and a note from the Foreign Office dated December 4, 1946, from which it emerged that the ministry, in a reply on November 8 to the national police chief, had written: "As far as he is concerned, there is no reason to recommend that fru Flagstad be given the opportunity to travel out of the country."[62]

The Ministry of Foreign Affairs and Ambassador Morgenstierne were the driving force behind the official decision to refuse Kirsten Flagstad permission to leave Norway. Morgenstierne did not want her to return to America. He put forward political arguments such as that she could "confuse people's ideas with respect to the difference between Norwegians and Quislings." For the moment, she had to answer her French agent and everyone else who asked for her that unfortunately she was not allowed to leave her homeland.

"The Voice of the Century" was confined to Norway. However, no charges were brought against her. Could she be regarded as a political prisoner? Flagstad's sheer presence was considered a challenge or threat to the authorities. Other factors would also be brought to bear. When an old enemy of Johansen's gained a central role in the case, it became even more complicated and dramatic.

### Old Enemy Appointed Prosecutor

To implement the compensation settlement, the Reparations Office appointed an inspector, a lawyer, in all cases of larger applications for restitution and those in which confiscated property had to be managed. There were four thousand "clean" lawyers in Norway after the war—and three thousand estates that had to be administered.

In May 1945, the former Home Front leader, then the newly appointed director of the Reparations Office and subsequently the minister of defense and minister of justice, Jens Christian Hauge, asked the legal expert Ingolf Sundfør to step in as official receiver and administrator in the case against Henry Johansen. Sundør was later also appointed by the director of public prosecution as official receiver for Flagstad's confiscated assets. Sundør's specialism was maritime law, and according to his legal colleagues, he had no experience in criminal cases of any significance. He was obviously not qualified to conduct what was presented as Norway's greatest economic treason

178 THE VOICE OF THE CENTURY

lawsuit. Moreover, it caused amazement that Henry Johansen's old foe was named as his official receiver and administrator.

There was a fierce enmity of long standing between Johansen and Sundfør. In 1933, the industrialist was involved in a bitter divorce wrangle. The wife of his business partner Fritz Mowinckel had engaged the services of Sundfør, who launched a violent attack on her husband and Johansen. The lawyer reported them to the police for withholding and falsifying evidence, but the public prosecutor had sent the report back to the police with a recommendation for partial shelving of the case. Sundfør became so outraged that he continued to pursue the matter in the tabloid press, and the case moved to the columns of the liberal newspaper *Dagbladet.*

Mowinckel and Johansen were accused of tax evasion on the front page of the newspaper. Sundfør had appealed against the public prosecutor's dropping of the case and threatened to blow his top if the appeal proved unsuccessful.[63] Johansen's lawyer replied to his allegations in the same newspaper, but this response merely added fuel to the flames. Sundfør immediately refuted his comments and amplified his accusations against Johansen, saying in conclusion that he felt morally indignant and furious.[64]

Several articles followed in which Sundfør accused Johansen of having had dishonest business dealings with a Swedish shipping concern, A/S Götaverken. Sundfør had written a number of letters to the company in an attempt to persuade them to his side. The letters eventually took on such a threatening character that the firm had to put their lawyer on the case. He defended the company by complaining about Sundfør's behavior to the Ministry of Justice. The ministry forwarded the complaint to the head office of the Norwegian Bar Association. They in turn expressed their sharpest condemnation of Sundfør's conduct and warned him against carrying out his threats. Thereafter, the Ministry of Justice dealt with the case and found that Sundfør had behaved in a manner inimical to sound legal practice.[65]

These rebukes did not change Sundfør's pattern of behavior. He continued to use heavy artillery. In a letter to public prosecutor Jak. E. Andersen, he wrote that Johansen was a thorough scoundrel with The King's Medal for Meritorious Services hanging on his chest. He was also a thief, a swindler, and a fraudster, and the prison gates should open wide to admit him. Once again, a complaint against Sundfør was sent in, and yet again the head office of the bar association unanimously spelled out that it contravened good legal practice to transfer his legal action from the prosecution services to the press and to use

Part 3: The Years of Struggle (1941–51)          179

unseemly descriptions when writing about his adversary. Sundfør answered by submitting a complaint to the head office about his opponent's lawyer, Sven Arntzen, who later became director of public prosecution. When the complaint led nowhere, he resigned from the bar association on December 4, 1933.[66] Arntzen was of the opinion that Sundfør had conducted a long-standing, tireless campaign to disgrace Johansen. The case was heard in the courts until as late as 1938, when Sundfør finally lost his appeal in the Supreme Court.

Seven years later, in May 1945, this same Sundfør was appointed as Johansen's official receiver and administrator and as the manager of Flagstad's assets. He writes that in May 1945 he was instructed by the then director of the Reparations Office, Jens Christian Hauge, to take on the oversight of Henry Johansen's estate. Three days later, a protest against his suitability came from Johansen's defense counsel, but Hauge informed Sundfør that the Reparations Office gave no credence at all to this protest. Another protest was made in June 1945 about the Reparations Office appointing Sundfør, and the case was heard in Oslo District Court. In a letter from July 13, 1945, Sundfør received further instruction from the Reparations Office to continue.[67]

Why did Jens Christian Hauge appoint Ingolf Sundfør in particular as supervisor and prosecutor in this case?

### Unknown Background to the Flagstad Case

In February or March 1945, a clandestine meeting was held in Oslo among the leader of the Milorg organization, Jens Christian Hauge, the top brass of the secret police, and the police chief who had come from London. They had doubts about the feasibility of setting up a police administration quickly enough to keep on top of the situation arising from the liberation of Norway. This led to the formation of a separate crime unit in Norway comprising men who had worked in the security service. In Oslo, they formed a separate group, calling themselves the Liaison Department, with their main office in Victoria Terrasse.[68]

The Soviets and the Western Allies were competing among themselves for the acquisition of valuable German prisoners of war as well as of war criminals. For a few months after the German capitulation, the British regarded Norway as its territory and so felt they had first claim on prisoners of interest, not least intelligence agents. The secret services became a commodity on the international market.[69] The forerunner to the Liaison Department was established during the war by illegal groups whose aim was to chart and uncover German and Norwegian agents and informers and also obtain all possible information about measures taken by the occupying forces and the Norwegian Nazis against the Home Front in order to warn the Norwegian illegal organizations about them. They investigated the network of spies and informers the Germans had left behind in the population. The Liaison Department was not under British command but worked in cooperation with the Task Force (groups involved in the war effort) to locate former Abwehr (Defense) agents, members of the former German security police (Sipo), and sabotage groups called Varulver (Werewolves).

The department was to monitor illegal activity aimed at undermining the settlement—in short, the plans that traitors could make to create unrest in society. The department was given wide powers since rumors were circulating about planned acts of violence and sabotage from so-called Nazi underground movements. The Liaison Department's activities were strictly classified. It functioned as a closed unit that only a few of those in the know in the government and in the military intelligence service were told about. In Parliament, only the Justice Committee knew of its existence. When its activities were later revealed in the press, no official person took responsibility for what had gone on there. The inexperienced staff and lack of oversight and control from other elements in society explain why the department's activities gradually took on such a degenerate character. The department's corps of provocateurs consisted of prisoners arrested for treason, prisoners suspected of war crimes, and prisoners with criminal backgrounds. The department used a long series of informers, and the staff were unable to sort out truth from lies in the steady stream of diffuse information that flowed in.

The Liaison Department became a place for planting false accusations and conspiracy theories, most of these produced by criminals with diagnoses of serious personality disorders, criminals with whom the Liaison Department slipped into cooperation. These people operated as provocateurs and were, for instance, installed in cells with prisoners they were to spy on. The department arranged several prison escapes. They operated with hiding places in private homes for escapees and planted false information among the prisoners. The result of this activity was overwhelmingly tragic for all concerned and, in some cases, led to miscarriages of justice.[70]

Linked to the Liaison Department, there also existed a legal office for assignments more related to police work. A legal office of this nature was established at Ilebu, and Henry Johansen was held there. This is where countless informers and provocateurs carried out their activities.

## Part 3: The Years of Struggle (1941–51)

## Henry Johansen Pointed Out as Conspiracy Leader

The most notorious of all the Gestapo agents was Bernt Somdalen. He was arrested on June 4, 1945, and transported to the Ilebu prison camp for traitors, where he was held until July 25 of the same year. He knew his war crimes were so serious that he would be transferred to Akershus fortress and that the prosecuting authorities would recommend the death penalty for him. In Norway, the most significant war criminals were held at Akershus fortress in Oslo, where they were subjected to brutal, in-depth interrogation by British and Norwegian police. Somdalen had many lives on his conscience. He had served as a soldier for the Norwegian Viking division on the eastern front and subsequently operated as one of the most important agents in the Gestapo's infamous unit IV N. This was the Gestapo's most dangerous headquarters for spies and agents in Norway, notorious for the major inroads they made into the resistance movement and for their ability to harm the civilian population through the intelligent use of passive and active agents. The unit recruited dehumanized frontline soldiers, people with alcohol and psychological problems, and also arrested resistance fighters, who through long hours of brutal torture were turned into agents for the other side.

Somdalen went from being the Gestapo's most active agent and provocateur to being the most active investigator, informer, provocateur, and witness for the Norwegian authorities after the war. With the help of a strong survival instinct and an incredible shrewdness, he maneuvered his way into the legal purge and became a notable person of influence within both the police and the legal system. In the postwar period, the former Gestapo agent traveled around as an investigator for the Norwegian legal authorities under the alias *Superintendent Bang.*

While a lower court condemned the war criminal Somdalen to death, as *Superintendent Bang* he was an active player in uncovering treason. His reports, with details of agents and crimes committed during the war, were included as attachments from the prosecuting authorities to the court in every single treason case of any magnitude. The exposure of his activities was the greatest legal scandal in Norway in the aftermath of the war.

Somdalen was the one who first gave the police the idea that an "Economic Ring" or an "NS opposition" existed. According to him, this was composed of wealthy, imprisoned traitors with an organized network on the outside and considerable hidden capital.[71] Henry Johansen was eventually pointed out as the leader.

Somdalen enlisted in the Liaison Department and began his report writing at the beginning of June 1945. The information he gave was undoubtedly sent to Jens Christian Hauge, who established the Liaison Department and left his post as head of the Reparations Office to become secretary and legal adviser to Prime Minister Einar Gerhardsen when the coalition government took office on June 25, 1945. Did a secret, conspiratorial network such as Somdalen suggested actually exist? The police and prosecution authorities began to lean in that direction. Somdalen's "information" to the police led to several extended investigations. One aim of these was to appropriate all the assets this ostensible organization possessed.

Somdalen's reports from Ilebu, signed by the prison governor, were sent to Sundfør, the prosecutor in Johansen's case, at the end of June 1945. These reports informed him that Johansen was a member of an underground movement. The demand for compensation from Johansen being set as high as 750 million kroner can be explained when set against the background of this information from Somdalen, alleging that Henry Johansen led a Nazi underground group called the Economic Ring.

## The Conspiracy Theory Expands

This narrative would be further developed by another former Gestapo agent, Hans Westby, who also worked as an informant for the police investigating treason in the postwar period. Westby was an agent for the Gestapo during the war, an informant for the Norwegian secret police after the war, and a notorious thief. He was placed under judicial observation and declared a person with inadequately developed mental faculties, someone who could not distinguish fantasy from reality.[72] Nevertheless, the secret police swallowed his fanciful information about the Economic Ring.

Westby said that the Economic Ring had drawn up long lists of people who were to be cleared away, and the lawyer Sundfør was on this list. Through middlemen in Sweden, the ring had apparently also come into contact with the Ethiopian government for the purpose of depositing capital there. In Ethiopia, the traitors would be granted good positions so that they could run the economic affairs in that country. The ring had four hundred members and more than one thousand supporters known only to the leaders. The organization was divided into two groups, the prisoner group and the free group. The task of the organization was to obtain economic means that would be placed at the disposition of "the Secret Council." This council would only operate

## Part 3: The Years of Struggle (1941–51)

through front men, and the president was Henry Johansen. He held the council's dangerous card files, which contained explosive information about men in prominent positions. This would be used against them, and the archive was hidden in the prison where Johansen was incarcerated.[73]

This information led to an overnight police raid with Westby as guide. No such card file was found. According to Westby, Henry Johansen also planned to liquidate his prosecutor, Sundfør. From prison, he had obtained a hired killer who would be paid for the assignment.

Westby's story was also made public after Johansen's death. On October 22, 1947, the newspaper *Verdens Gang* stated that the murder plans were set in motion to save Kirsten Flagstad's fortune. The Liaison Department had later tasked Somdalen with investigating these assassination plans. Johansen's wife was also involved as a provocateur and went along with the plans so that her husband's time in prison would be reduced. In a subsequent interview, she was asked whether the police had abused her sexually. She denied this but felt they had taken part in really vile activity.[74]

### Investigation of Flagstad's Telegrams to Her Husband

In the postwar Norwegian legal purge, a punishment principle was adopted that until then had been regarded as unacceptable—namely, that the accused's spouse would be liable for the financial penalty if there were assets available. In practice, it was punishable to be married to someone who had been a member of the NS. That this was unreasonable eventually became obvious, and the legal paragraph allowing this action was repealed on August 3, 1945. The confiscation of Flagstad's total assets was founded on this rule. She and her lawyer therefore expected that the confiscation would be annulled, but they received no response from Sundfør, the prosecutor. Flagstad's perception was that he was trying to damage her as much as possible.

> Sundfør is appointed as administrative receiver for both my husband and me. He hates my husband because he lost a case against him and now he wants revenge. . . . He tries in every way to demonstrate that my money is actually money my husband transferred to me during the war. He does not believe I have earned this money myself. He is trying to reduce my income in the USA to next to nothing. I have proof that I had a large amount of capital in 1940 that has not increased since. Even though the law permitting confiscation of my money has been repealed, everything I own is still under arrest. My lawyer has appealed and written to the Ministry of Justice, but it

184 THE VOICE OF THE CENTURY

is taking such a long time in the legal system. Sundfør has said that it is not advisable for me to leave the country. My lawyer has had to write to my employers to explain the situation as to why I have to cancel my engagements.[75]

Somdalen's writings aroused a suspicion that the underground movement had hidden assets at their disposal. Intense police investigation was now initiated to search for them, and Flagstad was suspected of being involved. Sundfør applied to the telegraph company, requesting that they locate all the telegrams that had passed between Flagstad in the US and Johansen in Norway, all the way from 1935 to 1941 when Flagstad returned to Norway. The purpose of this was to investigate whether they contained any details about the transfer of assets.

The director of the telegraph company points out in a letter of reply that to take such steps, they would need the agreement of the sender or addressee or a suspicion of crimes against the defense of the realm, against the independent security of the state, or against the state administration of Norway. In addition, the director points out that the operation would be both expensive and complicated.

The police must have considered that these criteria had been fulfilled, as the Economic Ring was a threat against the state's security, and shortly afterward, the management of the telegraph company was ordered to confiscate the telegrams. The costs would be borne by the police.[76] The results were sparse: the telegrams between the spouses contained nothing other than purely personal messages.[77] For the rest of her life, Flagstad had no idea that her telegrams, sent from the US to her husband in Norway, had been seized and read by the police.

## A Central Figure in the Press Campaign against Flagstad

The intelligence section at the embassy in Washington had received information about what Johansen and Flagstad were now suspected of, as well as all the rumors that were in circulation. They requested a meeting with the American Treasury Department, which took place on November 9, 1945. The embassy's representatives then gave an account of Norwegian citizens who had collaborated with the Germans and against whom the Norwegian authorities were now taking action. Henry Johansen and Kirsten Flagstad were among these names. The intention as far as Flagstad was concerned was to gather information about her income and assets in America.[78]

Part 3: The Years of Struggle (1941–51)          185

At the same time, the embassy made sure to feed the press. A central figure here was Tor Myklebost, a Norwegian journalist, diplomat, and ambassador. From 1941 to 1945, he was the press adviser to the embassy in Washington; from 1946 to 1949, he was assistant editor of the Norwegian tabloid newspaper *Verdens Gang*; and from 1949 to 1956, once again he was press adviser at the Norwegian Embassy in Washington and head of the Norwegian Information Service in the US.

Myklebost was the one who wrote the embassy's announcement about Flagstad on June 14, 1945. He continued the campaign against her from his new position as assistant editor of *Verdens Gang*, working closely with the Ministry of Foreign Affairs and Ambassador Morgenstierne. Myklebost's loyalties lay primarily with the diplomatic service.

On September 22, 1945, he printed an account of a conversation he had had with the mayor of New York, Fiorello La Guardia. The newspaper relayed its view that Flagstad had no chance of resuming her career, and the editor was keen to have the mayor's reaction.

> "What about Kirsten Flagstad? We thought there was little prospect of her appearing on the stage again."
> "A loss for the world," he commented. "A son of a bitch like Quisling is of no consequence, but Kirsten, Kirsten. . . ."
> He was genuinely unhappy. It is scarcely necessary to add that he loves opera above anything else on this earth.[79]

On January 3, 1946, there was a huge splash on the front page of *Verdens Gang*. The headline claims that Kirsten Flagstad was an indirect war profiteer. At the end of the article, the paper refers to an interview with Sundfør. According to him, Flagstad had received commission on the sale of barracks to the tune of 111 million kroner.[80]

Myklebost had good contacts at the editorial desk of the *Nordisk Tidende* publication in Brooklyn. On February 28, 1946, *Verdens Gang*'s interview with Sundfør was printed on the front page of the *Nordisk Tidende*. The headline read, "Did Kirsten Flagstad Receive 111 Million Kroner in Commission from Barracks Building?" With that, the rumor that Flagstad had been a war profiteer who had earned vast sums of money from the war spread to America. The fake news was spread further to Americans through the details appearing in various forms in a number of newspaper columns.

Was there anything in these claims? Kirsten Flagstad had no ownership interests in Henry Johansen Ltd. from 1940 to 1945.[81]

## Illegal Confiscation

Several meetings had taken place between Sundfør and Johansen at Ilebu prison camp, but by 1946, the relationship between them had become so inflamed that these meetings stopped. In one of the interviews, Sundfør had said that he was unaware that Kirsten Flagstad had earned considerable sums through her singing, a comment that made Johansen exclaim ironically, "Then you're one of very few people. At any rate, it's well known by most people who have any interest in singing."

Flagstad had written to McArthur and told him that now she had to prove that she had earned her own money. So she asked him, as discreetly as possible, to obtain a summary from NBC of her income since 1935. She required the same from the Metropolitan and from the agent who had arranged her European engagements.

She had received requests from Paris, Monte Carlo, England, Spain, Portugal, Switzerland, and Belgium, and she had accepted because she desperately needed to earn money again. When her European agent Mr. Horwitz asked if she would sing Leonore at the Parisian opera house, she warned him that the wildest rumors had been spread about her. He replied that he was already familiar with them and that it would be an honor to welcome her to the opera house.

She was to begin her tour in December 1945 but had to cancel everything because the authorities would not let her out of Norway. They thought she was lying about her engagements in order to leave the country.[82] This led to a considerable loss of income, as well as hurting her personally.

On May 20, 1946, Agder District Court, with authorization from the Criminal Code § 36, paragraph 1, supported Sundbefore's claim that the total confiscation of Flagstad's assets be upheld. In the text of the code, it states that this forfeiture can be imposed on the guilty party or any person on whose behalf he has acted.[83]

The decision was appealed in the Supreme Court, but the case was dismissed on the grounds of an administrative error.[84] Flagstad was never formally charged under § 36, nor was any indictment produced against her with regard to suspicion of having committed any criminal act. The confiscation by the authorities, which lasted until as late as 1950, was therefore in contravention of Norwegian law.

## Husband Dies

In the late autumn of 1945, Flagstad heard through her lawyer that her husband was unwell and confined to bed. She initiated a lawsuit in an effort to have him brought to a location where he would receive good care, but the case had to go through Sundfør, who said no. Her repeated applications were met with the same response. Christmas 1945 and New Year's 1946 passed without him sending her a card. Not until the spring of 1946 did she receive any news of him, when the office manager, Stake, phoned to tell her that Johansen was now in the hospital. Flagstad realized that her husband must be extremely ill, and she traveled to Oslo immediately. She heard from a friend the sad news that he was suffering from cancer and that he had been given only a short time to live.

From people who had visited him, she learned that he was in pain from large tumors in his throat and gullet. His lawyer said it was nearing the end for Johansen and asked Sundfør if Flagstad could visit her husband before he died. Sundfør gave permission for this but on condition that there had to be a police guard in the room who could hear what they were talking about. He had written to the police and asked them to confer with the senior consultant in the ward to prevent any witnesses or family talking about his business interests.

The couple felt it was humiliating to have a police guard in the room at their final parting, so they refrained from meeting. Johansen did not want Flagstad to see him in such a condition. Throat cancer is often a far from pretty sight, and he did not want her to remember him like that.

On Midsummer Eve, June 23, 1946, Henry Johansen died under police guard. Kirsten Flagstad told her American biographer about it: "The darkest moment of my life was when I went to the hospital to collect his body. When I cast my mind back to those days, when I was fighting Sundfør in court, knowing at the same time that my husband was dying, I don't know where my composure came from. It was some kind of proof that I had changed into a different person, that day. I hardly shed a tear when my husband died. Only a little. I'm afraid all my tears had dried up, because I haven't cried much since then."[85]

There were very few mourners at Henry Johansen's funeral, but there was an abundance of wreaths and flowers from his business contacts. Flagstad sat alone on the front pew in the Western Crematorium on June 27, 1946. No one reached out to her.

## Kirsten Flagstad's Mental Health

McArthur writes in his book that from 1945 onward, he began to worry about Flagstad's mental health. Accusations that she was a Nazi sympathizer, that she had met with Hitler in Berlin and had sung for Nazi troops there, that she was a war profiteer, all of this she took terribly to heart.

The day after her husband's funeral, the *New York Times* published a telegram sent to the newspaper from Oslo. This claimed that the Norwegian government had confiscated 16 million kroner from Johansen's estate. It was obvious that Flagstad had plans to return to the US, but the authorities had denied her an exit visa. They suspected her of having disregarded her husband's dealings with the Nazis.[86]

Flagstad was now faced with the task of proving to the authorities that her money was her own, saved from earnings in America and Europe. A great deal of her correspondence with McArthur had to do with clarifying the situation vis-à-vis her income and outgoings in the US. He received long weekly letters in which she, overwrought, gave an account of the tiniest details of her life. In all likelihood, Flagstad developed an obsessive-compulsive disorder during these years. She was dominated by a perception that everyone was against her, and she had begun to exhibit delusions that she was a dreadful person. These made her believe that no one wanted to have anything more to do with her. She was extremely afraid that the people she regarded as her nearest and dearest would abandon her.[87]

Flagstad found that no one dared show her any sympathy whatsoever. One of the few exceptions was a young Norwegian composer, Arne Dørumsgaard, who had sent some songs dedicated to her. She was now worried that he might be stigmatized as doubtful. She did not know him but hoped for his sake that he would not have to pay for having made contact with her.[88] She wrote to a female friend that she was knitting so nervously that she was getting cramps in her hands. On occasion she also received letters from friendly people in America who did not believe everything printed in the newspapers. This was a great consolation.[89]

In April 1946, she had received an invitation to visit the family of the composer Halfdan Cleve. In her letter of reply on April 29, Flagstad wrote that she was very taken aback to hear from them: "As I thought you disapproved of what I did and probably believed all the lies and slander about me. All the same, I think I won't pay you a visit with my situation as it is at present, but I really appreciate that you have been thinking of me."[90]

## Part 3: The Years of Struggle (1941–51)

The victimization of Flagstad and her closest associates was brutal. It is reflected in the drastic decision made with regard to the two children of her sister Karen-Marie. The press campaign led to Stefi and Knut being bullied at school since the pupils knew that Flagstad was their aunt. It had a severe effect on her that the children had to suffer, and the sisters therefore decided that the children would not go back to school in Oslo in the autumn of 1947. Stefi, aged nine, and Knut, aged eleven, were sent to a mountain farm farther inland, where Kirsten Flagstad was a less well-known name and the community did not know that the children were related to her.[91] Flagstad also sent her old housekeeper away on a temporary basis and refused to visit her. She did this to ensure that the elderly lady was not subjected to any unpleasantness.

### Authorities Send Police for Flagstad

While her husband lay on his deathbed, she had to appear at court hearings in Kristiansand with Sundfør, the prosecutor. These hearings took place on June 18 and 19, 1946, a few days before Johansen died. The confusion about Flagstad's role in the case was mirrored in the debate between the respective lawyers and the court administrator about her status before the court. Was she there as a witness or as a defendant in the case? "Since no case has been brought against her, she cannot be a defendant," said the administrator. "She may well become a defendant in the case," countered Sundør. "She is summoned in accordance with § 220 because there is an intention to bring a case against her, and it is not possible in a civil case first to be questioned as a witness and thereafter as a defendant," insisted Flagstad's lawyer.[92]

Flagstad told her American biographer she had hoped that, after these court hearings in June 1946, in which she had given an account of her income and assets, she would have her passport renewed. Sundør did not content himself with questioning her about her wealth; he also touched on the accusations directed at her by Ambassador Morgenstierne of unpatriotic conduct in America. After Sundør had come forward in the American press with the claim that Flagstad was a major war profiteer, he and Morgenstierne had been working together, and they now exchanged information.

It must have been offensive for her to have to defend her concert program to a Norwegian prosecutor who did not understand the first thing about music. She has said that this was the last straw for her, and she blurted out that the Norwegian Embassy in Washington had spread lies about her and her husband. Sundør reported this at once to the Ministry of Foreign Affairs, which then telegraphed the embassy in Washington.

190                    THE VOICE OF THE CENTURY

The case would have repercussions. On October 19, 1946, Morgenstierne wrote to the ministry that he had asked Sundfør for a transcript of Flagstad's statement, in which she, in addition to asserting that the embassy had spread lies about her, had insisted that the embassy had a distinctly hostile attitude toward her.

Morgenstierne requested assistance from the Foreign Office to obtain a further statement from Flagstad about this matter.[93] On November 21, 1946, Morgenstierne wrote a letter to Sundfør in which he posed a question about whether fru Flagstad, during questioning in court, could put forward such accusations without him having the opportunity to reject them or have them struck from the court record. He ended his letter thus: "I can now see what the Ministry of Foreign Affairs, to which I also wrote about this case, must undertake to do with reference to this matter."[94]

When it is taken into consideration that Flagstad was telling the truth, that the embassy had really publicized untruths about her, including in their announcement dated June 14, 1945, what later happened takes on the character of injustice.

On October 29, 1946, Foreign Minister Halvard Lange sent a letter to the director of public prosecution concerning Flagstad's accusations about the Norwegian Embassy in Washington, to which he attached Morgenstierne's letter.

The foreign minister stated that these were serious accusations and asked for the assistance of the director to obtain a more detailed statement from Kirsten Flagstad.[95] In a police report from Oslo Police Headquarters, it emerged that the police had tried to locate Flagstad to take her to the police station for questioning. The police in Kristiansand had attempted to call her on November 21, 1946. The accompanying endorsement from the Criminal Investigation Department states, "Fru Kirsten Flagstad Johansen—defamatory comments."[96]

The director of public prosecution considered the possibility of defamation proceedings regarding Morgenstierne and the embassy in Washington. It seems it was unclear whether Flagstad was living in Kristiansand and had "fled" to Oslo when she realized that the police were looking for her or whether she was already located in the capital. During their search for her, the Oslo police had called the Grand Hotel on November 23, 1946. She felt threatened and asked her lawyer to come to the Grand immediately to help her. Presumably, she was afraid that the police were about to place her under

Part 3: The Years of Struggle (1941–51) 191

arrest. She wisely answered that she would seek advice from her legal counsel before saying anything. Her lawyer's response to the police was that Flagstad would not give a statement. He would later write to the Ministry of Foreign Affairs and give an account of Flagstad's assertions. On May 5, 1947, A. L. Gullestad, a Supreme Court lawyer, sent the Foreign Office a twelve-page letter in which he listed the false statements the embassy made about Kirsten Flagstad.[97]

## Confidential Information from American Treasury Department

Through her lawyer, Flagstad had agreed to give a statement about her income and assets in America to the Reparations Office and prosecutor Sundfør. He did not accept this and now approached American banks and cultural institutions across the country to find out what Flagstad had earned. The embassy in Washington extended Sundfør's reach in this endeavor. On October 10, 1946, Lars J. Jorstad, an embassy adviser, wrote a letter to the Hannover Bank. He made reference to Henry Johansen's estate and businesses still being subject to criminal prosecution and noted that the Norwegian authorities wished to determine the division between the estate and fru Kirsten Flagstad's assets. He requested that the Hannover Bank provide printouts of accounts in the names of Henry Johansen and Kirsten Flagstad from 1936 onward.[98]

McArthur writes that Sundfør, with the assistance of the Norwegian Embassy, had also approached the National City Bank and the Metropolitan. Both turned him down with the response that he must first provide documentation to show legal authority to demand the release of such information.[99] Flagstad realized that these applications from the Norwegian authorities, forwarded by the embassy in Washington, placed her in a bad light. As early as January 19, 1946, she wrote a letter to Oslo Police Headquarters: "In this connection, I would like to make you aware that direct approaches from the police and prosecutor Sundfør to the American authorities may cause irreparable damage to my future career as a singer in the USA."[100]

Since the Norwegian authorities had hit a brick wall at the American banks, Secretary-General Colbjørnsen and press attaché Sven Oftedal at the Norwegian Embassy in Washington now turned to the American Treasury Department. They had a meeting in the department concerning this matter on November 9, 1945, and a similar meeting took place on October 9, 1946. The report in the *Nordisk Tidende* on February 28, 1946, suggesting that Flagstad

192 THE VOICE OF THE CENTURY

had received 111 million kroner in commission for the procurement of barracks buildings was used as an argument for the release of information.

The Norwegian Embassy succeeded in obtaining from the American Treasury Department printouts of the accounts in American banks belonging to Johansen and Flagstad.

However, the case would have embarrassing consequences for the embassy, something they attempted to hush up with the help of the Ministry of Foreign Affairs. Flagstad's lawyer must have got wind of the American Treasury Department's release of information about her accounts in American banks to the Norwegian Embassy. In a letter to the Treasury Department, Flagstad's lawyer disputes a few details of this information. An embassy memo of October 25, 1946, marked "confidential," states that an employee in the American Treasury Department had found it extremely regrettable that Flagstad had learned that the department had given the embassy information about her assets. It conflicted with departmental practice to release such information. What had been passed on to the embassy was intended as confidential information. The employee was keen to have the matter over and done with so that the staff in the department would not be faced with difficulties because they had deviated from normal practice. The Norwegian Embassy writes:

> I said it was regrettable if the Treasury's people suffered any "inconveniences" because of this and that the embassy would like to do whatever was within its power to smooth things out. I asked whether Mrs. Schwartz could suggest a procedure, but until now she has said that she must have still more time to think matters over. Nor was she willing, without further thought, to say what broadcasting companies here are involved. She will phone the embassy when she wishes a further conversation.
>
> These two conversations in the Treasury took place in a very friendly atmosphere and both Mrs. Schwartz and Miss Duff stated that they considered it all just one of those things. I have not yet heard anything further from Mrs. Schwartz.[101]

The memo was written by embassy adviser Jorstad. The following day, October 26, 1946, he wrote about the case to the Foreign Office on behalf of Ambassador Morgenstierne. On November 8, Foreign Minister Lange wrote to Sundfør, informing him that the Treasury found it unfortunate that the information the embassy had received from them about Kirsten Flagstad Johansen had been brought to her attention, as these details had been intended as entirely confidential.[102]

Part 3: The Years of Struggle (1941–51)      193

After this, the Norwegian Embassy did not have any more correspondence with the American Treasury Department regarding Kirsten Flagstad. On December 24, 1946, Sundfør wrote a letter to the Ministry of Foreign Affairs stating that he could not understand why it had become impossible to obtain any details whatsoever from the American authorities concerning Henry Johansen's estate and Kirsten Flagstad's assets. After all, this was a matter of the interests of the Norwegian state.[103]

## Support and Vile Slander

Flagstad asked McArthur if he could come and help her. He landed in Oslo on September 8, 1946, bringing several suitcases filled with business receipts. He had quite a shock when he met Flagstad. Admittedly, in her letters she had prepared him for her instability, but he had not expected to see a tearstained woman dressed in mourning who had put on more than two stones in weight.

Well in advance of McArthur's arrival in Norway, the Ministry of Foreign Affairs had been alerted about his journey and his support for Flagstad.

On September 9, 1946, Sven Oftedal, the ministry's press spokesman in New York, who had also been the editor of the *Nordisk Tidende* for lengthy periods, sent a letter to the director of the press office in the Ministry of Foreign Affairs, Jens Schive. Oftedal told Schive that he had a good friend in Kansas who had sent him a letter. He wrote that it was "a pretty interesting little document" that Schive could distribute to whoever "might need to be informed."[104] The letter was shown to Hans Olav, the head of the press corps at the embassy in Washington, and the secretary-general, the most senior administrator in the Ministry of Foreign Affairs in Oslo.

What were the contents of the letter from Oftedal's friend, who, incidentally, remained anonymous? The letter has been given the file number 032264 in the Foreign Office archives and is marked "confidential." This female friend writes that Oftedal had encouraged her to be more critical. She says that she met McArthur one evening, and he then told her he was going to Norway to visit Flagstad. He struck her as being a very arrogant man with no scruples. He wondered how he could obtain a passport when he intended to visit someone who was obviously not on good terms with the Norwegian government. He also wanted to know what status Flagstad now had. The friend's husband had said that McArthur behaved just as one would expect of a Nazi and that he would almost certainly attempt to bring Flagstad back to America so that he could earn money through her. This friend thought it paradoxical that someone who conducted such beautiful music displayed such bad manners.[105]

194 THE VOICE OF THE CENTURY

McArthur was fairly ignorant of the rumors that the Norwegian Foreign Office was spreading about him. He contributed greatly to bringing clarity to Flagstad's tax returns. As an old bureaucrat, he knew how to conduct conversations with lawyers. He also realized that Flagstad, who had never concerned herself with her own finances, was not in a position to produce adequate documentation. He made up his mind to stay in Norway longer than planned because of an important court hearing due to take place on October 10, 1946.

It was also of great value that McArthur helped Flagstad to judge the state of her voice. In the evenings, they went through parts of her repertoire. He was delighted that her voice was unchanged. On September 24, they celebrated McArthur's birthday at Amalienborg, and that same day, Flagstad received a telegram from her daughter in America to tell her she was now a grandmother. After the court appearance on October 10, McArthur traveled home. He writes that as soon as he had arrived home, he began to receive letters from Flagstad saying that she was feeling lonely and depressed. She fought against thoughts that she would never have another happy day in her life and would never get her passport back.[106]

## Quisling's Prosecutor Gets Flagstad Out of Norway

Even though Kirsten Flagstad's situation was cleared up in the autumn of 1946, she was still refused a passport. The central driving force in this was the Ministry of Foreign Affairs. It emerges from a "confidential" letter dated February 15, 1948, from Morgenstierne to Foreign Minister Lange that they had had a number of personal conversations about Kirsten Flagstad over the years. The rumors that had been put out by former war criminals now working as provocateurs for the police investigating cases of treason, saying that Henry Johansen had been an underground leader of a Nazi organization with huge reserves of capital held abroad, possibly also played a part in the case.

Flagstad's friend Arne Dørumsgaard, the young composer, had advised her to seek help from Annæus Schjødt regarding her passport. He was one of Norway's sharpest lawyers, and his work had included prosecuting the case against Quisling. Dørumsgaard's reasoning was that if Schjødt had managed to have Quisling condemned to death, he could also manage to liberate Kirsten Flagstad's passport. At first, Flagstad was reticent, believing that such a prominent figure as Schjødt would not want anything to do with her. However, Dørumsgaard succeeded in persuading her and even accompanied her

Part 3: The Years of Struggle (1941–51)

to Schjødt's office. Schjødt accepted the brief, and on November 23, 1946, the dispute about Flagstad's passport was finally heard at the Reparations Office in the presence of Flagstad herself. At this meeting, it was agreed that she would be granted a passport. On November 28, Schjødt escorted Flagstad to the Oslo Police Station, where the passport was issued.[107] Sundfør also came to the police station, still insisting that Flagstad must not leave Norway. With her passport safely in her handbag, she went to Kristiansand to pack her belongings. She wrote to a friend: "Now when I am able to travel at last, I feel very sad. I like the quiet life I've led here and am nervous and scared about meeting up with strangers in other surroundings. I'm obviously starting to grow old."[108]

Stake, the office manager, had now become one of her few confidants. He was to drive her to the Swedish border, where she would be met by Henry Johansen Jr., who would drive her onward to Stockholm. The only thing she had on her mind was leaving the country. Flagstad was filled with anxiety that Sundfør might dig up something else and manage to stop her yet again. She was also worried about the fact that she was absolutely broke, as Sundfør had also confiscated her travel checks. However, she was extremely relieved once she had passed the Swedish border and was on her way to Stockholm.[109]

## Ministry of Foreign Affairs Refuses to Give Up

A note dated December 4, 1946, from the office of the foreign minister argues that Flagstad should not be permitted to travel out of the country and on to America. The note refers to the *Verdens Gang* report of that same day, which stated that Flagstad proposed to travel to Sweden and America to perform there. Further, the note provides a reminder that the national police chief, in a letter from October 30, 1945, had argued against allowing her to leave the country because she could destroy evidence in the case against her husband or dispose of assets that should have been seized. The police chief had also added that her conduct would damage Norwegian interests. The note goes on to recollect that the ministry, in its reply to the police chief, had said that there was no reason to recommend that Flagstad be given the opportunity to leave the country. Furthermore, it says that on an earlier occasion, in June of the previous year, it had been decided that the question of the desirability of fru Flagstad's potential trip to America should be dealt with by the police department, since the messages from Morgenstierne were forwarded to both the Ministry of Church Affairs and the Ministry of Justice for information and possible action.[110]

196 THE VOICE OF THE CENTURY

Would the Ministry of Foreign Affairs recommend to the Ministry of Justice that an interim injunction be implemented? *Interim injunction* is a term in the civil process that refers to a provisional court decision. It means that the physical or legal person to whom the decision refers is obliged to refrain from, perform, or endure something, pending a more comprehensive court case on the subject. It is worth noting that interim injunctions are not applicable in financial claims. Arrest can also be a form of interim injunction.

So the Foreign Office was insisting that Flagstad should be forcibly held in Norway since they anticipated that she would face trial. The ministry referred to the charge against her later in the memo. It was solely based on Morgenstierne's belief that Flagstad in her present state of mind would inflict great damage if she returned to America. The ambassador felt that Flagstad would confuse people's ideas with regard to Norwegians and Quislings and the situation prevailing in Norway. The ambassador therefore requested most urgently that if at all possible they should seek to prevent her return to America.[111]

The Foreign Office may have sent this memo to the Ministry of Justice with a request for an interim injunction against Flagstad. In a later endorsement in pencil on the memo, principal officer Alfred Bredo Stabell of the Foreign Ministry wrote that Flagstad had left, and presumably, they should therefore simply shelve the case.

Kirsten Flagstad's intuition, that she had to leave Norway as quickly as possible, proved correct. She left before the bureaucracy had time to react. Once she had left the country, any decision about applying for interim injunctions would be far more dramatic. Such a decision would have meant her being declared a wanted person, to be arrested and brought back to Norway.

## We Will Stop Her

Kirsten Flagstad felt at a loss when she arrived in Stockholm, as all she owned was thirty kroner. She telegraphed McArthur to tell him about her desperate situation, and McArthur got in touch with a Norwegian American, Captain Torkild Rieber, who was an oil millionaire and had contacts all over the world. Flagstad had met him at the Grand Hotel just after Johansen's funeral and had told him her version of the story. Rieber took pity on her and provided Flagstad with start-up capital, a gesture she would never forget.

She spent Christmas 1946 in Zurich. From there, she tried, in cooperation with her impresario Frederic Horwitz, to obtain engagements throughout Europe. She gave two concerts in Cannes on January 18 and 19, 1947. After

# Part 3: The Years of Struggle (1941–51)

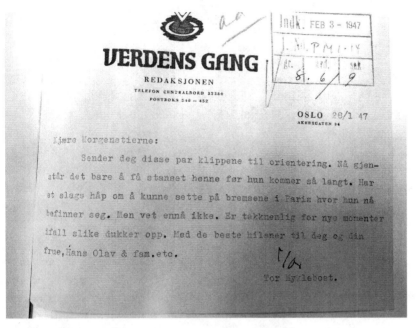

Telegram from Assistant Editor Myklebost to Ambassador Morgenstierne indicating that he is making every effort to have Flagstad stopped from returning to the US to resume her career. *Source: National Archives, Norway.*

that she headed to Paris, where she held two concerts with the Lamoureux Orchestra on January 25 and 26. Difficulties arose because the conductor would not allow Flagstad to sing Isolde's "Liebestod" (Erotic death). The orchestra played, but to begin with, she was not permitted to come out onto the stage. The snub was ineffective because the audience expressed their displeasure by shouting, "Flagstad, Flagstad," and then applauded her onto the stage for several curtain calls.[112] The *Sunday News* reported that it was American soldiers in the hall who led the protest against the boycott of Flagstad. Backstage, she was interviewed by the *New York Herald Tribune*, which also had a Paris edition. She said that the Frenchmen had insisted she should sing Wagner, but she had managed to include four songs by Grieg all the same. "Despite everything," she said, "I am Norwegian."[113]

From Paris, she applied for a visa to America, primarily to visit her daughter and grandson, Sigurd, whom she had never seen. She had long understood that this would prove difficult. American newspapers frequently wrote negative things about her. She had seen cuttings in which it was claimed that she had traveled home in Hitler's private plane. The newspapers had embellished the embassy's false accusations in the announcement about her on June 14, 1945, in which they wrote that Flagstad had been flown home from Berlin.

The embassy did nothing to correct such false stories. Many Americans may have genuinely believed that Flagstad was closely connected to the Nazi regime and to Hitler. The embassy received a letter from an outraged American who claimed that Flagstad was a good friend of Hitler's and that she had helped him in every way. Furthermore, the letter said, she had done everything she could to sabotage America, and so she should not be allowed to return to the country. The letter writer asked the embassy to deal with the matter at once.[114]

The embassy did not reply to these letters. The embassy and its ambassador wanted to prevent Flagstad from returning to America. It suited their purposes for such rumors to be spread. The day before the embassy received this letter, on January 28, 1947, Tor Myklebost had written a telegram to Morgenstierne on headed notepaper from the *Verdens Gang* newspaper. It expressed the situation succinctly: "Sending you these few cuttings for your information. Now it only remains to stop her before she gets that far. Have some hope of being able to pull on the brakes in Paris where she is located at present. But don't yet know. Grateful for fresh details if anything should come up. With best wishes to you and your wife, Hans Olav & family, etc."[115]

## They Want to Destroy Me

What specific actions did Morgenstierne and Myklebost undertake in their efforts to stop Flagstad? They circulated negative comments about her, including in stories planted in the tabloid newspapers. They did so to stir up public opinion against her, and they had the Foreign Office behind them. From the wording of the telegram, there can no longer be any doubt about their intentions. Everything the journalist wrote must be read in the light of his motive: to stop Flagstad from returning to America to practice her profession. Myklebost sent cuttings of his articles about Flagstad to Morgenstierne. If they had succeeded in their project to have her stopped, they would have destroyed Kirsten Flagstad not only as an artist but probably also as a person. She had a strong feeling that this was what they wanted: "The newspapers in Oslo have been extremely busy lately.... They must be furious because so far they haven't succeeded in their efforts to destroy me."[116]

Part 3: The Years of Struggle (1941–51)

Myklebost also launched an attack on a testimonial Kirsten Flagstad had received from Emil Stang, who was an old friend of the Flagstad family and, from 1946 to 1952, chief justice of the Supreme Court in Norway. Flagstad had realized she would need documentation to demonstrate that she had not acted in support of the occupying forces in Norway or in any other German-occupied country. In the autumn of 1945, she had asked Stang if he would write a testimonial for her. Stang had quite simply written that Kirsten Flagstad had shown a steadfast, patriotic attitude throughout the entire war.

On the same day that Myklebost's article "Emil Stang's Testimonial for Kirsten Flagstad" appeared in *Verdens Gang*, the newspaper printed a caricature of Flagstad and Stang under the heading "Tristan and Isolde," with Stang kneeling in front of Flagstad, handing her the testimonial. Underneath is the text "Beautiful Isolde, I hereby present you with this epistle on your loyalty."[117]

## The Cash Cow Returns

On April 30, 1946, Morgenstierne sent a letter to the Ministry of Foreign Affairs to which he attached the wording of the testimonial. He also sent a copy to Sundfør, the prosecutor. In this letter, Morgenstierne said that he could not agree that Flagstad had shown a steadfast, patriotic attitude while she was in the US. He referred to his previous letters to the ministry, including the many in which he talked about the concert that had an exclusively German program, and also pointed out that she had defied the Norwegian authorities by traveling home during the war. Because of the publicity surrounding Stang's declaration in Norwegian American circles, Morgenstierne urged the ministry to inform Stang of the reports he had submitted regarding Flagstad's conduct in America during the war. He felt that they should ask Stang whether, having read Morgenstierne's reports, he still maintained that Flagstad had shown steadfast patriotism throughout the war. In conclusion, he wanted to know whether Stang wished steps to be taken to prevent Flagstad from making use of a pronouncement that Stang found he could not uphold.[118] Such was Morgenstierne's reasoning.

On January 22, 1947, the head of the press corps at the Norwegian diplomatic service in America sent a letter to his counterpart in the Foreign Office. Here he writes that he had heard on a radio station that Flagstad was coming back to America for a concert tour, armed with Stang's testimonial. The diplomatic service press chief writes:

## THE VOICE OF THE CENTURY

This is not exactly happy news, but we're prepared for further unpleasantness going forward. The commercial interests that have secured their cash cow will certainly stop at nothing to increase their output.

It would be pretty useful to see the wording of Emil Stang's "blessing." The date may be of interest. It sounds extraordinary that the Chief Justice should issue the kind of recommendation mentioned.[119]

### Male Chauvinism and Contempt for Women

The discussion of Kirsten Flagstad as a "cash cow" refers to the commercial exploitation of her as an artist, but at the same time, it may indicate contempt for women. A man who operated lucrative business practices would scarcely be described in such terms. The diplomatic and political life of that time was totally dominated by men. That a woman had distinguished herself and gained such a powerful, independent position in the international arena, exclusively on the grounds of her accomplishments, was rather unusual.

The early Christian tradition, through its interpretation and definition of the hierarchy of creation, condemned woman to be a subordinate creature. Only man was created in God's image. Women were primarily sexual beings, reproductive organs and mothers, formed to be man's helpmeet. The mothers of the church in the Middle Ages were the first to use feminine metaphors to describe God to show that women, too, are created in God's image. The feminists of the nineteenth century took up this aspect in their battle for women's civil rights; one of them was the Norwegian feminist Aasta Hansteen, who in 1878 published the book *Woman Created in God's Image*, an attack on the Lutheran single-sex church. Activists for women's rights demanded that women should also be defined as human beings, as individuals with specific talents and characteristics. She was a soul but also a spirit—an eternal human spirit on the same level as man. From the 1900s, human rights were extended to apply to both sexes, but feminist thinking was not incorporated as a global reform until the UN's Women's Convention and Committee on the Elimination of Discrimination against Women (CEDAW) in 1979. By then, Flagstad had already been dead for seventeen years.[120]

The persecution of Flagstad had a misogynistic aspect. If we look more closely at the composers and singers who were members of the NS, many of the men resumed their positions, but the women never came back.[121] It seems as if they were subjected to an even greater hatred than the men. Norwegian

## Part 3: The Years of Struggle (1941–51)

women who were suspected of having had social and sexual relations with German soldiers were given the brutal label of "German slut" after the war. Between three thousand and five thousand were unlawfully interned in camps established by the Norwegian state. The state regarded this as a measure to protect *Norwegian men* from sexually transmitted diseases, for example. These women were subjected to witch hunts, having all their hair chopped off, their bodies painted with slogans, and psychiatric experimentation performed on them. A politicized form of psychiatry worked on the basis of guidelines that stigmatized them and their children with German soldiers en masse as individuals with impaired mental faculties. This was to serve as an explanation for them having "betrayed" the Norwegian state. The women were regarded as the property of the nation and the state.

The men were in a different position. In April 1942, the Norwegian government-in-exile in London, which consisted only of men, passed changes in the Norwegian marriage laws making it possible for Norwegians overseas to marry again without informing their spouses in Norway of it. The law was called Lex Nygaardsvold, or the bigamy law. This legal change was of short duration because of its absurdity. Equally harsh was the decision that wealthy industrial magnates and capitalists who had earned good money from the war and used slave workers were allowed to keep their profits. After the war, several of them were elevated as Norwegian nation builders. They were all men.

### Collective Effort in the Foreign Office

The victimization of this powerful woman continued. On January 24, 1947, the embassy in Washington sent a confidential urgent letter to the Foreign Office with three duplicate copies. One of these was addressed to the prosecutor, Sundfør, who was far from pleased with the contents. On February 14, 1947, Sundfør replied that in previous letters to the Ministry of Foreign Affairs, he had asked for Morgenstierne to draw up a compilation of everything he knew about Kirsten Flagstad's conduct in America. The lawyer wrote that her position with regard to a patriotic attitude could possibly come up in any trial resulting from the criminal case. Sundør regretted that Kirsten Flagstad was now "armed" with a declaration about her steadfast patriotic attitude.[122]

In a letter dated January 24, the ambassador reminded the ministry of the reply to the letter Morgenstierne had sent in April 1946, saying that Stang had to be confronted with his testimonial. They wrote that the embassy and consulate general in New York had received several inquiries from journalists

202          THE VOICE OF THE CENTURY

asking in particular for the basis on which fru Flagstad had been granted an exit permit from Norway. The embassy asked to be telegraphed at the earliest opportunity with the most extensive information possible on this subject.[123]

Now the Foreign Office reacted. The next day, January 25, 1947, press chief Schive wrote a letter to the secretary-general. He did not believe it expedient to try to put barriers in the way of Flagstad's performances, since she had now been granted a passport. Nor did he believe that it would succeed, since she had such a huge audience. Stang's testimonial was another matter, however. Schive could well understand that Morgenstierne was surprised by it, since the Norwegian authorities had refused Flagstad help for her journey home. Schive suggested to the secretary-general that he should write a friendly letter to Stang. If that led nowhere, then they would have to entrust the matter to the Ministry of Justice.[124]

On January 25, Schive also wrote a letter to Stang, stating that the Foreign Office's press service had received inquiries from abroad about the extent to which his declaration also covered the period of Norway's war against Germany, when fru Flagstad was living in America, and her journey home to Norway through Germany.[125]

It is doubtful whether the press service had received so many inquiries: this was really an excuse for the approach. Above all, the Ministry of Foreign Affairs was fighting its own battle, and Morgenstierne's, against Stang's testimonial. On January 28, Schive wrote another letter to the secretary-general. He said that Stang had answered the letter from the press service by phone. The chief justice had asked to be excused from writing, as he was unwell: "Stang, who was very courteous, was obviously ill at ease and repeated several times that he had gone too far in his testimonial. Besides, it had been written before he was appointed Chief Justice, he said."[126]

*Verdens Gang* followed up with articles by Myklebost about the matter, articles that quickly found their way into the *Nordisk Tidende*. *Verdens Gang* also included an editorial that vehemently took Stang and his testimonial to task.[127] In Schive's final letter to the secretary-general, the one with information about Stang's qualification, there is a postscript saying that the letter should be shown to the foreign minister.

## Case Comes Up at Foreign Minister Level

The campaign led to Emil Stang being rebuked in the media, and NTB, the Norwegian News Agency, received a statement from Stang on January 27, 1947. In this message, Stang stated that many spiteful rumors had been circulating

## Part 3: The Years of Struggle (1941–51)

about Kirsten Flagstad. He had investigated these and discovered that they were untrue. He confirmed that he had given her a testimonial about her steadfast patriotic attitude in Norway. Now, however, he saw that she was being attacked for her position in America before she returned to Norway. Stang was not able to say anything about this. He wrote that he had no knowledge of whether there was any truth in the accusations being advanced against her, and he concluded: "I now see that my testimonial was too comprehensive. It ought to have been more explicitly confined to her conduct in this country, as I could not give an opinion on anything else."[128]

On January 31, 1947, Foreign Minister Halvard Lange wrote a letter to the embassy in Washington about the matter. The letter was sent by airmail, and telegrams with fairly similar contents were also sent there from the Ministry of Foreign Affairs. Lange writes:

> On Monday 27 January, the Chief Justice issued a statement—which is attached—through the Norwegian News Agency. The statement was immediately telegraphed to the information office in New York with the request that it be forwarded to the embassy.
>
> After this, the position should be clear as far as the testimonial is concerned, since the Chief Justice openly admits that he should have confined his declaration to cover the time after her return home. It goes without saying that the embassy can give this correction all possible publicity. Moreover, in the opinion of the Foreign Office, it is scarcely feasible to take any action with respect to fru Flagstad's tour abroad, since she does not have any criminal questions left unsettled with the Norwegian authorities and has received a passport in the normal way.[129]

The Foreign Office had lost the battle over Flagstad's entry to America, but Stang's modification would be given all possible publicity in the US, on the instructions of the Norwegian foreign minister.

### Still a Rolls-Royce of a Soprano

At the end of January, while she was still in Paris, Flagstad received a visa for America. At the same time, the embassy in Washington and Myklebost were ensuring that Stang's modification was given as much publicity as possible in Norway and the US. It was published in a number of American newspapers and breathed new life into several gossip columns. The publication led to quite a few angry readers' letters from Americans. They wondered why, if the Norwegian authorities had given such a clear indication that they wanted rid

204 THE VOICE OF THE CENTURY

of her, America should be saddled with Kirsten Flagstad. The conclusion in many newspaper items was that she should not receive American citizenship. Flagstad had of course told a newspaper she would like to apply for this.

After her stay in Paris, Flagstad traveled to London. On February 6, 1947, she was to give a Wagner concert at the Royal Albert Hall with the London Philharmonic Orchestra and with Karl Rankl on the conductor's podium. The concert was to be broadcast on radio via the BBC to around ten million listeners. She was dreading this, but in London she met only an educated, music-loving audience who behaved in a dignified manner. The city and its people were greatly affected by the ravages of war, but the Royal Albert Hall was unscathed. It must have been cold both inside and out on that evening, as a critic relates that he was wearing a double layer of duffle coats and had brought a warm blanket with him. He was not alone in defying the freezing conditions—a crowd of as many as six thousand people had ventured out into the snowy weather and found their way to the Royal Albert Hall to hear Flagstad sing.

Ambassador Prebensen at the Norwegian diplomatic service in London considered whether or not he should try to put a stop to the concert by approaching the BBC. In a letter dated January 30, 1947, marked "confidential," he wrote to the Foreign Office: "With his knowledge of fru Flagstad through material in the Ministry of Foreign Affairs, especially through reports from Ambassador Morgenstierne, Ambassador Prebensen does not intend to be present at the concert or to support it in any way whatsoever. . . . In the event that the Norwegian authorities do not regard the lady's past record to be acceptable, Ambassador Prebensen feels there is reason to take a diplomatic step to prevent the BBC from broadcasting the concert. He would like to hear the Ministry's opinion on the matter."[130]

The Ministry of Foreign Affairs called the embassy in London on January 30, instructing them not to take any action in this case. However, Ambassador Prebensen spoke to the *Morgenposten* newspaper about it, saying that the Norwegian diplomatic service had no wish to be present at the concert. *Morgenposten* made further comment: "The Norwegian colony in London, with the embassy at the forefront, were conspicuous by their absence."[131]

The audience rose to greet Flagstad with a whole minute's applause, with some weeping loudly all through the concert, so moved were they that this voice had survived the war. One described the concert as "a taste of butter, after having had nothing but margarine for ten years." Another said it was "like seeing the ocean again."[132] They were able to hear a mighty voice that sang with a sparkling lightness, and they saw a woman who with simple dignity stood motionless as a sentinel on the stage. The critics decided that Flagstad was still a Rolls-Royce of a soprano. Each note was of pure gold. The orchestra never once succeeded in drowning out her voice, which carried perfect control and enormous power.

## Traveling as Fru Johansen

Flagstad experienced her reunion with the English public as heartfelt and without any trace of negativity. Tense and under a great deal of stress, she was dreading her onward journey. She was to sing in three performances of *Tristan and Isolde* at the La Scala opera house in Milan. On March 5 and 6, she would be back in London to hold two more concerts before she finally headed for America.

In Milan, the people had a delicate emotional relationship with German opera. As many as two hundred police officers were placed among the audience, and outside, considerable forces were standing by. They patrolled the street in front of posters proclaiming, "*Tristan and Isolde* starring the world's greatest singer." The head of Milan's partisan organization had demanded that the performances be canceled, and it was anticipated that riots might break out. The partisans had nothing against Kirsten Flagstad but did not want

Flagstad with a police officer outside La Scala in 1947.
Source: *Flagstad Museum*.

German opera and the German language to be heard. The very idea brought their frenzy to a fever pitch.[133]

The critics did not mention this aspect in their columns. Instead, they concentrated on the music and agreed that it would be almost impossible to find a better Isolde. Her voice had a tremendous dramatic power and moved with precision at every modulation. It flowed like a ribbon of gold over the hundred-strong orchestra, up to triple forte. The sound was like organ music in its depth and trilled exquisitely on the high notes, carrying into the farthest corners of the hall. "She completely dominated the stage, from the first to last act," wrote *Il Popolo*. The performance would go into the annals of La Scala as the greatest ever, predicted *Time* magazine. It helped Flagstad's self-confidence to have it confirmed that her voice was still equal to the most challenging roles. It had become deeper in sound and even richer in tone.[134]

In every other way, she was not so good. The stress caused an increasingly troublesome psoriasis to break out, and her body was in a constant state of alert. She had received a so-called clean bill of health from the American authorities. Even though this was a standard expression, she reacted badly to it: "I felt it was stigmatizing and humiliating. As if I had been through disinfection and was now ready to rub shoulders with people again."[135]

Her yearning to see her daughter and meet her grandchild propelled her across the Atlantic, but Flagstad's continued career in America would follow a thorny path. Her impresario had arranged a number of concerts, and she knew there were several cities that no longer wanted to hear her. From McArthur, she had received a discouraging telegram to say that a planned tour of South America had to be canceled. Erich Kleiber had refused to have her as a soloist.[136] Her experiences in Norway during the past few years had made her consider American citizenship. This had emerged in the press and had been met with strongly negative reactions. She had not heard a single word from her old employers at the Metropolitan. In the press, it was written that the Metropolitan was awaiting the opinions and reactions of the public. They would trim their sails to the wind and let Flagstad paddle her own canoe. She felt that this was going to be difficult. For her own self-protection, she chose to use the name that was printed in her passport. Flagstad traveled across the Atlantic as fru Johansen since no one knew who that was.[137]

## Mudslinging Continues

A columnist in the *Nordisk Tidende* newspaper, Magny Landstad-Jensen, wrote about Kirsten Flagstad on February 20, 1947, in her column "Our

Women and Our Homes." She felt it was evidence of a complete lack of decorum as well as any understanding of human behavior for Flagstad to flaunt a testimonial that ran counter to public opinion in many countries. She ought to remain in quarantine for a while longer.

Landstad-Jensen wrote: "People would prefer to forget now, but I believe many people still harbour bitterness in their hearts towards fru Flagstad, but they prefer to sit on the sidelines. However, out of respect for those who are buried in common graves, and those who had their nails pulled out and most of the bones in their bodies smashed to pulp, people have no wish to stand in line to present bouquets and applaud her 'steadfast patriotic attitude.'"[138]

The day after the article was printed, Ambassador Morgenstierne sat down to write a letter to the author, Magny Landstad-Jensen. The letter is marked "personal." Morgenstierne says here that he felt the need to thank her for what she had written about Kirsten Flagstad. "It's as if it were written from my own heart," he writes. Morgenstierne rounded off with a wish that everyone would adopt a similarly unambiguous standpoint as her, that they would show their moral indignation.[139]

To those who wrote negative comments about Flagstad, it seemed encouraging to receive such an expression of support from the Norwegian ambassador and the embassy in Washington. That same day, Morgenstierne also wrote a letter to Myklebost at *Verdens Gang*, to which he attached a cutting of the Landstad-Jensen article from the *Nordisk Tidende*. He believed that Myklebost would certainly be interested in the material and want to quote the columnist in *Verdens Gang*. Morgenstierne wrote to Myklebost that this was one of the best opinion pieces he had seen.[140]

On February 28, 1947, Morgenstierne sent another press cutting from the *Nordisk Tidende* about Kirsten Flagstad, this time to the Ministry of Foreign Affairs. This stated that the Norwegian students at the University of Minnesota had written to the principal of the university's arts faculty, James Lombard, thanking him for refusing to permit Flagstad to sing there. Morgenstierne writes, "As you will see, the students are thanking Mr. Lombard for his decision not to arrange a concert for Flagstad at the university."[141]

## Kirsten Flagstad Arrives in America

The New York newspaper the *Daily News* ran a report on January 23, 1947, about an opera singer, Kirsten Flagstad, who had traveled on Hitler's private plane and whose husband had been a Nazi collaborator. This woman was now in America.[142] False news of this type created expectations. Flagstad

208                    THE VOICE OF THE CENTURY

relates that she arrived in New York on March 14, 1947. The next day, a group of journalists had assembled for a major press conference with her, arranged by McArthur. After all she had been through, she had grown suspicious of journalists. She mentions in particular a reporter who subjected her to what she considered to be the third degree, as if she were a criminal who had been smuggled into the country. She got the impression that many people were keen to spin her life story into a detective yarn.

A journalist had asked her why she did not protest against all the negative things being written about her. She answered that she had done so, but no one had been willing to print what she said.[143] She was convinced that in the main, nothing but misunderstandings would emerge from this prearranged press conference, so she asked McArthur not to organize any further meetings of that kind with the press. After a few days in New York, she went to Montana to meet her daughter and grandchild: little Sigurd was now six months old.

Two days after Flagstad's press conference in New York, Morgenstierne wrote again to the Ministry of Foreign Affairs, enclosing a cutting with details of an interview with Flagstad in the *New York Times*. He pointed out that she had referred to Stang's testimonial without mentioning that he had qualified his statement to cover only her time in Norway. The ambassador had therefore felt duty bound to inform the press about the facts of the situation. Morgenstierne wrote that he had done this in accordance with departmental instructions. He was afraid that Flagstad would damage Norway's cause in America and that it would therefore be necessary to counter her statements. The matter had of course taken on a different character now that the lady in question had gone on the offensive. Morgenstierne writes about Flagstad's departure from America in 1941, "She also mentioned that her true destination was Sweden, not Norway. This is the first time the embassy has heard of that."[144]

This was not the first time the embassy had heard of that. Reference should be made to the urgent telegram Morgenstierne sent to the Foreign Office in London on April 14, 1941, in which he wrote about Flagstad: "Her intention is to meet her husband in Stockholm."[145] It was actually Morgenstierne who, in all probability, managed to stop her entry into Sweden by also telegraphing the legation in Stockholm about the matter.

### Embassy's New Statement

Flagstad was living on borrowed money and had to earn her daily bread. It was no longer possible to check into expensive hotels, so she had rented two simple rooms in New York for four months. A two-month concert tour was arranged for her before she would once again sing at the June Festival in

Part 3: The Years of Struggle (1941–51)

Zurich. The concerts in America involved fresh confrontations with her opponents. Pictures taken of Flagstad at this time show a lady with wide-open eyes, most likely a sign of the tension and anxiety she was feeling. For the moment, she knew nothing of how dramatically the situation would evolve. However, Flagstad had good powers of intuition and felt physically that great danger was approaching. She began to receive threats about the horrendous things that would happen during the planned concerts. The first of these was to take place in Boston on April 6, 1947, and ticket sales were disappointing. Several organizers had canceled, as they did not want her to appear. Moreover, a Flagstad concert would constitute a considerable security risk that many of the organizers refused to take.

The Norwegian authorities did not make things any easier. On March 17, 1947, the *New York Times* printed a statement from the Norwegian Embassy in Washington. They wrote that the embassy would not take a stance in the controversies swirling around Flagstad, nor would they reply to her complaints in the interview, when she said that Norwegians had treated her badly. However, the embassy did want to bring the following facts to light:

1. The Norwegian authorities had not found sufficient evidence to provide a basis for a criminal prosecution of Flagstad. She had therefore been issued a passport. She could leave Norway and travel wherever she wanted.
2. Flagstad left the US on April 19, 1941. At the time, Norway was at war with Germany, and the Norwegian Legation in Washington, acting under instructions from the Norwegian Foreign Ministry in London, refused to assist her. She therefore had to seek help from other quarters to travel via Portugal and Germany to Norway. Until the end of the war, she lived there with her husband, the late Henry Johansen, who was a member of Quisling's traitorous party, the National Samling. Until his death, he was being prosecuted for treason.
3. The American press had published a testimonial from Chief Justice Emil Stang, stating that Flagstad had a steadfast patriotic attitude during the war. Chief Justice Stang provided this testimonial before he became chief justice, and on January 27, 1947, he modified his statement. He said that it was too wide-ranging and only covered the period of her stay in Norway during the war, not her conduct while she was in America. Stang said he had no knowledge of the time from the invasion of Norway on April 9, 1940, until fru Flagstad traveled home to Norway from the US in April 1941.

The embassy's "facts" about Flagstad. Facsimile *New York Times*, March 17, 1947.

These are the facts.[146]

Morgenstierne told the newspaper that he would not object to her plans to become an American citizen. According to McArthur, this statement gave the impression that Flagstad had committed crimes while she was living in America. It stirred people up, and for her adversaries, this was grist to the mill.[147]

## Vilified by Walter Winchell

On March 19, 1947, Myklebost included in *Verdens Gang* a report about an article by Leonard Lyons, repeated in several hundred American newspapers. It claimed that Flagstad's representative had submitted an offer to Columbia Records to make a recording. They argued that she had gone back to Norway during the war only because she wanted to be a good wife. To this, Columbia replied, "Frau Göring was probably also a good wife, but we've no wish to enter into any business dealings with her either."[148]

Part 3: The Years of Struggle (1941–51)

The gossip columnists understood instinctively that Flagstad was now easy game and provided good material for further spin. The Norwegian authorities would not lift a finger, no matter what was written about her. On the contrary, they would enjoy it. McArthur relates that a gossip columnist and radio presenter by the name of Walter Winchell had immediately reacted to the embassy's statement by filling his column in the *Daily Mirror* and his radio program with Flagstad slander for three weeks in a row.[149]

Winchell had the reputation of being the inventor of gossip columns in the US, and dishonesty was ingrained in the system. In his own radio show, he had made hanging celebrities out to dry into a popular sport. He was arrogant, cruel, ruthless, and notorious for not having particularly trustworthy sources for his information. He said himself, "Usually I get my material from people who have promised someone else not to breathe a word to anybody."[150] By legitimizing the use of gossip as mainstream media, Winchell paved the way for modern celebrity-focused journalism. By breaking the main rules of journalism, of not using unconfirmed sources, he also came to be regarded as the father of a trend that led to American journalism losing respect and credibility among the general public.

His activities were wide-ranging, and he made use of ghostwriters. Winchell's columns and radio programs were spread to more than two thousand newspapers and read by millions every single day. Material from his columns was also taken up in the most popular radio stations in the US. Everything he broadcast about Flagstad in 1947 was negative, and most of it was downright lies. The embassy was a principal source of information. The Metropolitan's chief archivist, Robert Tuggle, succeeded in locating one of Winchell's ghostwriters, Herman Klurfeldt. On being asked who at the Norwegian Embassy had given them information about Flagstad, he answered that it had been everyone who worked there. They were all against her.[151]

In his columns and radio shows, Winchell used Morgenstierne and Myklebost as corroborating witnesses; he quoted both of them and cited them in support of his portrayal of Flagstad. Their points appeared in his columns in block capitals. Winchell drew far-reaching conclusions. He wrote that Flagstad had stayed in Kristiansand during the war as the loneliest woman in the world and that people had treated her as if she did not exist. Norway was her prison. She had betrayed the Norwegian people, and she had also betrayed the proud tradition of great Norwegian men and women—Ibsen, Bjørnson, Nansen, and others. Now this woman wanted to become an American citizen. When her application landed on the desk, the immigration authorities ought

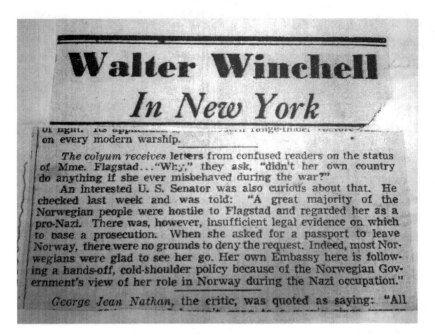

Hate campaign against Flagstad. Walter Winchell in New York. Facsimile.

to have the *New York Times* of June 1945 in front of them, in which the president of the Norwegian Parliament, C. J. Hambro, was quoted. He had said that for Norwegians, Flagstad was dead.[152] Here Winchell was referring to the conclusion of the Norwegian Embassy's official statement about Flagstad on June 14, 1945.

He added that readers had become confused. Why did her own country do nothing if she had behaved badly during the war? An American senator had also become interested in this question. He had made inquiries about it and learned that the vast majority of the Norwegian people were hostile to Flagstad because of her Nazi sympathies. However, at present there was insufficient evidence to prosecute her. This was why she had been granted a passport, and most Norwegians were glad that she had left the country. Winchell wrote, "Her own embassy here is following a hands-off, cold-shoulder policy because of the Norwegian Government's view of her role in Norway during the Nazi occupation."[153]

In one of his columns, Winchell reproduced a letter from a captain on the American cargo ship *Young Man of Manhattan*. Before the war, the captain had accompanied Flagstad on a walk around Harlem. He said that he could remember how she had used expletives when complaining that non-Aryans had access to the subway and boasted of the joy it would be for an artist to shake the dust of the Jewish Communist America off her feet and set out for places where the Third Reich now ruled. The captain emphasized that it would have been impossible for Flagstad to go home to Norway against the wishes of her government had it not been for the aid and approval of the Nazis.[154] On March 24, 1947, Winchell pointed out that Flagstad's forthcoming concert in Carnegie Hall would take place on Hitler's birthday, April 20.

Such reports led to an increasing number of negative comments in newspapers and inquiries at the embassy with questions about Flagstad—in particular because Winchell, in his columns, strongly emphasized that the embassy was his source and that Norway was keen to get rid of her. This also increased the number of anonymous threatening letters. Several Jewish organizations now applied to the embassy posing questions about her past. The embassy made no comment, at least not officially, beyond their statement dated March 16, 1947. No letters of thanks from Morgenstierne to Winchell exist, but his articles were sent from the embassy to the Foreign Office marked "for the dossier." In Norway, *Verdens Gang* and *Dagbladet* characterized Winchell as a powerful man and also recounted some of what he had written.

## Rejected by the Metropolitan

Kirsten Flagstad waited for a reply to her application for a work permit in the US. Her impresario, George Engles, had sent it to the American Guild of Musical Artists (AGMA). The reply was a long time in coming, and when it eventually arrived, it was a great disappointment to her. On March 28, 1947, the organization wrote: "The AGMA management feel that they do not have the authority to readmit Kirsten Flagstad as a full member, considering that such serious accusations have been made against her in the press. However, since these have not been confirmed by official sources in Norway, they will nevertheless consent to the granting of a work permit."[155]

This response shows the magnitude of the impact the anti-Flagstad press campaign was having. She was refused membership in her own professional organization because unsubstantiated claims about her had appeared in the media. AGMA's reply was mentioned in many American newspapers as well as in *Verdens Gang* in Norway. Without a doubt, it fed suspicions and stirred people up even further. It was a crushing blow to Flagstad that her professional association rejected her.

214 THE VOICE OF THE CENTURY

The Metropolitan season was still running, and Flagstad thought they might have given her a role or two in the remaining performances. An invitation from the Metropolitan would have made it easier for her: she felt that being connected to the institution would have protected her. Despite what their former star soprano had meant for the opera house, they now chose to trim their sails to the wind. As an independently financed organization, they were dependent on public opinion. Several people expressed the view that Flagstad could hire premises herself and hold concerts. Then the general public could decide for themselves whether or not they wanted to attend. At the Metropolitan, the public had bought tickets for the season and therefore had to accept the singers the management offered.[156] Flagstad received no communication from the Met. However, she read in the newspaper that the manager, Edward Johnson, had made it clear that he did not want her back at the opera. Flagstad says, "This rejection came as a shock. I was deeply hurt by it and I'm not ashamed to admit it.... They shunned me as if I were contaminated and unclean. Not a single phone call, not even from the people who had been my closest colleagues for many years."[157]

## An American Diplomat Intervenes

Immediately before Flagstad returned to America, Florence Jaffray Harriman wrote a letter to Eleanor Robson Belmont, who was on the management board at the Metropolitan. Belmont was a well-known English actress who married the enormously wealthy American banker August Belmont in 1910. He died in 1924, leaving a colossal fortune to his widow. Mrs. Belmont joined the Metropolitan's board in 1933 as the first woman to do so and founded the Metropolitan Opera Guild in 1935. She was therefore a woman of great influence over the institution.

The letter from Harriman was about Kirsten Flagstad. Harriman, a diplomat who was America's minister in Norway from 1937 to 1940, knew Belmont from social life in high-ranking circles. When Germany attacked Norway on April 9, 1940, Minister Harriman was evacuated to Stockholm along with the rest of the American Legation. Due to her post, Harriman also had close connections to Morgenstierne.

Harriman wrote in a letter to Belmont that her Norwegian friends were extremely upset about rumors circulating that the Metropolitan would take Flagstad back. She reminded Belmont of what the embassy had said and told her that Flagstad had performed in Germany during the war. Flagstad loved her husband and wanted to be near him. Harriman did not understand how

## Part 3: The Years of Struggle (1941–51)                215

Flagstad could do so, since Johansen was a coarse and vulgar person, completely unlike all the other Norwegians she had met. Her impression was that Norwegians would feel resentful if a traitor was accepted into an Allied country. It would be regarded as a hurtful and antagonistic act toward Norway.[158]

Belmont answered this letter on March 7, 1947, but the reply was not found in either Harriman's or Belmont's papers. A typewritten copy, however, was found in the archives at the Norwegian Embassy in Washington.

Belmont did not take a stance on the accusations against Kirsten Flagstad. She wrote that at that time, Flagstad had not yet received an entry permit to America (clean bill of health), so it was premature to discuss her return to the Metropolitan. Belmont refrained from comment on the Norwegian situation but said she wholeheartedly agreed with Harriman's assessment of Henry Johansen. However, she promised to bring the contents of the letter to the attention of the opera house management. No matter what the Metropolitan's board might decide in the future, at this particular juncture, as far as she was aware, the opera house had no obligations to Flagstad. Her fate when she did return to America was something Belmont left for the gods to decide.[159]

On March 20, 1947, Ambassador Morgenstierne wrote to Mrs. Harriman to thank her for letting him in on this correspondence. At the same time, he sent her the embassy's statement about Flagstad to use as she wished. He also thanked her for the wonderful dinner she had hosted for him and Trygve Lie: they had enjoyed sharing a meal and meeting all the interesting people present.

Harriman's letter is worth dwelling on. To whom was she referring when she wrote about "her shocked Norwegian friends"? Was it Ambassador Morgenstierne and his circle, with whom she was often photographed? She had recently invited him and Trygve Lie to dinner. Was Kirsten Flagstad a topic of discussion on this occasion? Who told her that Flagstad had been refused a visa because Henry Johansen had collaborated with the occupying forces?

It had been Lie, in his capacity as foreign minister, who had given this order from London. Harriman received this information long after she had left Norway in 1940. Who told her the untrue story about Flagstad giving one or two concerts in Germany on her way home in 1941? Who were the Norwegians who had told Harriman that Flagstad had a close, friendly relationship with the occupying Germans in Norway during the war? Who told her that Flagstad was a traitor? Why did Harriman report back to Ambassador Morgenstierne concerning her correspondence with Belmont? What did the Norwegian Embassy and Ambassador Morgenstierne have to do with this question?[160]

Ambassador Florence Jaffray Harriman and Ambassador Wilhelm Torleif von Munthe af Morgenstierne, 1937. *Source: United States Library of Congress Print and Photographs Division.*

Harriman's letter may have influenced the Metropolitan's board with regard to Flagstad. Nevertheless, in March 1946, Belmont said that it was up to the American authorities to decide whether Flagstad was allowed to return to the US. However, the Metropolitan would want to have her wonderful voice back. The comment was referenced in the *New York Times* on March 20 and gave Flagstad some flicker of hope.[161] Incidentally, she was totally unaware of the diplomatic game taking place behind the scenes about her future fate in America.

### Norwegian Prime Minister Asked to Step In

An American officer, Alfred Gerhard Dehly, clearly saw that the Norwegian diplomatic service was acting as a destabilizing factor in America with regard to Kirsten Flagstad. Through its campaign, the embassy was playing a part in riots and unrest that were damaging to society. This brought him to write a letter on March 17, 1947, to the Norwegian prime minister, Einar Gerhardsen. During the war, Dehly had trained military divisions, shock troops preparing for an invasion of Europe to topple the Nazi regime. In his work, he had met people from the Norwegian resistance movement who had made a good impression on him. However, Norway's good reputation was now in danger if this persecution of Kirsten Flagstad was allowed to continue.

Dehly, who after the war seems to have been employed as a director in the American Food and Drug Council, previously had been in correspondence

Part 3: The Years of Struggle (1941–51)          217

with the Norwegian prime minister about this affair. He had then inquired about Flagstad's fate and asked whether the Norwegian authorities had any scores to settle with her. Gerhardsen had forwarded the letter to the Ministry of Justice, and Dehly had received the answer that Kirsten Flagstad was not the subject of any criminal prosecution.

In his letter to Prime Minister Gerhardsen on March 17, 1947, Dehly explicitly requested that the smear campaign against Kirsten Flagstad, being run from the Norwegian Embassy in Washington, be stopped. He asked the prime minister to step in to prevent a prominent Norwegian artist being treated in this fashion.[162]

The prime minister forwarded this letter to the Ministry of Foreign Affairs, with an accompanying letter that has proved impossible to trace. This overture led to some internal correspondence within the Foreign Office. After this, the embassy made no more official statements about Flagstad, but the unofficial mudslinging continued with full force. On April 11, embassy adviser Hans Olav wrote a letter of rebuke to a reporter in the *New York Herald Tribune*. The journalist, Virgil Thomson, was a great Flagstad admirer and had made favorable comments about her that the adviser was keen to correct. He stressed in his letter that Flagstad was "the wife of a Nazi collaborator."[163]

## Her Life under Threat

Kirsten Flagstad was now left high and dry, with the exception of a few faithful friends and colleagues. From this position, she had to build her postwar career. She had been forced to swallow her pride by allowing an admirer to pay for her lodgings in New York. The worst was still to come, however. All the threats that had come her way necessitated a major security presence at her forthcoming performances. The first of these was to take place in Boston on April 6, 1947. The entire premises were thoroughly searched in advance. The police were looking for explosives and firearms, among other things, and a huge turnout of police was tasked with guarding the building. She was allocated her own detectives to escort her around.

Outside, she saw booing and yelling pickets waving placards accusing her of collaborating with the Nazi regime and telling her to leave. Two detectives took her by the arm, and a number of plainclothes police officers followed every step she took. In front of the stage door stood a row of uniformed police officers. The hall was packed, but she was so anxious and confused that she thought it was only half-full. The audience rose to their feet to give her a warm welcome. This was too much for her, and she was on the verge of

The hate campaign in the press stirred up large numbers of the public.
*Source: Flagstad Museum.*

dissolving into tears. McArthur sent her a warning look. She must not break down now.

The concert proceeded without incident, and there was no more trouble at this time. The critics noted that her voice had developed since they had heard it last. She sang like an angel and was still the most amazing voice of the age.[164]

The next day, Flagstad and McArthur arrived in Milwaukee, where they were faced with a concert hall daubed with swastikas. Angry demonstrators, carrying placards with Hitler, swastikas, and demands for her to leave, were gathered around the entrance. Flagstad's impresario had worked hard to find a secret entrance to the concert venue so that she could avoid walking past the pickets. The police presence in front of the hall was considerable, since so many threats had been received. Three other concerts in the Midwest went the same way: audiences were sparse, and the finances of the project were about to collapse, despite the fantastic reviews.

On April 20, 1947, her first concert back at New York's Carnegie Hall took place. The concert was sold out since Flagstad was still a draw for the music

*Source: Flagstad Museum.*

lovers of the city. Three thousand New Yorkers moved past the demonstrators and into Carnegie Hall. The organizers had slipped Flagstad and the detectives surrounding her in through a back door so that they did not have to be confronted with the demonstrators outside. McArthur warned her that the public in New York would give her a warm welcome and that she must be careful. She must not burst into tears as she had been on the brink of doing in Boston.

Kirsten Flagstad sat in the performers' foyer, listening to the shouts of the demonstrators out on West Fifty-Sixth Street. She was now fifty-two years old, but she knew that the power and brilliance of her voice were still intact. The yells reached into the room: "Hitler is singing in Carnegie Hall"; "Kirsten Flagstad entertained the Nazis; we fought against them"; "Let freedom sing, not Flagstad"; "Quisling's voice is in Carnegie Hall"; "Send Brunhild back to Valhalla"; "It's not on view now, Flagstad, but your swastika is shining." The demonstrators had been out in full force since 1:00 p.m., and the ones in the first row were chanting, "Norway doesn't want her, so why do you?"

Flagstad had developed a sense of paranoia on the basis of her life experiences. She was convinced that her enemies were monitoring her every step and trying to drive her to the precipice. They were just waiting for something to happen, for something to go wrong: for her to forget the music and humiliate herself in public. After all the threats, she had begun to look over her shoulder everywhere she went. She often glanced up at the fly loft to make sure nothing could come loose and fall down on her, and she listened for the least sound. Being under constant surveillance was unpleasant, but she had made up her mind to keep a grip on herself and sing like never before. Plainclothes police officers accompanied her onto the stage at Carnegie Hall.

What met her there was a standing ovation, whistling, and enthusiastic cheers. This overwhelming ovation brought a blush to her cheeks, but she controlled herself. The first two songs were performed in a shaky voice, but then she got into her stride and sang her heart out for two hours. The evening ended in triumph.[165] The critics wrote that Flagstad was still the noblest singer in the whole world. The sound of her voice was quite simply godlike, from the top notes to the lowest register.[166]

## In Norway, She Is Dead

Two days later, on April 22, 1947, the terrible concert in Philadelphia, described in "Post Festum" in this book, took place. *Verdens Gang* reported on this concert, using the headline "In Norway She Is Dead."[167] On May 5, 1947, Myklebost sent a telegram to Morgenstierne, enclosing copies of negative Flagstad material from *Verdens Gang*. He wrote that he had also had the information included in the *Nordisk Tidende*. The telegram with its enclosures was forwarded to the embassy's press adviser, Hans Olav. Myklebost also alerted him to the fact that he had written an article that would be printed in the *Reader's Scopes* publication's August edition.[168] This article brands Flagstad a traitor and contains a series of dishonest claims.

At the end of May 1947, Flagstad traveled to Europe. Several American newspapers wondered why Flagstad was never criticized there. An obvious reason was that no malevolent press campaigns were waged against her in European countries and no Norwegian ambassador there had it in for her. Morgenstierne knew that Flagstad planned to return to America around October or November. He therefore continued his zealous campaign, but not all newspaper editors were willing to put themselves at his disposal in this persecution. In May 1947, Ambassador Morgenstierne began to put pressure on Norway's largest newspaper, *Aftenposten*. The newspaper had been reticent about printing negative material about Flagstad. The editors inserted news

## Part 3: The Years of Struggle (1941–51)

about the riots and trouble surrounding the singer in America discreetly in their news coverage and gave these incidents scant, balanced comment. Morgenstierne was unhappy about this and urged the newspaper to print the embassy's press release of March 16, 1947, as well as an article about her alleged unpatriotic behavior in America. On this point, Ambassador Morgenstierne encountered unaccustomed resistance from the journalist Theo Findahl.

Findahl, who was in Berlin from 1939, had been able to follow the run-up to World War II. On April 7, 1940, he had telegraphed *Aftenposten* to tell them that the German invasion of Norway was underway. The newspaper's editor had shown the message to the admiral in command, who had refused to believe it and stopped them from publishing it. Throughout the war, Findahl had been involved in a British intelligence operation, and after the war, he was *Aftenposten*'s New York correspondent. He was unwilling to submit the material Morgenstierne was requesting, since he had not been able to reach Flagstad's impresario. He was keen to hear his version of the story. "You hear all sorts of different opinions," Findahl wrote to Morgenstierne.[169] At that, the ambassador complained to the newspaper's management about what the journalist had written about Flagstad in America. The communication must almost be regarded as an attempt by the authorities to control the free press, in this case Norway's most important newspaper.[170]

### That's Enough Now

In May 1947, Flagstad traveled to Europe for concerts in London and The Hague. As usual, she was a star attraction at the festival in Zurich, as Isolde and Brunhild in *Götterdämmerung*. She enjoyed the peace and harmony of her surroundings there but at the same time longed to go back to the US. Her family had sent her cuttings from Norwegian newspapers, and she read that a number of cultural figures and artists as well as music organizations had come together to write a petition protesting her victimization. This was printed in all the major newspapers in Norway on June 17. The artists in Norway who had betrayed their country had by now been out of quarantine for a long time and were back at work. The signatories found it both unfair and prejudiced that the persecution of Flagstad had still not come to an end. They urged their fellow compatriots to stop these shameful attempts to undermine Kirsten Flagstad's name and reputation.[171]

Myklebost had previously answered one of them by saying that it was Flagstad herself who had provoked all these attacks against her. He concluded:

"And with reference to the Norwegian newspapers reproducing telegrams and pictures that convey what is happening at her concerts, they are simply doing their duty as communicators of news."[172]

It was not quite so straightforward as far as Myklebost himself was concerned, in his position as assistant editor at the newspaper: in a telegram to Morgenstierne dated January 28, 1947, he stated that his purpose was to stop Flagstad. This was the aim of all his writings about the case. His newspaper, *Verdens Gang*, printed a simultaneous counterstatement to the petition. They felt it was unfortunate and incomprehensible that any adult persons could put their name to such a document.[173] They added that several prominent cultural figures in Norway lacked judgment when it came to Kirsten Flagstad.

Flagstad relates in her American biography that she did not appreciate such well-meaning defenses of her in the newspapers, as they merely provoked responses that hurt her even more and kept the debate going. She herself never spoke up to refute the allegations in the media because she found it served no purpose.[174]

In the Norwegian Foreign Office, the persecution of Flagstad had not ceased; it continued unabated, if in a more discreet fashion. The ministry opposed the public petition. On June 23, 1947, the Foreign Office's press chief, Jens Schive, sent a cryptic letter with two attachments to the press adviser, Hans Olav, at the embassy in Washington. He writes:

> I am sending you an anonymous leaflet with accompanying envelope that was received by the Foreign Minister.
>
> If you have a discreet Sherlock in Seattle, it would be good if you could get his little grey cells moving. However, it would not be expedient to give the product any further publicity.
>
> A little letter about how public opinion views the Flagstad case and the possible attitude of Norwegian- and Swedish-Americans would not go amiss. As you have seen from the newspapers, there is now quite an uproar about a campaign by Norwegian artists in support of fru Flagstad and the discussion may well flare up again as a result. But we have no wish to have things screwed up by disputes between Norwegian- and Swedish-Americans à la 1905.[175]

It is a mystery what anti-Flagstad steps the Foreign Office, with the foreign minister in the vanguard, were planning here. It has been impossible to find the leaflet and envelope in the archive.

Part 3: The Years of Struggle (1941–51)                    223

## "Shall We Stop Flagstad from Singing at the Royal Wedding?"

The deceased Queen Elizabeth II married Prince Philip in London on November 20, 1947. The planned celebrations were as magnificent as can only be expected of the British. On October 18, 1947, Prebensen, the Norwegian ambassador in London, wrote a letter to the Norwegian Foreign Office alerting them to the fact that a *United Press* report had stated that Flagstad would sing at a concert in the Royal Albert Hall in London on November 25 for the royal family and guests attending Princess Elizabeth's wedding. However, Prebensen had investigated the claim and discovered this was not the case. On October 23, a postscript to Prebensen's letter was added by the press adviser, Jens Schive: "Since then, the newspapers have received official denials, including one from Princess Elizabeth's personal secretary. It should therefore be unnecessary for us to take any action."[176]

Did the Foreign Office regard it as their function to try to stop a concert starring Flagstad for the British royal family? Morgenstierne also received information that the concert would not take place. He subsequently sent out several letters to private individuals informing them that Kirsten Flagstad would not be singing at the royal wedding in London. Why did he do that?

Flagstad's concert took place in the Royal Albert Hall on November 24, a charity concert to benefit the British Empire Nurses' War Memorial Fund. Sir Thomas Beecham conducted the Royal Philharmonic Orchestra.

"When you hear Flagstad singing Sieglinde again, it arouses impatience to hear *The Ring* again, despite all its awful Teutonic implications," wrote the *Times*.[177] Flagstad had regained a position in the UK that the Norwegian ambassador had no power to destroy.

### Another Setback

In the late summer of 1947, Flagstad had spent six weeks with her family, tickled pink with her grandchild. They lived in a primitive cabin beside a lake in Montana, avoiding both newspapers and radio broadcasts. She had written to her sister that what she wanted most was to disappear because she knew that the idyll had to end. She would have to force herself back onto the stage again to earn her living. "Oh how I wept when I had to leave," she writes.[178] Ahead of her, she had several concerts in Havana, Cuba, before setting out on a concert tour of the US. She was afraid to appear in public again.

224                    THE VOICE OF THE CENTURY

It had been difficult for her impresario to find engagements for her in the US. Only a few local organizers had taken a chance on holding a concert starring Flagstad. After she came back from London, she learned that protests had led to two planned concerts in Atlanta and Savannah being canceled. According to the *New York Times*, the organizer had been bombarded with messages from people accusing Flagstad of having been a Nazi fellow traveler during the war.[179] The cancellations caused financial damage, as did the newspaper headlines.

It was an extremely difficult situation. She took what was offered, even singing in school assembly halls, often to half-empty auditoriums. McArthur reflects on this phenomenon in his book. Flagstad was sought after in Europe, a continent that had been almost destroyed by the war. But in the US, which had not been occupied, and where not a single bomb had been dropped, she could scarcely get an engagement.[180] However, there were exceptions—Carnegie Hall was always full, and the number of demonstrators had dwindled since the previous season.

The Civic Opera House in Chicago hired her, and the Chicago Symphony Orchestra, under Artur Rodzinski's baton, agreed to play. Flagstad's first postwar appearance on stage in an opera house in the US took place on November 16, 1947. She sang Isolde with Set Svanholm as her partner. *Newsweek* reported on November 24 that this was a historic performance that no one would forget. The controversies swirling around her, about whether or not she had been a collaborator, continued, and the Metropolitan still refused to take a gamble on falling foul of their subscribers. These difficulties had caused Flagstad's Isolde to grow in stature, and the audience responded to her with overwhelming cheers. The Metropolitan's hesitancy became Chicago's triumph.

### Flagstad Season at Covent Garden

After spending the Christmas holiday with family, Flagstad traveled to London, where she had a number of engagements in the late winter and spring of 1947–48. She had rented two rooms with a bathroom. There were electric fires in both rooms, so she did not freeze. In London, they made no fuss and left her in peace. At the theater, they were kind and treated her like a queen. She enjoyed herself immensely, eating Danish rye bread and drinking gin. The windows were old and unpainted, but she had received so many flowers that she could barely see how shabby they were.[181]

Here, she did not lack for invitations. From February 19 until April 8, she sang a total of ten performances of *Tristan and Isolde* and six *Walküre*

## Part 3: The Years of Struggle (1941–51)

Brunhilds at Covent Garden. In itself, this was a frenzied schedule, but in addition, Covent Garden had insisted that the opera should be sung with English text. Opposition to the German language was still strongly felt within the populace. Learning the vast libretto in a different language from the one she was used to must have been time-consuming and challenging in every way. The critics did not mention the change of language and its consequences, apart from the *Daily Herald*, which contented itself with commenting that Flagstad had triumphed over the language.[182] The experiment was not repeated: they may well have felt that some of the vitality had been removed from Wagner's works—after all, he was no Englishman. Nevertheless, many critics concluded that Flagstad was still the world's greatest living soprano voice.

Reuters reported that Queen Elizabeth of Great Britain (later known as the Queen Mother) and her two daughters, Elizabeth and Margaret, the Duke of Edinburgh, and the Duke of Kent had had to have dinner sent in from Buckingham Palace. It was served in the lobby outside the royal box so that they could attend the almost five-hour-long performance of *Tristan and Isolde*, at which Flagstad sang.[183]

In addition to enduring all these performances, Flagstad also undertook five recordings for His Master's Voice and gave two concerts at the Royal Albert Hall. She writes that she rested as much as she could because she could feel that it had been seven years since she had had so much to do with opera.[184] It may have brought some small comfort that afterward she was heading to La Scala in Milan to sing in four performances of *Tristan and Isolde*, this time in German. However, here she encountered major problems with the conductor, Victor de Sabata. She thought he was conducting at the wrong tempo and making Wagner unrecognizable. Her partner, Max Lorenz, was terribly nervous, shaken by all he had been through during the war. He had lived in the cross fire of persecution against homosexuality and his marriage to a Jewish woman, as well as giving shelter to his Jewish mother-in-law. He was in no state to tolerate the brusque conductor, who did not concern himself about the singers onstage. Flagstad tried to give Lorenz self-confidence. She had never felt so angry onstage, but she held her tongue. The conductor is always right, her father had told her. The high C in the second act came automatically, and this amazed her because in recent years she had had to replace it with an A.[185] Her fury may have helped.

Then she went back to London and later to Zurich and Paris. One may well wonder when she ever had time for anything other than work. In London, several colleagues and admirers held intimate parties for her, something she actually enjoyed. One evening, she was sitting at the fire with a couple of friends when an actor came over to speak to her. Gesticulating wildly, he told her a story set in a small Italian town where *Tosca* was being performed one evening. The audience had insisted that it was the soprano, rather than the tenor, who should be shot.

The actor had hoped that Flagstad would laugh, but instead, he was given a cold look to signal that she found the story inappropriate. While this was going on, he was watching her because the man had a keen eye for human nature. He wondered whether this lady sitting here knitting a dark blue sweater, slurping black coffee, and wearing horn-rimmed glasses with a leg missing was the same person he had heard and seen at the Royal Albert Hall. No, he quickly discovered that this was the private individual he was faced with: onstage, Flagstad was a completely different person.[186]

## Flagstad Meets a Soulmate

Even though she had rejected him at first, this man had aroused her interest. They would meet again the following evening, at the home of the Covent Garden conductor, Karl Rankl. This man was the actor, singer, and comedian Bernard Miles. Miles had a long list of achievements behind him as an actor and was particularly famous for his portrayals of war heroes and his performance as Long John Silver in the film *Treasure Island*. In 1951, he founded the Mermaid Theatre in London, mainly to give Kirsten Flagstad a small and intimate stage. In 1953, he was designated Commander of the Order of the British Empire (CBE), and in 1969, he was knighted, taking the title Baron Miles of Blackfriars. This was an honor given to only one other English actor before him: Laurence Olivier (Baron Olivier of Brighton).[187]

Miles had heard about the nightmare Flagstad was living through, and he saw how sad and traumatized she was when he met her in 1947. And so he made up his mind to help her and cheer her up. The advice he gave may suggest that he had knowledge of psychoanalysis. The evening at Rankl's residence was convivial—Flagstad laughed so much she was in tears of merriment at all his stories about the characters in Wagner's operas. He accompanied her home and invited her to visit his family the next day. Miles also claims that he fell in love with her. Something at least must have clicked between them, and for Flagstad this unleashed an avalanche of letters. She desperately needed someone to confide in, and Miles accepted this role. She wrote to him constantly about her experiences, the people she met, their reactions to her, and her own feelings. This was unlike Flagstad: the meeting with Miles opened her up.

He relates that she once dreamed that he stooped over her bed and lifted her out of a pool of blood.[188] This dream was not only symbolic; it also refers to something very specific. Flagstad's bed linens could be covered in blood. After the war, her psoriasis flared up and was sometimes terribly inflamed. She scratched herself so much at night that she bled. One of the reasons for this suffering was undeniably the anxiety and stress she experienced. The fact that he was lifting her up says something about his ability to take her out of her pain and about her confidence in him.

## The Subjects of Intimacy and Sex

There has been a great deal of speculation about the nature of their relationship. After the death of Flagstad's second husband, it appears she did not seek out any new romantic relationships. She brushed off anyone who came too close and never spoke of intimate relationships. Her shyness and sensitivity allowed no space for amorous overtures, and she felt these to be both invasive and disrespectful. She could not bear for anyone to approach her in that way.

It is not easy to distinguish between jokes and seriousness in what Miles has to say about his relationship with Flagstad, making him a problematic source. Without a doubt, he was among the very few people who came close to her and who obviously also observed her almost as a psychoanalyst and confidential adviser would do. He came physically close to her, by applying her stage makeup. He carried out this process in a theatrical, flirting manner, making her laugh. In her younger days, Flagstad had been smitten with Norway's most talented comedian of the time, August Schønemann. He was, like Miles, a sanguine, playful man, a masculine counterweight to her melancholy nature, which with the passage of time had become traumatized and depressive. An alchemist would perhaps have called this a mixture of quicksilver and lead that created new life.

Flagstad apparently told Miles that when she walked down from her dressing room to the first orchestra rehearsals at the Metropolitan, she stopped on the stairs to listen to Lotte Lehmann, who was singing the role of Sieglinde onstage. She had blushed on behalf of her own sex because she thought it felt as if Lehmann had undressed onstage. Lehmann and most other singers had a sensual quality in their voices that Flagstad lacked, Miles claimed. But her voice had qualities of power and resonance that made up for that shortfall.

Rehearsals in the New Theatre, Oslo, 1953, where Flagstad sang Dido. Also pictured, the tenor Bjarne Buntz and stage director Bernard Miles. *Archive: Scanpix.*

The androgynous character of her voice was what made it so great. The lack of obvious female expression sprang from the extreme shyness of her personality. Miles, who wanted to bring out this side of her, emphasized to Flagstad that Isolde was pure sex. Her answer to this was evasive. Singing should be good and should help other people. She had never liked Isolde, except for the first act. Miles told her lightheartedly that he had fallen in love with her at first glance. The melodies she made, and the fact that her mouth and lips were involved in the operation, made her irresistible to him. She was a free woman, and he felt just as every man would. He felt he had the right to try to captivate her. He had two rivals, McArthur and her Danish friend Knud Hegermann-Lindencrone. They were all around the same age, and her answer to them was the same as to Miles—extremely direct, firm, and Lutheran: "I don't get involved with married men. In the theater, I've seen how much unhappiness that sort of thing brings with it. It's my voice you're in love with and not me. But don't be too upset about it, because I'll sing for you."[189]

This was the fate of her three great admirers. Flagstad's morals were incredibly Lutheran, according to Miles. The men were given roles as guardian angels, advisers, and managers, each strategically placed in the US, Scandinavia, and London, and they always lent her a hand. Flagstad became a friend of Miles's wife, just as she had also become a close friend of Edwin McArthur's

Part 3: The Years of Struggle (1941–51)

spouse. She also loved Miles's children and their home in North London. And since the house had a charming apartment annex and they had a fabulous big Bösendorfer grand piano, she moved in with them. She adopted them, and they returned the compliment. Later she became godmother to one of their daughters.[190]

## Inquiry from the United Jewish Relief Appeal

While Flagstad was in London, she received a letter from a representative of the United Jewish Relief Appeal, A. Schusterman. The organization collected and administered funds for the support of around seventy-five thousand Jewish children who had lost their parents in the concentration camps. Schusterman asked if Flagstad would give a concert to raise money for them. She invited him to tea. Before she made up her mind, she wanted to ask him a direct question. Did he have any idea of all the rumors circulating about her in the US, including those that said she was an enemy of the Jewish people?

To her amazement, he nodded, and the detailed answer he gave made her really prick up her ears: "I know all about you, Madam Flagstad. Before we approached you, we checked very thoroughly to see if this was indeed the case and discovered that the rumours were groundless. So we would like to help you as much as we can, both here and in America. We will let them know that you have done nothing wrong. We would never have asked anyone who was hostile to the Jewish people."[191]

Such a declaration from a representative of those who had suffered most during the war moved her deeply. At the same time, the request posed a difficult dilemma for her. If she agreed, it could be used against her, and if she refused, the same thing could happen. Schusterman left the decision up to her. She said yes, with the greatest of pleasure. In total, she held three concerts for them in London—in 1948, 1949, and 1950. They also invited her to a traditional dinner in London, with prominent Jewish rabbis and members of Parliament present.

Schusterman wrote to several influential contacts in America asking them to repudiate the rumors about Flagstad. He also showed her a number of replies they had received. In the autumn of 1948, Schusterman issued an official statement to American newspapers on behalf of the organization, in which he thanked Flagstad for her generosity and assistance to Jewish children who had lost their parents in death camps. The declaration certainly swayed the press in America. No one knew what it meant to be persecuted like the Jews.

## Must Manage Alone

In August 1948, Flagstad set out on an extended tour in South America, to Argentina, Brazil, Chile, Puerto Rico, Venezuela, and Cuba. At first, the intention was for McArthur to travel with her, but he discovered that this was impossible from a purely financial point of view. His decision came as a shock to her. To think that she would have to travel on her own. The anxiety it caused her made her reject him completely to begin with. She wrote a letter saying that from then on, she would have to manage by herself in the world. Flagstad felt let down: if she had known that he would not be coming with her, she would never have gone on such a tour.[192]

They were soon on speaking terms again, but after this episode, Miles took over the place as the most trusted man in her life, a position McArthur had previously held. She completed the tour in dazzling style and says that in Caracas the audience had never attended an opera production before. The first one was *Tristan and Isolde*. The work was clearly too much for the weary audience, and the applause was polite but restrained. In South America, she encountered no unpleasantness either.

Flagstad was not back in the US until November. On December 12, she rounded off the year with her customary concert in Carnegie Hall. Pickets with hateful slogans were yet again in evidence. This upset her so much that she lost her balance on the way in and fell. A few people rushed to help her up, and she soon composed herself and continued with the concert. After more concerts, she traveled to Europe in February 1949. In March, she sang Isolde for as many as eight performances in various European cities, and at one of these, she also performed a *Walküre* Brunhild. In April, she was onstage again in three performances of *Tristan and Isolde* and sang four *Walküre* Brunhilds. Her finances were looking up, and the newspapers vied with one another in their superlatives. In May, Covent Garden presented all the operas in *The Ring*, with the exception of *Das Rheingold*, in the original language. Many years had passed since this major work had been staged there. The eminent Wagner expert Ernest Newman was worried that there were hardly any people in Britain under the age of thirty who had heard this colossal work and that the audience thus had no background from which to judge what they were hearing. The singers came in for a great deal of criticism from him, and he made reference to the composer's ears, which must have been extremely sensitive to the purity and beauty of the music. The only person to pass his searching scrutiny was Kirsten Flagstad.[193] She sang the role of Isolde for the 150th time that spring.

Part 3: The Years of Struggle (1941–51)

Her voice was like Niagara Falls—it was just a shame that it could not go on flowing equally long, sighed one critic.

After meeting Miles, Flagstad tried to work in London as much as possible so that she could be with him and his family. Miles was a strong opponent of Wagner, but this served only to amuse her. Little by little, he exerted pressure to persuade her to change her repertoire, to McArthur's great annoyance. By now he had realized that Flagstad sought Miles's advice on most things.

Miles had encouraged her to accept Furtwängler's invitation to Salzburg to sing Leonore in *Fidelio*. This was a sensitive role for Flagstad. Both the reunion with Furtwängler and the fact that Leonore's husband was in prison brought many bad memories. Miles was undertaking some kind of exposure therapy with her: she had to subject herself to what she most feared. He would come to Salzburg and give her emotional support by his presence.

## Persecution Damaged Her Voice

Flagstad spent some of the summer of 1949 in Zurich, where she sang Isolde. It is said that she dominated the stage with her monumental, flamboyant dynamism. She was a vocal phenomenon that captivated the audience from the very first moment to the last.[194] She was disciplined and accomplished enough not to let her poor physical and mental condition affect what she did onstage.

Conflicts had accumulated again, and they had an impact on her body. Flagstad would soon be fifty-four years old, and she had lived in a state of terror ever since war broke out. After the war, she had had to live with incessant harassment, smear campaigns in the press, demonstrations, and threats against her life and health. She had been in a state of constant tension and lived in pervasive anxiety. This burden, which she had tried to suppress through hard work, as well as a certain amount of alcohol consumption and sleeping tablets, had broken her system. The perpetual weight of tension on her muscles and skeleton had induced chronic pain, and the inflammation of her skin was a barometer of inner stress.

McArthur received an ominous letter from Zurich telling him that her health was in a poor state. On July 8, she described terrible pains in one arm and a dreadful outbreak of psoriasis. Increased inner tension led to muscular cramps, for which she received special treatment while she was in Zurich. She was simply unable to tolerate any more stress and agitation.

The discussion about whether she should return to the Metropolitan had flared up again in the newspapers. In September and October, she was to sing Isolde and Walküre-Brunhild at the opera house in San Francisco, but the

Flagstad and Miles with his wife in Salzburg, 1949. It is clear that Flagstad is deeply worried about all the conflicts swirling around her. *Source: Flagstad Museum.*

opera season there was in danger of collapse because of the protests against her. She was aware of all this when she arrived in Salzburg. There, her colleagues were all friendly and sympathetic, but she was unable to sleep. The press in Austria was full of articles saying that she was not welcome to sing in San Francisco. Everyone around her knew about it. Everything she faced churned around in her head at night. The case against her late husband's estate had not yet been settled, and her assets had still not been released. She was waiting for this to happen at long last, because she longed to go home to her own house. She wrote to Miles that her difficulties seemed endless, but at the same time, she had to concentrate on work. She expected him to come: she needed his support and encouragement.

Furtwängler appeared with an array of star soloists and the Vienna Philharmonic for the production of *Fidelio*. Flagstad had stated several times that Beethoven was her favorite composer. His compositions demanded more refinement and sensitivity from a singer than Wagner's did.[195] The spoken dialogue in opera was a challenge, but it helped that she had Bodanzky's orchestral arrangement for the recitative in her ear. *Die Presse* noted that Flagstad

# Part 3: The Years of Struggle (1941–51)

might not have had the right degree of suppleness in the lyrical parts, but her command of the dramatic parts left the audience speechless. The final aria was met with effusive clapping and cheering from the audience. The production was such a success that it was repeated the following year with the same soloists, the only exception being Irmgard Seefried, who was replaced by Elisabeth Schwarzkopf singing Marzelline. Both productions were transmitted on radio, and in 1999, EMI Records released a CD of the performance in their "Festspieldokumente" series, which is based on thorough remastering of sound sources from various archives.

Reviews mentions a lack of suppleness in Flagstad's voice, a deficiency that was connected to her trauma. A Norwegian singing teacher, Sissel Høyem Aune, has written about this:

> In Flagstad's pre-war recordings, a relatively light embouchure can be heard, a bright, harmonic lustre: the sound is soft and round. Also, her phrasing draws us into the Wagnerian polyphony. In her interpretation of lieder and romances she cultivates all the facets of expression, both the delicately transparent and the full, resonant sound. The handling of the text is discreet but distinct.
>
> After the war, we hear an embouchure that is heavier. She begins the notes from below and glides into them: it takes longer before the initial notes are established at the correct pitch. This is a stylistic measure to compensate for a stiff, inflexible and rigid musculature. The sound still has an unusual carrying ability and brilliance, but is more metallic. The phrases are shorter because of the deterioration in the elasticity of her physique. Flagstad herself says in 1945 that a new feeling of ice and iron bars encircled her. Anxiety and sensitivity formed a kind of muscular armour in defence and this in turn created a psychological imbalance between her internal and external musculature. Flagstad's post-war interpretations, especially of Norwegian romances, are marked by a hardness, a coolness and an almost mechanical style that we do not find in the recordings she made before the war. The ageing process has had some effect, but the hate campaign against her also damaged her voice.[196]

## Mayor of San Francisco Demands an Answer

Even though her body and mind were fairly shattered, she kept things going and continued to garner great triumphs on the European stage. This was the price she had to pay, and she cannot have been particularly relaxed when she traveled to San Francisco in the autumn of 1949. In July 1949, a dispute had broken out between the management of the San Francisco Opera House and the management of the building in which the opera company was accommodated, War Memorial House. The opera company had engaged Flagstad for four performances in their autumn season, but War Memorial House, under pressure from the American Legion and the Veterans of Foreign Wars, decided to refuse permission for her to appear there. The conflict had come to a head because the opera company's season would fold financially if Flagstad were not allowed to sing. An American musicians' organization, the AGMA, wrote a letter threatening to boycott the War Memorial House if they discriminated against Flagstad, but the management of the opera house was adamant. To the opera-loving public in San Francisco, this was just as dramatic as the 1906 earthquake that had destroyed most of the city. Now, for the first time in twenty-seven years, it looked as if there would not be an opera season there.

On July 15, 1949, the Norwegian consul general in San Francisco, Jørgen Gabe, sent an urgent letter about the situation to the embassy in Washington. He had also called to get hold of Morgenstierne but had had to make do with Myklebost, who had now returned to the embassy as a press adviser. The consul general had received a call from Superior Judge Milton Sapiro, who also represented the American Legion. He wanted to know if Kirsten Flagstad had been decorated with the Order of St. Olav. The consul general confirmed that she had received this honor in 1937. The consul general had read in the newspapers that there had been a huge fuss in the management of the opera house and that they had unanimously agreed to refuse her permission to sing there. He had received various phone calls and inquiries wanting to discuss

"A traitor to Norway"?
Source: Flagstad Museum.

## Part 3: The Years of Struggle (1941–51)                    235

Kirsten Flagstad, but he had, however, said that the official Norwegian representation in San Francisco preferred to make no comment on the dispute. The Norwegian diplomatic service regarded this as an entirely internal American issue.[197] It emerges from a telegram sent later that Gabe had received a message to send the embassy's statement about Flagstad, dated March 16, 1947, to anyone who inquired about Flagstad at the consulate general.

In a letter on July 21, Gabe thanked Morgenstierne for his assistance. He wrote that the situation had been overinflated in the San Francisco press. In truth, all the articles had reported that the management was strongly criticized for their decision not to allow Flagstad to sing. Even though the embassy's official policy was to refer to its statement, Morgenstierne was still running his semipersonal campaign to influence matters. On July 19, 1949, he wrote a letter about the issue to a Norwegian Flagstad opponent, Chas R. Pedersen, in San Francisco. Here he stated quite explicitly that Flagstad had betrayed Norway. He wrote that only the people who had been active in the Home Front should have traveled home during the war. The more important the position a person held, the more reason to remain in post.[198]

The Norwegian Embassy received several telegrams about the matter. A clear statement about Flagstad's criminal record as a Nazi collaborator was called for. On July 21, the major of San Francisco, George Christopher, telegraphed Morgenstierne asking to be informed of Flagstad's status in her homeland. Were the rumors of her activities in Norway during the war true? Did the Norwegian authorities have information confirming that she had been involved in some kind of proactive Nazi operations during the war? The meeting to make a final decision on her engagement was to take place that same evening. The mayor would therefore request a response from the Norwegian Embassy in Washington that afternoon.[199] Morgenstierne telegraphed back that same day, answering that he could not say anything more about this other than the embassy's statement of March 16, 1947.[200]

The mayor had taken on a mediating role in the dispute. In his office, there had been several meetings between the concerned parties. He was determined to resolve the disagreement to reach the final result of allowing Kirsten Flagstad to sing at the opera house if he received clear confirmation from the Norwegian authorities that she was not being prosecuted and had not taken part in proactive Nazi collaboration in Norway during the war. Since his first approach to the Norwegian Embassy did not bring a clear answer, he now turned to the Norwegian Consulate General in San Francisco. On the afternoon of July 21, 1949, Consul General Gabe called Morgenstierne to tell him that Mayor Christopher had sent him a telegram at 4:30 p.m. local time

236 THE VOICE OF THE CENTURY

in which he had requested answers to three questions within one hour. In fact, the mayor was to make a decision that same evening about whether the entire opera season in the city should be canceled. His questions were the following:

1. Is fru Flagstad held to be unpatriotic as far as Norway is concerned?
2. Would the Norwegian authorities have any objection to her holding concerts in Norway?
3. Can the Norwegian authorities produce information for us to show that fru Flagstad has been involved in any form of pro-Nazi activity?[201]

The mayor did not receive a reply to his inquiry, either from the Norwegian Consulate General or from the Norwegian Embassy. This unquestionably led to uncertainty and confusion. The mayor had called in Thomas H. Swindol, who had been America's vice-consul in Norway in 1946–47, to the meeting with the other interested parties. Swindol stated at the meeting and also to the newspaper the *San Francisco Chronicle* that there had been no opposition to Flagstad in Norway just after the war. The only report he had heard of was something printed in a communist newspaper.[202] The mayor of San Francisco wanted unambiguous answers to his questions from the Norwegian authorities so that the War Memorial House could make the right decision. He therefore sent an express telegram from the management meeting to the American ambassador in Oslo, Charles U. Bay, asking for his help. Bay immediately contacted the Ministry of Justice requesting an urgent response to the mayor's questions. The minister of justice, Oscar Chr. Gundersen, replied that Kirsten Flagstad had not broken any Norwegian laws. There was no proof that she had collaborated with the occupying power. She had been issued with a passport and could travel back to Norway freely whenever she wished. The Norwegian authorities had nothing against her holding concerts in her homeland.

Ambassador Bay passed this response from the Norwegian minister of justice, that Flagstad was not being prosecuted in Norway and therefore could not be prevented from performing anywhere, on to American newspapers for publication.[203] In this he was taking upon himself a task that was really the function of the Norwegian Embassy in Washington. The consul general in San Francisco sent Morgenstierne a newspaper cutting of Bay's statement to the press.[204] On August 2, the American League and the Veterans of Foreign Wars decided by six votes to five to overturn their previous decision not to let Flagstad sing in the opera house. Even though they had reached this conclusion,

## Part 3: The Years of Struggle (1941–51)                    237

there was still a great deal of apprehension that her performances would attract demonstrations and other unrest. This fear turned out to be groundless.

When Kirsten Flagstad arrived in San Francisco, she met with an opera management that was afraid and nervous. She herself was filled with dread and paranoid delusions that she might be injured. They were scared of all sorts of sabotage against the opera house, everything from cut electricity wires to more targeted attacks. A series of threatening letters had come, from both anonymous and named persons, and had been handed over to the police. The first performance was a baptism of fire, not a situation that allowed her musculature to relax. She stayed with friends in San Francisco who did not know how to protect her.

On the evening of the premiere on September 30, 1949, she was escorted in through a double police cordon and even had to show ID to enter the premises. Once inside the War Memorial House, she was not able to take a single step on her own outside the dressing room.[205] Anxiety took hold of her, her psoriasis smoldered, and her joints and muscles ached, but she had to go onto the stage. The police had thrown a security ring around it in case anyone planned to dart forward and attack her. The audience was ecstatic after the performance and cheered her to the rafters.

A steely character and genuine artist had managed the unthinkable. After a few hours and a few drinks, she would slump down into herself again, once again feeling the disquiet and pain from her body, overexerted in every way, and from a deeply traumatized psyche.

### On Heading for Home

In the autumn of 1949, Flagstad wrote to Miles that she wanted to end her opera career the following year and sing only concerts from then on. When the legal position in Norway was settled, she wanted to stay at home as much as possible. On September 8, 1949, she had received a telegram from an old friend, the singer Egil Nordsjø, who was also the chair of the Norsk Tonekunstnersamfund (Norwegian Society of Music Artists). He wrote that they had unanimously nominated her to be an honorary member. This nomination triggered an avalanche of protests and letters in newspapers. A question mark was placed on the committee's mental capacities, and a list of its members was published in several newspapers. There was good reason for the general public to demand an explanation of them for this nomination, which conflicted with everything Norway stood for. There was no reason to reach out a conciliatory hand to Flagstad.[206]

238 THE VOICE OF THE CENTURY

Flagstad may have picked up on some of these criticisms, written by well-known cultural figures. They may have had quite a distressing effect on her. Now, however, it was the battle to return to the Metropolitan that took its turn. Flagstad's impresario had contacted her and asked her to meet with Rudolf Bing, who was to succeed Edward Johnson as general manager of the Metropolitan. Bing had Jewish parents and had grown up in Vienna, where he had worked as an impresario. In 1927, he had moved to Berlin to work as the manager at the opera house there. In 1934, he had fled from the Nazi regime to England, where he had been in charge of major music festivals. In 1949, he was appointed general manager at the Metropolitan and moved to New York. Bing saw it as his task to get Flagstad back to the opera.

She met him for the first time in her hotel room, under a cloak of secrecy. This was not an easy encounter, but Flagstad liked him from the first minute. They were well aware that a positive decision would bring fresh controversies for them both. She relates that he asked her to sing Isolde and two *Ring* cycles in addition to *Fidelio*, the last of these with Bruno Walter as conductor. Flagstad was not keen to sing any more than one *Ring*, mainly because she did not want to push out Helen Traubel, the Wagner soprano at the Metropolitan throughout the war years. They agreed to keep this decision to themselves until the New Year.[207] Bing did not yet have authorization from the board.

The first six months of 1950 were heavily laden with both Brunhilds and Isoldes in Paris and Barcelona, as well as concerts in Brussels, Geneva, and Lausanne.

A major event in the history of music was *The Ring* at La Scala in Milan with Wilhelm Furtwängler in March 1950. In contrast with many others, Flagstad found working under Furtwängler to be the easiest thing in the world. They had a similar understanding of how it all should be, and this made them both happy. In Milan, what was possibly the most monumental production of *Götterdämmerung* ever was staged and broadcast on radio. Here the audience heard the old retrospective Brunhild, who from the depths of her existence proclaimed an imperious, eternal peace over the world.

The director of EMI, Walter Legge, was also in Milan to convince her to take on two *Ring* cycles the following year in Bayreuth, but she turned him down. Wieland Wagner sent her a letter asking her to reconsider the proposition, and she promised to think it over again.[208] After the war, Winifred Wagner had been removed from all the work of administering the festival because of her fraternization with Hitler and the Third Reich. This job was transferred to her eldest son, Wieland Wagner.

Part 3: The Years of Struggle (1941–51)    239

For Flagstad, the major Wagner roles would soon belong to the past, as she was exhausted and depressed about all the mudslinging about her that still continued in America. In the end, she said no to Bayreuth: she could not bear the thought of any more arduous roles. It had also become known that the Metropolitan had engaged her, and this had stirred up the debate again. Walter Winchell came back to life and issued yet another lie, saying that she had sung in Germany during the war years.[209]

Flagstad's sister was with her in Milan, singing in a minor role. It was good to have her there, to have someone to talk to. Flagstad's psoriasis had flared up angrily, and she was covered in sores, which her sister treated every day with a sun lamp.[210]

She had been sent a newspaper article reporting that both Helen Traubel and Lauritz Melchior had resigned from the Metropolitan because she was coming back. A journalist called from London, asking her to comment on this. Later she discovered that this was not the situation at all. She had received more cuttings with very unflattering things about her. The living hell had started up again, and now she regretted agreeing to return to the opera house.[211]

## Deliverance from Pain—Richard Strauss's *Vier letzte Lieder*

There was little or nothing in German lieder that Flagstad could connect to the Nazism toward which she was accused of being sympathetic. Quite the opposite—in Beethoven and Brahms, the most sublime, tender emotions were expressed. In the music of Mahler and Strauss, she captured the lamentation of suffering and the deliverance of metaphysics. Flagstad had developed a strong relationship with the German language through her concert repertoire. She often felt a sense of loneliness onstage, something that had to do with the language barrier. When she sang German lieder outside German-speaking countries, hardly anyone could follow her interpretation. They did not understand the language, and this created a distance between performer and public.

As late in her career as the season of 1947–48, she discovered how much she had missed such closeness to her audience. During a concert in Zurich, there was nothing but lieder on the program. All of a sudden, it dawned on her that she was now singing for an audience that understood every word. This was stimulating but at the same time made great demands in terms of correct pronunciation, as mistakes would be spotted. For the first time, she felt completely exposed as an interpreter of German lieder, and this challenged everything she had to give. If she exaggerated a word or tempo because of

240 THE VOICE OF THE CENTURY

the meaning, the audience would follow her and also experience the poetry in the work.[212]

On April 24, 1949, Flagstad gave another lieder evening in Zurich, and the program included four of Strauss's songs, including the breathtakingly difficult "Befreit" (Released), with text by Richard Dehmel. In the final verse, the subject is death and liberation from suffering.

> Es wird sehr bald sein, wir wissen's beide,
> wir haben einander befreit vom Leide,
> so gab' ich dich der Welt zurück!
> Dann wirst du mir nur noch im Traum erscheinen
> und mich segnen und mit mir weinen;
> O Glück!

> (It will be very soon, we both know it,
> we have released each other from suffering,
> so I returned you to the world.
> Then you'll appear to me only in dreams,
> And you will bless me and weep with me—
> O happiness!)[213]

In the last line, above the word *weinen*, Strauss added a curved legato line that almost leads into what follows. It brings the music up to the absolute, extreme limit of what a human voice can express, in terms of both sound and physical ability. Next to no performers have ever been able to follow the composer completely, and Flagstad probably came nearest when she stretched the note over almost three bars. Her rendition of "Befreit" must have made a strong impression on Strauss's biographer Willi Schuh. He reviewed the concert and even conveyed his impression to the composer, the eighty-five-year-old Richard Strauss, who then lived in Garmisch, particularly stressing Flagstad's interpretation of "Befreit." Strauss had something on his mind, something he wanted to ask Flagstad about. On his writing desk, he had a collection called *Vier letzte lieder* (Four last songs). He had orchestrated three poems by Herman Hesse: "Frühling" (Spring), "Beim Schlafengehen" (When I go to sleep), and "September." The final poem, "Im Abendrot" (At sunset), was by Joseph von Eichendorff.

In April 1938, Strauss had completed the first draft of "Im Abendrot." A professor of music, Timothy L. Jackson, was convinced that as early as the summer of 1938, Flagstad must have received the first original version of "Im Abendrot" sent to her by Strauss. It could not be found within the composer's

# Part 3: The Years of Struggle (1941–51)        241

family circle, who had kept all similar drafts of his music, and it was also not in the Garmisch collection. In addition, a search was made for it in the residence of Furtwängler's widow, but it did not turn up there either. Jackson believed Strauss gave this version to Flagstad, asking her to study it.[214]

The song picks up the same motif as "Befreit," a theme to which the composer continually returned. As far back as 1894, Strauss had written his famous song "Ruhe, meine Seele!" (Rest, my soul!). Between this song and "Im Abendrot," there is a subtle and vital musical and poetical affinity, according to Jackson. Strauss did not orchestrate "Ruhe, meine Seele!" until after he had orchestrated "Im Abendrot." He had considered a motif in "Ruhe" unfinished, and it was something he wanted to settle before his death. The music links the motif to the word *Not* (need). The *Not* motif, which was anticipated in "Ruhe," first received its expression in the final part of "Im Abendrot." The German word *Not* has a religious and philosophical ring to it, in the sense of the fundamental existential pain of life itself. Liberating oneself from this is a metaphysical task and a deep yearning within us.

Strauss slipped into a deep depression in the years after the war: it may be that he had begun to take in all the atrocities and tragedies of Nazism in his homeland. He knew he was the last composer in the long tradition of German Romantic music.[215] Now he was faced with the reality of death, and what did he have left to redeem him as a human being and composer? "Im Abendrot" reflected his state of mind. The poem is about two old people, probably a couple, who are wandering through a darkening valley in the sunset. They have come to the end of the road in their long lives and are tired after their interminable journey. Two larks flit dreamily around them in the night air.

> Tritt her, und laß sie schwirren
> Bald ist es Schlafenszeit,
> Daß wir uns nicht verirren
> In dieser Einsamkeit.
>
> O weiter, stiller Friede!
> So tief im Abendrot,
> Wie sind wir wandermüde—
> Ist das etwa der Tod?—
>
> (We let their soaring flight delight
> Us, then, overcome by sleep
> At close of day, we must alight
> Before we fly too far, or dive too deep.

The great peace here is wide and still
And rich with glowing sunsets:
If this is death, having had our fill
Of getting lost, we find beauty—no regrets.)[216]

This was the great human philosophical question, the final redemption from *Not* that Strauss had wanted to suggest in his music. It speaks for itself that both the composition and the demands on the performer lie at an incredibly advanced, subtle level. It was quite natural, then, for him to approach the greatest, most exquisite-sounding and experienced contemporary dramatic soprano, Kirsten Flagstad. On May 13, 1949, Richard Strauss wrote to her:

Dear Madam,

For many years I have been absent from operas and concerts, ill and confined to bed for months beside the beautiful Lake Geneva and so I have never had the pleasure of admiring you. I was also forced to miss your Lieder evening in the Zurich Tonhalle, but my biographer, Dr. Willi Schuh, who is also the music critic in the *Neue Züricher Zeitung* newspaper, has told me in the most glowing terms about your fantastic Lieder concert and about your thrilling performance of Dehmel's lied.

This brings me to the idea I have of recommending some of my orchestrated songs especially for you. Your interpretative abilities are beyond those of ordinary concert singers. Like most of my songs, they demand an opera singer of greater substance, but someone who can also feel at home in a concert hall.

Since these songs in particular are divided up at different publishers, I have had copies made of all these lieder and now take the liberty of sending them to you. I have marked in blue the ones I think would suit you best, and I have spoken to my publisher in London, Boosey and Hawkes, to say that they must place them at your disposal with the accompanying orchestral material. If you would be so kind as to let me know which of my songs you do not have, because they are not easy to obtain. At the same time, I would like to tell you that my "Four Last Songs" with orchestra, which are being printed in London at present, are addressed to you. If you could think of performing them for the first time with a top-class conductor and orchestra? It would bring me great pleasure if you of all people would adopt some of these difficult, but also extremely rewarding, songs into your program. They are excellent encore items. [The songs he sent her include "Frülingsfeier" (Rite of spring), "Cäcillie" (Cecily), and "Wiegenlied" (Cradle song).]

My respectful greetings.

Yours faithfully, Richard Strauss

Part 3: The Years of Struggle (1941–51)          243

## Premiere Performance of *Vier letzte Lieder*

Richard Strauss never heard his four last songs performed. He died almost four months after he had written this letter, on September 8, and rumors of his new composition reached the London press immediately afterward. "New Songs by Strauss Can Only Be Sung by Kirsten Flagstad" ran the headline in the *Daily Mail* of September 19, 1949. Flagstad had been given the exclusive rights to sing them for a period of one year. However, some time elapsed before they could be performed. A mundane but crucial problem, then as now, was to obtain financing for the event. Not until May 1950 did Flagstad go to London for this major event in the history of music, the premiere of Richard Strauss's *Vier letzte Lieder.* The concert took place on May 22, 1950, in the Royal Albert Hall with the Philharmonia Orchestra, with Wilhelm Furtwängler wielding the baton.

The critics in attendance were far from effusive. Ernest Newman wrote that there was no proof that the songs had originally been intended as a cycle. Therefore, there was no indication of the order in which they should be sung. Flagstad sang:

1. "Beim Schlafengehen"
2. "September"
3. "Frühling"
4. "Im Abendrot"

The notes recently published gave a different order: 4, 3, 1, and 2. Strauss had not himself given a collective title to the work, nor had he laid down the order in which they should be sung. Newman felt that the order 2, 4, 3, and 1 was more psychologically correct. He emphasized that the songs are extremely difficult to sing and that Flagstad was not entirely comfortable with them.[217]

Newman had no knowledge of Strauss's letter to Flagstad. Later, Strauss's collaborator and music publisher, Ernst Roth, changed the order to the one we are familiar with today: "Frühling," "September," "Beim Schlafengehen," and "Im Abendrot."

Yet another reviewer wrote that Flagstad's voice had more heroic magnificence than romantic fervor. He felt that a voice such as Lotte Lehmann's would have been better suited to the task.[218]

Elisabeth Schwarzkopf, who was married to EMI's record producer Walter Legge, had herself studied the work and followed the rehearsals in London

244 THE VOICE OF THE CENTURY

with great interest. She says that on May 13, the day Strauss's widow, Pauline, died, there was a notice in the *Times* about a world premiere of four songs by Strauss.[219] One week later, two days before the concert, the text of the advertisement was changed to say that there would only be three lieder by Strauss. They had experienced great difficulty with the extreme complexity of the work and had had far too little time for rehearsals. The work, which resembled an opera, had never been played with an orchestra seated onstage. It was to be presented as concert pieces.

Legge was worried that Strauss's inner ear had heard something beyond the capabilities of an orchestra. The composer was dead and could not give any guidance, and there were no reference points. What Furtwängler elicited from the orchestra did not satisfy Legge, and neither did Flagstad's singing. Schwarzkopf says it was very clear that Flagstad doubted her own ability to do the work full justice.[220] She did not want to include "Frühling." Not until the dress rehearsal, at the very last minute, was she willing to perform it. It had been Schwarzkopf who persuaded her and gave her moral support. Furtwängler required three hours of rehearsal alone with the orchestra, and still it was not enough. It was unusual for both Furtwängler and Flagstad to be so dependent on the sheet music, even during the concert itself, which was also to comprise a Wagner section that would have to be done impromptu.

At the final rehearsal, the Indian maharaja of the Kingdom of Mysore was present. He was an expert in both Indian and classical music, the president of the Philharmonia Concert Society, and the orchestra's patron. He had been the one to finance both the rehearsals and the premiere of the work. He asked Legge for a recording of the rehearsal, but then the orchestra objected and demanded payment. Schwarzkopf claims that three discs were pressed,[221] one of which was given to the maharaja and another to Legge. At the premiere, a number of pirate recordings were made, and some of these were released in 1994, but the sound quality is so bad that they do no justice to either the orchestra or the soloist. However, the recording bears the sublime, unmistakable mark of both Flagstad and Furtwängler.

The audience was unhappy that there was no program to give details of the songs. It had all taken everyone by surprise, as if a completely unknown major composition had suddenly dropped from the skies.[222]

Flagstad performed the songs again the following year, in Cologne, Brussels, and Paris, to name but a few, but each and every time, she did so without "Frühling."

Part 3: The Years of Struggle (1941–51)          245

## Ernest Newman's Criticism of Kirsten Flagstad

Ernest Newman, the music critic and musicologist, is described as the most famous English music critic of the first half of the twentieth century. His knowledge of Richard Wagner, first displayed in a four-volume biography and later in a single volume about his operas, made Newman the foremost expert of his day. He had listened intently to every corner and every bar of Wagner's operas. Newman had also undertaken detailed studies of Franz Liszt and Richard Strauss, as well as a number of other eminent composers. He wrote reviews and articles about musical topics for several major English newspapers. He had followed Flagstad since her debut at Covent Garden in 1936 and had received various inquiries connected with her interpretations of Wagner's characters over the years. In 1950–51, he wrote quite a few articles in which he analyzed this in more depth.

He estimated that around 70 percent of the artists who sang Wagner in the time of the composer would not have been recognized by Wagner himself. Newman pointed out that, no matter how much he admired Flagstad's voice, he was not able to accept her as Isolde and Brunhild. He wrote that the paradox with Flagstad was that her advantage was also her limitation. The individuality and quality of her voice prevented her from producing the psychological nuances in the characters of the roles.[223]

Newman felt that the question of Flagstad's Wagner interpretations could not be detached from the frame of reference in which the interpretations were placed. There were people who thought it was simply a matter of closing your eyes, leaning back, and listening to the music. By doing that, one reduced the world's most foremost opera composer. In Wagner, the words, music, and action are inextricably linked. People who do not understand German do not appreciate the meaning of what is being said and sung. They do not have the remotest idea of what is going on or what the characters are conveying. For a select few, such as Newman, this question of interpretation cannot be distinguished from imitation. The most outstanding song in itself can at the same time be an incorrect interpretation, if the coloring is not in agreement with the psychology of the character and the situation at that moment. On this particular point, Flagstad's Isolde and Brunhild did not sufficiently convince Newman.

The reason lies entirely in the psychological aspect. It lies in the nature, in the individuality, of Flagstad's fantastic voice. It is impossible for her to

246 THE VOICE OF THE CENTURY

add color to certain notes in a high register, even in the darkest and most somber situations. Instruments such as oboe and flute change character and tone, causing different emotional suggestions and expression to follow. In low, middle, and high registers, composers continually employ these possibilities to express their objectives at that juncture.

Flagstad's voice, in its deeper register, is exquisite in itself, direct and simple and unusually expressive. From the low F to the upper E of the soprano range, it has a different tone color, in which Flagstad can interpret a certain number of characters. But from F-sharp upward, her voice has enormous power, and when she is at her best, she projects this part of her register with a perfect purity and dazzling brilliance. All her high notes are characterized by a blinding, white light and so are unable to express certain psychological situations and moods that the operatic scenes require.

A specific example is the great scene in which Brunhild parts from Wotan in the final act of *Die Walküre*. Here the phrase begins with "War es so. . . ." In the first four bars, Flagstad comes out with all the beauty to be found in her lower registers. Here she is Brunhild. The next two bars are placed in the center of the middle register and are still in harmony with the words being sung. But in the last F-sharp, she can only radiate out like the sound of a splendid silver trumpet. The vocal phrasing is introduced by the orchestra alone for about twenty bars. Wagner moves softly and sorrowfully, first with the bass clarinet, then the cellos, and then mainly with the oboes, then the bassoons, and finally the bass clarinet, which yet again brings forth what Brunhild expresses in words. By using the optimum choice of instruments for his purpose at that point, Wagner bathes the tragic stage in an atmosphere of poignant sorrow that is absolutely unrivaled. By listening, the audience is drawn into the atmosphere, until Flagstad's overly clear F-sharp shines and flashes like a sunbeam in a dark cave. The illusion that Wagner creates is broken, Brunhild disappears, and only Flagstad the singer is left.

The same thing happens in the second act of *Tristan and Isolde*, when her high clear notes are unable to convey the mystery and mysticism behind the mood of night in the garden. Despite her fantastic singing, Newman cannot accept her as Brunhild and Isolde, whose souls have been revealed to him through Wagner's text and score.[224]

With this, Newman says that Flagstad's voice in high registers had something completely superhuman about it. This was why it could not express anything other than itself—it had no knowledge of the human, psychological level. Here he has probably called attention to the true individuality of her

Part 3: The Years of Struggle (1941–51)

voice. In response to his assertion that she did not manage to give personal characteristics above high F-sharp, it can be said that a singer's training to a large degree consists of learning to give maximum resonance to all the individual notes. At this resonance, the harmonic series—tones that form intervals other than our equal-tempered scale and that accommodate certain pitches in the upper registers—will unavoidably be present. This criticism was perhaps due to Newman's dislike of these natural intervals. Anyway, Newman concluded that we should be grateful for Flagstad's voice, in what he perceived as our dreadful modern world.[225]

## Director of Public Prosecution Dismisses the Conspiracy Theory

Flagstad had an increasing need to establish a home for herself at last on this earth, not only in her art. In January 1950, she received a letter telling her that the treason case against Henry Johansen's estate and businesses was at an end. The estate, to which Flagstad was heir, was acquitted of treason and liability for damages. In his will, Johansen had written that Flagstad should have the right to reside at Amalienborg until her death. Given that the case was now settled, her own assets that had been illegally confiscated since 1945 were now also released. She had her legacy from her husband transferred, and this made Flagstad into a very affluent woman. It was no longer necessary for her to work.

Also in 1950, a parliamentary report was issued in which the Norwegian director of public prosecution, Andreas Aulie, following through on the investigation, concluded that the rumors about a Nazi underground movement in Norway with Johansen in charge were false. It had been former Gestapo agents, used by the Norwegian secret police as provocateurs and informers, who had invented this.[226] It was all shelved as a conspiracy theory.

The conclusion of these cases brought Flagstad a certain relief and at last opened the way for her to return to Norway. After an extended tour of Europe, she traveled home to her house for a few weeks. The fixtures and fittings there now belonged to her once again, and as many as nine cases of personal possessions had arrived from America. She experienced great pleasure in unpacking them and finding places for everything. Her furniture from another house that had also been confiscated had arrived. Some kind of feeling of home crept over her. To protect herself, she had refused all contact with the Norwegian press.

Nor did she want to meet anyone in Norway except for her family.[227] Flagstad had resolved never to sing in her home country again and only to have her private home and place of refuge there. Miles disagreed with this: he continued to believe that she should confront what she was most afraid of.

The faithful old housekeeper, Beret Stabben, had returned to her and ensured meticulous order in the house. The chauffeur, Karl Nilssen, saw to punctuality in matters of transport, and Stake was her absolute stalwart in all questions of business. This provided a fixed framework, but nevertheless, it could not soothe her devastated state of mind. Every morning, fru Stabben changed her mistress's bed linens, which were covered in flakes of skin and bloodstains from the many lesions and sores she had on her body. The heat beneath the quilt made Flagstad itchy, and she had to scratch. She knew she mustn't, but she did it in her sleep. Her scalp was covered in crusted skin, and her hair irritated it: she was far from well. All the same, she continued with her hectic life as a vocal artist for several more years. She felt that it took time to wind down a business such as hers.

## Smear Campaign against Rudolf Bing, Manager of the Metropolitan

Bing, who had been forced to flee Nazi Germany in 1934, was not unfamiliar with the fatal consequences stemming from ideological and political encroachment on art. However, he anticipated that the controversies around Flagstad would come to an end once they had her onstage. He said to Bruno Walter that she was without a doubt one of the vocal phenomena of the age and so it would be ridiculous to exclude her.

In January 1950, he persuaded the Metropolitan's board to agree with his decision, but at the same time, he was prepared for pandemonium to break out. His viewpoint was that it was not right to overlook a great artist, one to whom the American authorities had granted a residence permit. The Metropolitan was an artistic rather than political institution.[228] It was their mission to offer the best international talent if they were available.

At the same time, the institution had a responsibility not to offend the general public's understanding of human rights. The Metropolitan had waited for several years after the war had ended and undertaken thorough investigations before reengaging Flagstad. They were happy to make it known that there was no proof that she had been morally disloyal to the fundamental values of the US or of her own country. She had not supported Nazism, either actively or passively. The Norwegian government had freed her from suspicion of any involvement in such activities during the war.[229]

## Part 3: The Years of Struggle (1941–51)          249

Bing had delved deeply into the case, studying a number of documents and interviewing a few people who were familiar with the story. In March 1950, he nevertheless received a formal complaint from representatives of Norwegian officialdom in Washington. This cited the concert she had held there in 1940, which had consisted of only German music, as evidence against the Metropolitan's statement. An official intervention from another country was not something that any cultural institution could take lightly. Bing approached McArthur, who admitted he had been the one to draw up the program. Bing felt that this had not been particularly wise, with regard to what was going on in Europe at the time. He also requested a statement from Flagstad.[230]

She was still unable to understand that a concert program could be interpreted as a political act. For her, this element was absent, and she clearly lacked the ability to see the issue from any perspective other than her own. Once again, she explained the complete absence of any political motives in the choice of her repertoire. Morgenstierne was still obsessed with obstructing her, now by protesting against Bing's decision to reengage her at the Met. The ambassador was also unable to see this from any perspective other than his own emotionally inflamed standpoint.

Bing received hundreds of letters about the matter: people from all walks of life became impassioned about it. Many of the letter writers had formed an image of Flagstad as something evil, or as someone allied to something evil. Because he was taking her back, Bing was also harassed to some extent. This may well have been more wearing for him than he admitted. He was also keen to engage Furtwängler as musical director at the Metropolitan, but when the opposition grew, he gave up. Presumably, Bing could not face subjecting himself to the same rigmarole all over again.[231] Given the amount of abuse and threats, that can be easily understood. He had his own memories of flight and persecution in his personal baggage. Bing also fought on behalf of African American artists. In 1951, the first Black ballet dancer, Janet Collins, was given a permanent contract at the Metropolitan, and in 1955, Marian Anderson was also employed. The Metropolitan was among the last bastions of serious music to engage Black artists in leading roles. Their inclusion there at long last was very much thanks to Bing's willingness to deal with controversy.[232]

His courage made him an object of hate. A letter to Bing says that having Flagstad back at the Metropolitan was an affront to Americans.[233] The graves of young American boys who had died in the war were still fresh in people's minds. Other letters were of a more threatening character: Bing did

250 THE VOICE OF THE CENTURY

not deserve the American title of Mr. when he sided with that lousy, wanton whore Flagstad, when he allowed the infiltration of such garbage. Bing should not take the warning lightly: "If you book the damn Nazi Flagstad YOU WILL BE SORRY AND SO WILL THE BITCH."[234]

## The Golden Curtain Falls

Nervousness, obsession, and demands drove Flagstad through a concert tour of Europe at breakneck speed in the spring of 1950, and in the autumn, she returned to the US. From September 25, 1950, until January 14, 1951, she sang a total of forty concerts there. On January 22, 1951, she was to appear again as Isolde on the Metropolitan stage after an absence of ten years. McArthur relates that threatening letters had poured in.[235] He hoped he had managed to hide the worst of these from her, but she knew of some of them at least. Flagstad was off balance and grew irritated at the least thing when she arrived. The fresh deluge of threats made her afraid and paranoid. She thought most people were out to get her, and she trusted only a very few people. The sensitivity and suspicion she felt also made her reject old friends.

The management at the opera house was worried about security. Before she stepped onto the stage, the building was searched, and the lights were kept brighter than usual so that the New York police chief could keep an eye on what was happening inside the auditorium. A number of police officers were stationed all around. Flagstad sat in her dressing room, possibly fearful that the letter threatening that someone would throw acid at her when she went onstage would come true.

Flagstad has always claimed that had she let her opponents win, they would have been proved right. She had set herself the aim of recapturing this fortress, and so she must go out onstage. She knew she was still an artist of some stature, but she felt no pleasure in finally being back at the Met. Her disappointment at having been excluded from the opera house for so long was too great. The anxiety she felt on venturing onto the stage and her steely concentration on what she had to do there may have overshadowed everything.

The audience not only reacted to her as an artist but also clapped as if she had come home from a well-won victory. As the stage curtain went up after the prelude, an unusually tumultuous applause broke out. The same thing happened after every act, and in the end, the golden stage curtain was lowered five times for her. A group of young men had taken up post around the orchestra pit, booing loudly at her for ten whole minutes.[236] The critic Olin Downes observed a significant stiffness in her high notes as well as some

Flagstad as Isolde at the Metropolitan again, January 22, 1952. With regal authority, she sings the Irish princess's first line of text, "Wer wagt mich. Zu hohnen?" (Who dares to mock me?), and there is such tumultuous applause that the performance has to stop for several minutes. *Source: Flagstad Museum.*

inaccurate intonations, something that he put down to the nervous stress she must have been under. Virgil Thomson wrote in the *Herald Tribune* that Flagstad received a total of nineteen curtain calls. She still had the ability to set the Metropolitan alight with her unique vocal power and dramatic talent.[237]

On the other hand, McArthur remembers little of the performance. All evening, he had relived the torture they had been through. A woman of less courage and more guilt would never have survived a smear campaign of such dimensions, he believed. But tonight, tonight it was all over. From now on, there would be no more threatening letters, no more pickets, and no more malicious stories. Flagstad had been forced down into the deepest abyss, but here and now, she had made a triumphant return. Naturally enough, he had tears in his eyes by the end of the first act. After the last fall of the curtain, Kirsten Flagstad came forward alone to receive the greatest ovation ever given at the Metropolitan, but her heart was still cold.[238]

## Notes

1. Biancolli (1952), pp. 120–21.

2. Morgenstierne to the Norwegian Legation in Stockholm, April 22, 1941, Archive code 38.8.15, vols. 1–2, file: Kirsten Flagstad, Ministry of Foreign Affairs archive, National Archives, Norway.

3. Morgenstierne to the Ministry of Foreign Affairs in London, April 21, 1941, Archive code 38.8.15, vols. 1–2, file: Kirsten Flagstad, Ministry of Foreign Affairs archive, National Archives, Norway.

4. Biancolli (1952), pp. 120–27.

5. "Demma sin barndom med ei verdensstjerne" [Childhood memories of an international star], in Åmli mållag og Åmli historielag (2010).

6. "Demma sin barndom med ei verdensstjerne."

7. Herresthal (2019), pp. 16–21.

8. *The Confessions of Winifred Wagner, Parts I–II*, dir. Hans Jürgen Syberberg, 1977.

9. Herresthal (2019), p. 42.

10. Herresthal (2019), pp. 126–27.

11. Herresthal (2019), pp. 39–40.

12. Herresthal (2019), p. 234.

13. Herresthal (2019), p. 169.

14. Herresthal (2019), p. 201.

15. Herresthal (2019), p. 156.

16. Herresthal (2019), p. 92.

17. Herresthal (2019), p. 182.

18. Bruland (2017); "Holocaust i Norge," Wikipedia, https://no.wikipedia.org/wiki/Holocaust_i_Norge.

19. Herresthal (2019), pp. 146–49.

20. Herresthal (2019), pp. 272, 284.

21. Herresthal (2019), p. 168.

22. Herr Daubenmeier, the Dolder's manager, in discussion with the author, 2002.

23. Schmid-Bloss (1943); Solbrekken (2003), p. 313.

24. *Neue Züricher Zeitung*, June 13, 1942.

25. A. Bakke, Trade Envoy, to the Ministry of Foreign Affairs pro tem in London, June 23, 1942, Archive code 38.8.15, vols. 1–2, file: Kirsten Flagstad, Ministry of Foreign Affairs archive, National Archives, Norway.

26. Finn Koren to the Royal Ministry of Foreign Affairs pro tem in London, June 23, 1942, Archive code 38.8.15, vols. 1–2, file: Kirsten Flagstad, Ministry of Foreign Affairs archive, National Archives, Norway.

Part 3: The Years of Struggle (1941–51)

27. Trygve Lie, Foreign Minister, to the Royal Legation, Bern, July 13, 1942, Archive code 38.8.15, vols. 1–2, file: Kirsten Flagstad, Ministry of Foreign Affairs archive, National Archives, Norway.

28. Finn Koren, Minister, to the Ministry of Foreign Affairs, August 17, 1942, reproduced in Ole Kolsrud, "Eksil-Norge og jødene under 2. Verdenskrig" [Norway in exile and the Jews during World War II], *Historisk Tidsskrift* 3 (1994), in Westlie (2011), pp. 87–89.

29. Trygve Lie to A. I. Easterman, Political Secretary, British Section, World Jewish Congress, London, December 1, 1942, Ministry of Foreign Affairs archive, reproduced from Samuel Abrahamsen, "Norway's Response to the Holocaust," Holocaust Library, New York, 1991, in Westlie (2011), pp. 87–89.

30. Westlie (2011), pp. 88–89.

31. Morgenstierne to Ministry of Foreign Affairs, August 5, 1942, Archive code 38.8.15, vols. 1–2, file: Kirsten Flagstad, Ministry of Foreign Affairs archive, National Archives, Norway.

32. A. Bakke, Trade Envoy, Bern, to the Ministry of Foreign Affairs, "Personal Message Fru Kirsten Flagstad," September 25, 1942, Archive code 38.8.15, vols. 1–2, file: Kirsten Flagstad, Ministry of Foreign Affairs archive, National Archives, Norway.

33. Birgit Nilsson, interview by Torstein Gunnarson, May 5, 1979, NRK.

34. Biancolli (1952), pp. 134–35.

35. Kraus (1942), p. 232.

36. Herresthal (2019), pp. 206–17.

37. "Wagner Concert," *Aftenposten*, December 1, 1942.

38. Harald Herresthal, email, June 6, 2019; Odd Langballe, Norwegian Musicians' Union, in discussion with the author.

39. *Neue Züricher Zeitung*, May 28, 1943.

40. A. Bakke, Trade Envoy, to Ministry of Foreign Affairs, March 5, 1947, Archive code 38.8.15, vols. 1–2, file: Kirsten Flagstad, Ministry of Foreign Affairs archive, National Archives, Norway.

41. Norwegian Embassy in Washington to Ministry of Foreign Affairs pro tem in London, November 29, 1943, Archive code 38.8.15, vols. 1–2, file: Kirsten Flagstad, Ministry of Foreign Affairs archive, National Archives, Norway.

42. Karlsen (2020).

43. Øyvind Riberg, witness interview, March 27, 1947; Ragnar Siegel, witness interview, October 2, 1947; Einar Orderud, witness interview, September 1, 1947, Oslo Police Headquarters: Misc, Anr. 3194—Henry Thomas Ingvald Johansen.

44. Einar Orderud, witness interview, September 1, 1947.

45. Karlsen (2015).

46. Leif Stake, interview, January 22, 1946, Oslo Police Headquarters: Misc., Anr. 3194—Henry Thomas Ingvald Johansen.

47. Finn Støren to Oberführer Fehlis, February 9, 1945, National Archives, Norway.

48. "Johansen Arrest Sifted," *New York Times*, February 24, 1945.

49. Royal Norwegian Information Service, New York office, Royal Norwegian Embassy, Washington, DC, to Mrs. K. M. Hall, March 7, 1945, Flagstad Museum archive.

50. Rushprint (2015).

51. Storeide (2014), pp. 194–97; Anette H. Storeide, in discussion with the author, August 10, 2015. Storeide reported in a telephone conversation on February 23, 2016, that the total sales value and profit amounted to 118.9 million kroner, not the 118.9 billion kroner that is erroneously cited on p. 412 of her book.

52. Karlsen (2015).

53. Kirsten Flagstad to Kathrine, February 10, 1946, Flagstad Museum archive.

54. Kirsten Flagstad to Kathrine and Jack, September 5, 1945, Flagstad Museum archive.

55. *The Confessions of Winifred Wagner, Parts I–II*, dir. Hans Jürgen Syberberg, 1977.

56. Gunnarson (1985), pp. 165–66.

57. Irving Spiegel, "Flagstad's Career Put Up to U.S. as Norwegians Here Attack Her," *New York Times*, June 15, 1945.

58. McArthur (1965), pp. 163–65.

59. "The Flagstad Story," *Newsweek*, June 25, 1945.

60. Kirsten Flagstad to Peggy and Edwin, July 22, 1945, Flagstad Museum archive.

61. Morgenstierne, Ambassador, to Ministry of Foreign Affairs, June 20, 1945, Archive code 38.8.15, vols. 1–2, file: Kirsten Flagstad, Ministry of Foreign Affairs archive, National Archives, Norway.

62. Ministry of Foreign Affairs, memo, December 4, 1946, Archive code 38.8.15, vols. 1–2, file: Kirsten Flagstad, Ministry of Foreign Affairs archive, National Archives, Norway.

63. "Case against Henry Johansen and Fritz Mowinckel Partially Abandoned," *Dagbladet*, June 13, 1933.

64. "Sundfor Amplifies Accusations against Henry Johansen and Fritz Mowinckel," *Dagbladet*, July 15, 1933.

65. Sven Arntzen, "Ingolf Sundfør's Conduct towards A/S Götaverken, Gothenburg," *Norsk sakførerblad* [Norwegian lawyers' journal], no. 10 (December 1934): 175–77.

## Part 3: The Years of Struggle (1941–51)

66. "Ingolf Sundfør—Sven Arntzen," editorial article, *Norsk sakførerblad* [Norwegian lawyers' journal], no. 10 (December 1934): 173–75.

67. Ingolf Sundfør to Agder Court of Appeal, process writ, October 1, 1945; Trygve Bendixen to the Director of Public Prosecution, letter with attachment, January 28, 1946, Treason Case against Henry Thomas Ingvald Johansen, H3194.

68. St. meld. nr. 64 (1950), p. 81.

69. Pryser (1994), pp. 38–40.

70. St. meld. nr. 64 (1950), p. 86.

71. Report to Criminal Assistant Erik Andressen, July 19, 1946, Oslo Police Headquarters, transcripts of judgments in A no. 4489—Bernt Gustav Somdalen.

72. Forensic psychiatry declaration, December 30, 1946, Romerike Police Station: files, no. 360/45—Hans Ottar Westby.

73. Hans Ottar Westby, interrogation, January 17, 1950, I:S 1555, Director of Public Prosecution's treason archives, series D—case files, box 52.

74. May-Britt Somdalen, interview, March 5, 1948, I:S 1555, Director of Public Prosecution's treason archives, series D—case files, box 52.

75. Kirsten Flagstad to Edwin McArthur, October 24, 1945, Flagstad Museum archive.

76. Ingolf Sundfør to the management of the telegraph company in Oslo, August 7, 1945; Police Chief in Oslo to the telegraph company's management, August 23, 1945, Oslo Police Station: Misc, anr. 3194—Henry Thomas Ingvald Johansen, National Archives, Norway.

77. Henry Johansen and Kirsten Flagstad, 27 telegrams from April 9, 1940 to April 27, 1941, Oslo Police Station: Misc, anr. 3194—Henry Thomas Ingvald Johansen, National Archives, Norway.

78. Reference from a conference held in the American Treasury Department with participants Finance Secretary Colbjørnsen and Embassy Secretary Oftedal from the Norwegian Embassy in Washington, November 9, 1945, Archive code 38.8.15, vols. 1–2, file: Kirsten Flagstad, Ministry of Foreign Affairs archive, National Archives, Norway.

79. "With *Verdens Gang* in America. We Interview and Are Interviewed by Mayor La Guardia," *Verdens Gang*, September 22, 1945.

80. "Premiere på brakkebaroner i februar" [Premiere of barracks barons in February], *Verdens Gang*, January 3, 1946.

81. Oslo Police Station: Misc, anr. 3194—Henry Thomas Ingvald Johansen, National Archives, Norway.

82. Kirsten Flagstad to Edwin McArthur, September 28, 1945; Kirsten Flagstad to Kathrine, October 14, 1945, Flagstad Museum archive.

83. Penal Code, May 22, 1902.

84. Transcript of court record, Agder District Court, appeal case B no. 930/45, fru Kirsten Flagstad.

256 THE VOICE OF THE CENTURY

85. Solbrekken (2003), p. 338.

86. "Oslo Bars Flagstad Exit, Seizes Husband's Estate," *New York Times,* June 29, 1946.

87. McArthur (1965), pp. 174–82.

88. Kirsten Flagstad to Kathrine, February 10, 1946, Flagstad Museum archive.

89. Gunnarson (1985), pp. 169–70.

90. Kirsten Flagstad to Berit Cleve, letter no. 366, April 29, 1946, National Library Letter Collection, Norway.

91. Stefi Tyrihjell, in discussion with the author, 2004; Solbrekken (2003), pp. 339–40.

92. Gunnarson (1985), p. 174.

93. Morgenstierne to the Ministry of Foreign Affairs, October 19, 1946, Archive code 38.8.15, vols. 1–2, case: Kirsten Flagstad, Ministry of Foreign Affairs archive, National Archives, Norway.

94. Morgenstierne to Ingolf Sundfør, Supreme Court Lawyer, November 21, 1946, Archive code 38.8.15, vols. 1–2, case: Kirsten Flagstad, Ministry of Foreign Affairs archive, National Archives, Norway.

95. Foreign Minister to the Director of Public Prosecution, October 29, 1946, Archive code 38.8.15, vols. 1–2, case: Kirsten Flagstad, Ministry of Foreign Affairs archive, National Archives, Norway.

96. Accompanying endorsement in report to Oslo Police Station, November 26, 1946, Archive code 38.8.15, vols. 1–2, case: Kirsten Flagstad, Ministry of Foreign Affairs archive, National Archives, Norway.

97. A. L. Gullestad, Supreme Court Lawyer, to the Ministry of Foreign Affairs, May 5, 1947, Archive code 38.8.15, vols. 1–2, case: Kirsten Flagstad, Ministry of Foreign Affairs archive, National Archives, Norway.

98. Lars J. Jorstad, Counselor at the Norwegian Embassy, to the Central Hannover Bank, October 10, 1946, Archive code 38.8.15, vols. 1–2, case: Kirsten Flagstad, Ministry of Foreign Affairs archive, National Archives, Norway.

99. McArthur (1965), p. 172.

100. Kirsten Flagstad to Oslo Police Station, January 19, 1946, Kirsten Flagstad's folder, Oslo Police Station: Misc, anr. 3194—Henry Thomas Ingvald Johansen, National Archives, Norway.

101. Norwegian Embassy in Washington to Ministry of Foreign Affairs, October 25, 1946, Archive code 38.8.15, vols. 1–2, case: Kirsten Flagstad, Ministry of Foreign Affairs archive, National Archives, Norway.

102. Foreign Minister to Ingolf Sundfør, Supreme Court Lawyer, November 8, 1946, Archive code 38.8.15, vols. 1–2, case: Kirsten Flagstad, Ministry of Foreign Affairs archive, National Archives, Norway.

## Part 3: The Years of Struggle (1941–51)    257

103. Sundfør to the Ministry of Foreign Affairs, December 24, 1946, Archive code 38.8.15, vols. 1–2, case: Kirsten Flagstad, Ministry of Foreign Affairs archive, National Archives, Norway.

104. Oftedal to Schive, Ministry of Foreign Affairs, September 9, 1946, Archive code 38.8.15, vols. 1–2, case: Kirsten Flagstad, Ministry of Foreign Affairs archive, National Archives, Norway.

105. T to Sven Oftedal, September 3, 1946, Archive code 38.8.15, vols. 1–2, case: Kirsten Flagstad, Ministry of Foreign Affairs archive, National Archives, Norway.

106. McArthur (1965), pp. 180–97.

107. Gunnarson (1985), p. 192.

108. Kirsten Flagstad to Kathrine, December 1, 1946, Source: Flagstad Museum archive.

109. Biancolli (1952), pp. 159–61.

110. Ministry of Foreign Affairs, memo, December 4, 1946, Archive code 38.8.15, vols. 1–2, case: Kirsten Flagstad, Ministry of Foreign Affairs archive, National Archives, Norway.

111. Ministry of Foreign Affairs.

112. Chronological overview of all Kirsten Flagstad's performances, https://dms-cf-02.dimu.org/file/022wazLzTnja.

113. "Flagstad Returns to the Stage," *New York Herald Tribune*, January 26, 1947.

114. "An Outraged American" to the Norwegian Embassy, January 29, 1947, Archive code 38.8.15, vols. 1–2, case: Kirsten Flagstad, Ministry of Foreign Affairs archive, National Archives, Norway.

115. Myklebost to Morgenstierne, January 28, 1947, Archive code 38.8.15, vols. 1–2, case: Kirsten Flagstad, Ministry of Foreign Affairs archive, National Archives, Norway.

116. Kirsten Flagstad to Norbert, February 10, 1947, Flagstad Museum archive.

117. *Verdens Gang*, January 25, 1947.

118. Norwegian Embassy in Washington, Report to the Ministry of Foreign Affairs, April 30, 1946, Archive code 38.8.15, vols. 1–2, case: Kirsten Flagstad, Ministry of Foreign Affairs archive, National Archives, Norway.

119. Oftedal to Schive, January 22, 1947, Archive code 38.8.15, vols. 1–2, case: Kirsten Flagstad, Ministry of Foreign Affairs archive, National Archives, Norway.

120. Apollon (2011).

121. Herresthal, email, August 6, 2020.

258      THE VOICE OF THE CENTURY

122. Sundfør to Morgenstierne, February 14, 1947, Archive code 38.8.15, vols. 1–2, case: Kirsten Flagstad, Ministry of Foreign Affairs archive, National Archives, Norway.

123. Norwegian Embassy in Washington to the Ministry of Foreign Affairs, January 24, 1947, Archive code 38.8.15, vols. 1–2, case: Kirsten Flagstad, Ministry of Foreign Affairs archive, National Archives, Norway.

124. Schive to the Secretary-General, January 25, 1947, Archive code 38.8.15, vols. 1–2, case: Kirsten Flagstad, Ministry of Foreign Affairs archive, National Archives, Norway.

125. Schive to Stang, January 25, 1947, Archive code 38.8.15, vols. 1–2, case: Kirsten Flagstad, Ministry of Foreign Affairs archive, National Archives, Norway.

126. Schive to the Secretary-General, January 28, 1947, Archive code 38.8.15, vols. 1–2, case: Kirsten Flagstad, Ministry of Foreign Affairs archive, National Archives, Norway.

127. "Aktsomhet" [Due diligence], *Verdens Gang*, January 29, 1947.

128. Emil Stang, statement, January 27, 1947, Archive code 38.8.15, vols. 1–2, case: Kirsten Flagstad, Ministry of Foreign Affairs archive, National Archives, Norway.

129. Lange, Foreign Minister, to the Norwegian Embassy in Washington, January 31, 1947, Archive code 38.8.15, vols. 1–2, case: Kirsten Flagstad, Ministry of Foreign Affairs archive, National Archives, Norway.

130. Norwegian Embassy in London to the Foreign Office, January 30, 1947, Archive code 38.8.15, vols. 1–2, case: Kirsten Flagstad, Ministry of Foreign Affairs archive, National Archives, Norway.

131. Gunnarson (1985), pp. 196–98.

132. Shawe-Taylor, "Kirsten Flagstad," *New Statesman*, February 15, 1947.

133. "Isolde at La Scala," *Time*, March 10, 1947.

134. Lecture by Eva Gustavson, sound b/689, Norwegian National Library sound collection. Gustavson was a Norwegian singer who studied in Milan at that time.

135. Biancolli (1952), p. 170.

136. McArthur (1965), p. 205.

137. Kirsten Flagstad to Miss Norbert, February 10, 1947, Flagstad Museum archive.

138. "Våre kvinner og våre hjem" [Our women and our homes], *Nordisk Tidende*, February 20, 1947.

139. Morgenstierne to fru Magny Landstad-Jensen, February 21, 1947, Archive code 38.8.15, vols. 1–2, case: Kirsten Flagstad, Ministry of Foreign Affairs archive, National Archives, Norway.

Part 3: The Years of Struggle (1941–51)

140. Morgenstierne to Myklebost, February 21, 1947, Archive code 38.8.15, vols. 1–2, case: Kirsten Flagstad, Ministry of Foreign Affairs archive, National Archives, Norway.

141. Morgenstierne to the Foreign Office, February 28, 1947, Archive code 38.8.15, vols. 1–2, case: Kirsten Flagstad, Ministry of Foreign Affairs archive, National Archives, Norway.

142. "I Have News for You," *Daily News*, January 23, 1947.

143. Biancolli (1952), pp. 171–72.

144. Morgenstierne to the Foreign Office, March 17, 1947, Archive code 38.8.15, vols. 1–2, case: Kirsten Flagstad, Ministry of Foreign Affairs archive, National Archives, Norway.

145. Morgenstierne to the Ministry of Foreign Affairs in London, April 14, 1941, Archive code 38.8.15, vols. 1–2, case: Kirsten Flagstad, Ministry of Foreign Affairs archive, National Archives, Norway.

146. Norwegian Embassy in Washington, statement, March 17, 1947, Archive code 38.8.15, vols. 1–2, case: Kirsten Flagstad, Ministry of Foreign Affairs archive, National Archives, Norway.

147. McArthur (1965), pp. 210–11.

148. "Kirsten Flagstad angripes fortsatt i U.S.A." In: VG March 19, 1947.

149. McArthur (1965), pp. 210–11.

150. Lund (2008), p. 356.

151. "War against Flagstad," Unpublished article, Robert Tuggle's personal archive, New York.

152. "Meet the Madam. Walter Winchell in New York," *Daily Mirror*, April 11, 1947.

153. "Walter Winchell in New York," *Daily Mirror*, January 23, 1948.

154. Dossier Erstatningsdirektoratet, Archive code 38.8.15, vols. 1–3, case: Kirsten Flagstad, Ministry of Foreign Affairs archive, National Archives, Norway.

155. McArthur (1965), p. 214.

156. "The Flagstad Case," *Time*, April 14, 1947.

157. Biancolli (1952), pp. 184–85.

158. Robert Tuggle, "Belmont Harriman Essay," Robert Tuggles personal archive, New York; Mrs. J. Florence Harriman to Mrs. August Belmont, February 25, 1947, Columbia University Rare Book Room.

159. Mrs. Belmont to Mrs. Harriman, March 7, 1947, Archive code 38.8.15, vols. 1–2, case: Kirsten Flagstad, Ministry of Foreign Affairs archive, National Archives, Norway.

160. "Belmont Harriman Essay."

161. McArthur (1965), p. 175.

162. Dehly to Einar Gerhardsen, Prime Minister, March 17, 1947, Archive code 38.8.15, vols. 1–2, case: Kirsten Flagstad, Ministry of Foreign Affairs archive, National Archives, Norway.

163. Hans Olav, Embassy Adviser, to Thomson, April 11, 1947, Archive code 38.8.15, vols. 1–2, case: Kirsten Flagstad, Ministry of Foreign Affairs archive, National Archives, Norway.

164. "Flagstad, Voice and Issue," *Newsweek*, April 28, 1947.

165. Solbrekken (2003), pp. 352–53.

166. "Isolde's Homecoming," *New Republic*, May 5, 1947.

167. "In Norway She Is Dead," *Verdens Gang*, April 24, 1947.

168. Myklebost to Morgenstierne, May 5, 1947, Archive code 38.8.15, vols. 1–2, case: Kirsten Flagstad, Ministry of Foreign Affairs archive, National Archives, Norway.

169. Theo Findahl to Morgenstierne, April 5, 1947, Archive code 38.8.15, vols. 1–2, case: Kirsten Flagstad, Ministry of Foreign Affairs archive, National Archives, Norway.

170. Morgenstierne to Findahl, April 8, 1947, Archive code 38.8.15, vols. 1–2, case: Kirsten Flagstad, Ministry of Foreign Affairs archive, National Archives, Norway.

171. "Forfølgenlsene av Kirsten Flagstad" [Persecution of Kirsten Flagstad], *Verdens Gang*, June 18, 1947.

172. Tor Myklebost, "Kirsten Flagstad," *Verdens Gang*, May 6, 1947.

173. "Kirsten Flagstad," *Verdens Gang*, June 18, 1947.

174. Biancolli (1952), pp. 176–77.

175. Jens Schive to Hans Olav, Press Adviser, June 23, 1947, Archive code 38.8.15, vols. 1–2, case: Kirsten Flagstad, Ministry of Foreign Affairs archive, National Archives, Norway.

176. Gunnarson (1985), p. 210.

177. "Wagner Concert," *Times*, November 26, 1947.

178. Kirsten Flagstad to Karen-Marie, November 10, 1947, Flagstad Museum archive.

179. "Flagstad Concerts in Georgia Cancelled," *New York Times*, December 16, 1947.

180. McArthur (1965), pp. 220–21.

181. Kirsten Flagstad to Ellen, February 23, 1948, Flagstad Museum archive.

182. "Flagstad Triumphs over Language," *Daily Herald*, March 4, 1948.

183. "Royalty at Opera," *New York Times*, February 25, 1948.

184. Kirsten Flagstad to Ellen, February 23, 1948, Flagstad Museum archive.

185. Kirsten Flagstad to Miles, April 16, 1948, Flagstad Museum archive.

186. Bernard Miles, unpublished biographical sketch, Flagstad Museum archive.

Part 3: The Years of Struggle (1941–51)          261

187. Wikipedia, s.v. "Bernard Miles," last modified April 17, 2015, https://en.wikipedia.org/wiki/Bernard_Miles.

188. Bernard Miles, undated notes, Flagstad Museum archive.

189. Bernard Miles, lecture on Kirsten Flagstad, sound b/692, Norwegian National Library sound collection.

190. Miles.

191. Biancolli (1952), p. 186.

192. McArthur (1965), p. 230.

193. Ernest Newman, "Singing Wagner," *Sunday Times*, May 29, 1949.

194. "Züricher Juni Festwochen," *Neue Züricher Nachrichtung*, June 25, 1949.

195. "Flagstad and Fidelio," *Opera News*, March 5, 1951.

196. Sissel Høyem Aune, "The Smear Campaign against Kirsten Flagstad and the Penalty Paid by Her Voice," in Solbrekken (2007), pp. 135–39.

197. Consul General Gabe to the Norwegian Embassy in Washington, July 15, 1949, Archive code 38.8.15, vols. 1–2, case: Kirsten Flagstad, Ministry of Foreign Affairs archive, National Archives, Norway.

198. Morgenstierne to Chas Pedersen, July 19, 1949, Archive code 38.8.15, vols. 1–2, case: Kirsten Flagstad, Ministry of Foreign Affairs archive, National Archives, Norway.

199. Christopher, telegram, July 21, 1949, Archive code 38.8.15, vols. 1–2, case: Kirsten Flagstad, Ministry of Foreign Affairs archive, National Archives, Norway.

200. Morgenstierne to Christopher, July 21, 1949, Archive code 38.8.15, vols. 1–2, case: Kirsten Flagstad, Ministry of Foreign Affairs archive, National Archives, Norway.

201. Christopher to Gabe, Consul General, July 21, 1949, Archive code 38.8.15, vols. 1–2, case: Kirsten Flagstad, Ministry of Foreign Affairs archive, National Archives, Norway.

202. "More about the Decision Due on Kirsten Flagstad," *San Francisco Chronicle*, July 26, 1949.

203. "Flagstad Dispute," *San Francisco Chronicle*, July 26, 1949.

204. Gabe, Consul General, to the Norwegian Embassy in Washington, July 27, 1949, Archive code 38.8.15, vols. 1–2, case: Kirsten Flagstad, Ministry of Foreign Affairs archive, National Archives, Norway.

205. Biancolli (1952), pp. 193–94.

206. Solbrekken (2003), p. 373.

207. Biancolli (1952), pp. 194–95.

208. Kirsten Flagstad to Miles, March 20, 1950, Flagstad Museum archive.

209. McArthur (1965), p. 254.

210. Kirsten Flagstad to Miles, March 20, 1950.

211. Biancolli (1952), pp. 195–96.

212. Biancolli (1952), pp. 222–23.

213. Oxford International Song Festival, April 25, 1949, https://www.oxford lieder.co.uk/song/1815.

214. Timothy L. Jackson, "'Ruhe, meine Seele!' and the Letzte Orchestra Leider," in Gilliam (1992), p. 105.

215. Jackson in Gilliam (1992), pp. 90, 94.

216. Cabrera (2020).

217. Ernest Newman, "Strauss' Last Songs," *Sunday Times*, May 28, 1950.

218. "The Last of STRAUSS," *New Statesman*, June 2, 1950.

219. Jefferson (1996), pp. 147–48.

220. Jefferson (1996), pp. 147–48.

221. Jefferson (1996), pp. 147–48.

222. Jefferson (1996), pp. 147–48.

223. Newman, "The Flagstad Question," *Sunday Times*, July 9, 1950.

224. Newman, "Voice and Character," *Sunday Times*, July 16, 1950.

225. Newman, "The Oracle," *Sunday Times*, July 23, 1950.

226. St. meld. nr. 64 (1950).

227. Kirsten Flagstad to Miles, June 9, 1950, Flagstad Museum archive.

228. Rosenberg (2019), pp. 224–25.

229. Rudolf Bing to Bernice Nece, April 9, 1950, Flagstad Museum archive.

230. McArthur (1965), pp. 258–59.

231. Ardoin (1994), p. 62.

232. Metropolitan Opera (n.d.).

233. Letter, February 4, 1950, Tuggle files, named MOA. See also Rosenberg (2019).

234. Letter, February 4, 1950, Tuggle files, named MOA. See also Rosenberg (2019), pp. 225–29.

235. McArthur (1965), p. 270.

236. "Met Crowd Hails Singer in Unprecedented Ovation," *New York Times*, January 23, 1950.

237. Biancolli (1952), pp. 276–77.

238. McArthur (1965), p. 270.

# PART 4

# Postlude
## (1951–62)

### A Flagstad Era Ends

The first half of 1951 marked the start of Flagstad's farewell to Wagner roles and audiences throughout Europe and America. On March 26, she sang Isolde for the last time on the Metropolitan stage with Set Svanholm as her partner. Hundreds of people had stood waving their handkerchiefs and programs as the Norwegian singer kept coming onto the stage to receive clamorous applause for her great performance of Isolde. Men and women stood for twenty-two minutes giving rhythmic applause and yelling at the top of their voices. They knew this was her last performance at the opera house. Some members of the audience had their doubts, but a journalist had visited her at the intermission and had it confirmed. General Manager Bing was present at the interview and interrupted to say that the lady had the privilege of being able to change her mind. They would keep hoping. She wondered whether he had not understood the way she had stressed a phrase in the duet "Nicht Mehr Isolde" (No more Isolde). She thought he had caught that. The photographer asked Bing to stand beside her for a photo.

> "This is the first time we've been photographed together," says Mme. Flagstad.
> "Won't you give her a kiss on the cheek?" the photographer asks.
> "Oh no, nothing like that," Mme. Flagstad replies. "But what about a handshake?"[1]

Present backstage that night was also Miles, who saw it as his mission to lead her away from the Wagner repertoire. She still had several more Isoldes left in Europe before she could say a final goodbye to the role. Her colleague Nan Merriman, the American soprano, had flown from California to New York to hear her farewell performance. Merriman had never experienced anything like it. For her, Flagstad was the most beautiful voice God had ever created. The applause she received when she appeared onstage was like a never-ending thunderstorm. Merriman sat so close to the stage that she could see the blush spread slowly over Flagstad's neck and face as she battled to control herself. How difficult it must have been for her to start singing afterward. What an artist she was, standing there, erect and dignified, as she sang. Merriman had often asked herself, "I wonder if the Norwegians know how magnificent she was!"[2]

## Ventures onto a Norwegian Stage Again

The farewell tour of Wagner roles headed first to Paris and then to Covent Garden and the festival in Zurich. On May 31, she sang Sieglinde in *Die Walküre* at Covent Garden. In fact she was a bit too old for the role, but her appearance was a gesture to a successor, Astrid Varnay, who sang Brunhild. Varnay relates that they were standing in a row taking the applause when Flagstad suddenly patted her on the shoulder, took her by the hand, and led her out to the center of the stage to receive a special round of applause. And all of a sudden, Flagstad was gone. She had left Varnay standing there and gone back to the row with the rest of the cast. In a beautiful, symbolic way, it was as if she had said, "You take over." For Varnay, this secret authorization was like being knighted.[3]

Not until later that summer was Flagstad back in her own home, where Miles was now a regular guest. He described Amalienborg as one of the least homely and most unoccupied houses he had ever visited. Most of all, it resembled a museum, in which the housekeeper had put everything neatly back in place to satisfy Flagstad's pedantic sense of order. In the mornings, she removed all the visible specks of dust from the Persian rugs before her mistress came down. The house also bore signs that Flagstad had lived in hotels for the last thirty years of her life.[4]

Without a doubt, Miles brought a great deal of life and vigor into the house. When he was present, the housekeeper found that many things were different. The actor liked to kneel before Flagstad in the garden and recite poetry. If she called out that the food was ready, the meal just had to wait until the poems were done. And then he said that in England it was always the man of the house who did the washing up on Sundays. And so he should wash up. She was worried about the fine, elegant glasses, afraid that he would break them.

# Part 4: Postlude (1951–62)

But he knew his stuff, he probably knew what he was doing, and everything always went well.

He had challenged Flagstad, saying that there still remained one last, unconquered bastion. She had to stand face to face with what she feared most, a Norwegian audience. Wouldn't she, as Norway's greatest singer of all time, also capture the stage there? She had vanquished the American public through her singing, so could she not do the same in Norway? He reminded her of how liberating it had been to reconquer *Fidelio*. The same thing would happen here. Reluctantly, Flagstad went along with his suggestion, and on September 5, 1951, she held a concert in Calmeyergatens Mission House in Oslo, a hall with seating for three thousand. The not inconsiderable proceeds of the concert would go to the Oslo Philharmonic's pension fund.

*Aftenposten* asked her if she was looking forward to it. "I don't know" was the answer. Her knees were shaking when she stepped onto the stage, so terrified was she of performing in Norway. Her psoriasis had flared up. She had chosen a flesh-colored gown with a lace pattern that resembled her patches of psoriasis so that they would not be so noticeable to the audience. Outside the hall, talk of her "Nazi tendencies" could be heard. Some of the old slogans were still shouted and spoken, but these were quickly hushed by other members of the audience. She opened with Grieg's "Guten" (The Boy), to a text by Aasmund Olavsson Vinje.

> Du ferer vidt og du verdt trøytt
> og Foten skjer.
> Du græt, so Puta ofte bløytt
> af Taarer er.
> Med dette Salt du vaskas ut,
> til dess du fær
> i deg den sleipe, hvasse Lut,
> som Livet tvær.
>
> (You travel far and you are tired
> And your feet ache.
> You weep, so that your cheeks
> Are often wet with tears.
> You are washed with their salt
> Until you acquire
> The slimy, biting caustic
> That life brings.)[5]

This song was a deliberate choice to convey to the audience what she had gone through and probably also an outlet for the pain and bitterness that lies within the text. It is not known whether Miles had accompanied her to Norway and was seated in the audience. She came directly from his safekeeping in London and was to return there the next day. The care, understanding, and affection she received there made it possible for her to return to the Norwegian stage. At every Flagstad concert in Norway before the war, the royal family had been present since it had been a major cultural event. That was not the case on this occasion. The upper classes of Norway were absent from the Calmeyergatens Mission House on September 5, 1951. She probably noticed this, but as far as she was concerned, the concert was primarily a matter of crossing a barrier of fear: singing in Norway for Norwegians.

## World's Greatest Opera Singer on the World's Smallest Opera Stage

After the concert, she headed straight to London, where *Dido and Aeneas* was to have its premiere on September 9 at the Mermaid Theatre at Miles's residence in St. Johns Wood. England had experienced a golden age of music in the seventeenth century, thanks not least to the genius of Henry Purcell (1659–95), who must undoubtedly be considered the *Orpheus Britannicus* of the baroque period. He lived a century before Mozart and has in common with him that they both died extremely young, at around thirty-six years of age. Among Purcell's stage works, his masterpiece is *Dido and Aeneas*. Although simple, it has a captivating, dramatic undertow, such as in Dido's famous lament and the closing elegies of the chorus.

At the end of her career, Flagstad chose the role of Dido, which was far less demanding than Wagner's Brunhilds. This is music that carries the entire piece, but there are no major action scenes. Flagstad could sit for most of the performance, since she was suffering from increasing hip pain. She describes this time as one of the happiest periods in her life.

Miles tells of the background to this production of *Dido and Aeneas*. Once when they were strolling out in the garden, she asked him what the large building beside his apartment was. Miles explained that it had been a boys' school that was badly bombed during the war. The classroom with seating for two hundred pupils was still intact, and he had had a vision of converting it into a theater. Flagstad said she would sing there, but what production should they stage? Miles suggested Handel, Gluck's *Alceste*, or what about Purcell? He told

Part 4: Postlude (1951–62) 267

her about the opera *Dido and Aeneas* and found the score for her. She took this with her when she left London in January 1950. At that point, she had several productions of *Tristan and Isolde* as well as both the *Walküre* and *Götterdämmerung* Brunhilds ahead of her at the Gran Teatre del Liceu in Barcelona. Above all, Flagstad was to sing an entire *Ring* cycle with Furtwängler at La Scala in Milan, and these performances were to be recorded for later release. She stayed in Milan for more than a month, but after a while, she wrote to Miles about Dido's lament, saying, "This is so beautiful that I'd really like to sing the whole score. Can you send it to me?"[6]

Miles felt she was the incarnation of Dido. She was fifty-six when she sang it at the Mermaid Theatre: she should probably have sung it when she was forty, since the role demanded a type of oratorio singing, which is a lighter style. It was not easy for her to make this change. Inside the small theater, they observed her enormous musicality and her total ability to concentrate. All of this was based on her breathing. She had enormous force behind her breath and an amazing ability to control it. And she knew the moment she had read a phrase how much breath she needed to take in. If it was a long phrase, from experience and instinct she inhaled the exact volume of breath needed for the notes. In Miles's opinion, the fortunate thing about her singing was that there were more notes per cubic inch of breath than for any other singer he had heard.

*Dido and Aeneas* had its opening night in London on September 9, 1951. The orchestra was seated on a small balcony at the back above the stage. The conductor, Geraint Jones, England's eminent harpsichordist, wielded the baton from his place at the harpsichord and played all the recitative parts. To allow the singers to see the orchestra and conductor, Miles had rigged up a huge mirror on the back wall.

It is unnecessary to draw attention to the sensation this production caused in London. Apart from the initial performance, which was restricted to the theater workers, people connected to culture and music in London scrambled to obtain tickets. Since the performance lasted no longer than an hour and a half, it was presented twice a day. That little hall, with its packed audience of rapt listeners, gave a completely unique, compact ambience.

Flagstad was treated well at this little theater, as is evident from the contract, which Miles, Furtwängler, and Lorenz had witnessed. It stated that the singer must be dealt with in accordance with her great name and renown. That she had to be cared for, nourished, applauded, praised, idolized, and exalted.

The world's greatest opera singer with a miniature of the world's smallest opera stage. *Source: Flagstad Museum.*

## Part 4: Postlude (1951–62)     269

She had to have half liters of dark beer at preordained times and receive un-expected, pleasant surprises, flowers and fruit. They should write letters with little poems to her and take every opportunity to make her laugh. Only a re-ally charming and devoted man could have brought himself to draw up such a contract, which must have seemed like balsam to her wounded soul. Flagstad also gave solo performances in the tiny theater, including Bach cantatas. The experience of being loved and taken care of made her blossom. Miles was later knighted for his efforts at the Mermaid Theatre, which would scarcely have seen the light of day without Flagstad's participation. His creative genius had managed to spin a little cocoon around her. He lifted her out of Wagner's great universe and led her into the smaller space of the baroque.

The record company EMI was farsighted enough to have the production preserved for posterity. Geraint Jones Orchestra and Singers, Kirsten Flag-stad, Elisabeth Schwarzkopf, Thomas Hemsley, and others made a recording that is still mentioned on music lovers' lists of what they would bring to a desert island. The recording took place in March 1952 in London. Fortunately, there were some people in Norway who had their eyes open to the worth of this production—the stage setting was not so large that it could not be repeated in Oslo, and in February 1953, Miles was brought to the Oslo New Theatre, where the performance was staged twenty-five times, until March 28. Aksel Otto Normann, the manager of the theater, was extremely interested in opera. He was keen to bring the production to Oslo and gave the conductor Øivind Fjeldstad the task of persuading Flagstad to come. The conductor was eager to make a contribution to Norwegian music and willing to use the pow-ers of persuasion he must have had to induce Flagstad to come to Norway. But before he began his offensive, she had cast a glance at the bag he had brought along, which contained the score, and said quite calmly, "I think I know what you have in that bag of yours. It's all right, I'll come!"[7]

### Farewell to Carnegie Hall

The New York public and the concerts in Carnegie Hall held a special place in Flagstad's heart. The high point every single season had been the concert in this splendid, spacious hall. And so it was entirely natural that she should give her farewell lieder concert, with piano accompaniment, there. She an-nounced from the stage that this concert was of a very special nature, as it would be her last. After these words were spoken, an atmosphere of solemn silence hung over the twenty-seven-hundred-strong audience. Every last seat in the hall was taken.

270     THE VOICE OF THE CENTURY

Once Flagstad had sung her way through a brilliant program of romantic music, there was a deathly hush in the hall before applause broke out. The audience could not quite take in that this was a farewell to the singer they had listened to for seventeen years, interrupted only by the years of war. They shouted requests for Wagner as encore numbers, and at this prompt, she reminded them that it had been exactly seventeen years since she made her debut at the Metropolitan as Sieglinde. In memory of that day, she sang "Du bist der Lenz" (You are the spring), without youthful joy and vigor but in gratitude for the wheel having come full circle. In a heartfelt speech of thanks to McArthur, she pointed out that they had made music together for seventeen years and given more than five hundred concerts. Now that had come to an end.

The ovations were thunderous, even after the lights onstage had been switched off. Beneath the grand piano lay a red rose, fallen from a bouquet, and a small white handkerchief she had dropped. A man in a brown suit, who had sat in the audience in the gallery, forced his way through, jumped onto the stage, and snatched the handkerchief up. Sometime in the future, he may well have shown this treasure to his grandchildren and told them he had picked it up from the stage in Carnegie Hall on February 1, 1952, when the great Flagstad gave her last lieder concert.[8] Perhaps it was a comfort that she would give several more concerts there as early as March with a symphony orchestra under the baton of Bruno Walter.

### A Judas Kiss at the Very Last Minute

Even though Flagstad had made up her mind not to sing any more opera, she had nevertheless given in to the Metropolitan's insistent requests to hear her in five performances of Gluck's *Alceste*, from March 4, 1952, to the final performance on April 1. Finishing at the Metropolitan in the role of a queen on her way to the realm of the dead may have stirred old memories. Alcestis has a sick, dying husband, whom she saves by sacrificing herself. When Flagstad stepped onstage on the last night, it was her 193rd performance at the Met. The box office was sold out, and people had lined up outside from 8:30 a.m. until 7:30 p.m. just to get standing room spots for the three-hour-long production. The audience clapped for twenty-two minutes and brought her forward onstage for standing ovations a total of thirteen times while confetti and programs were showered on the heads of the people sitting in the stalls.

Bing had invited New York's longest-serving governor, Thomas E. Dewey, and his wife, as well as the Metropolitan's president, Lowell Wadmond, to the management box. Bing probably had no idea that he had also invited one of

Flagstad's persecutors, Trygve Lie, who was now the first secretary-general of the UN. After the performance, the singers and the Metropolitan's board, with Bing in the lead, went backstage to congratulate Flagstad. On stage, she had been presented with a loving cup engraved with all the roles she had sung at the Metropolitan. Flagstad has said that she had no sentimental feelings or regrets about leaving the Metropolitan for good. She says in her authorized biography that returning to the Metropolitan gave her no pleasure. It was simply something she had to do to demonstrate that she was back where she should have been some years earlier. The only satisfaction was that it gave her a sense of triumph over her enemies. She was able to punish them by showing that she had survived their hate campaign.[9]

McArthur writes that during all this, she felt bitter because the opera house had left her to fight a desperate battle for survival on her own. He relates that Flagstad, at her final performance at the Metropolitan, was extremely proud that the secretary-general of the UN had visited her backstage to congratulate her.[10] Would she have been if she had known that he had been central in the campaign to destroy her postwar career? How would the audience in the auditorium and the press have reacted to the information that he, as the Norwegian foreign minister in 1942–43, had asked the intelligence services to keep her under surveillance? And that he had publicly expressed suspicions that she was unpatriotic? That in December 1946, he had approached the Ministry of Justice in an effort to prevent Flagstad from leaving Norway? That he had instigated a negative letter about Flagstad from Mrs. Harriman to a leading member of the opera house board of management? If Trygve Lie had had his way, Flagstad would never have returned to America. This fact places the mark of Judas on his presence in the theater and his express wish to go backstage to congratulate her. Flagstad's total ignorance of his previous behavior toward her also says something about her innocence and naivete.

### When the Top Notes Falter

Flagstad still continued with recordings of Wagner's operas. The sublime studio recording of *Tristan and Isolde* with Furtwängler, Flagstad, and Ludwig Suthaus was the conductor's first complete recording. It was also the first major complete opera recording for the Philharmonia Orchestra, EMI, and the producer Walter Legge, making it a milestone in the history of music. It was to take place in London in June 1952. Flagstad was hesitant about taking on such a strenuous task, in which she would have to stand for hours in front of a microphone. She was also worried about whether she would manage, in recording after recording, to sing the top notes. Her voice extended from low to high C, even high C-sharp. In her youth, she had sung in the operetta *Die Bajadere* and had hit the high C-sharp every evening, more than two hundred times in all.[11]

She was painfully aware that the high notes would become difficult with age. In a letter to Miles from Paris on February 6, 1949, she had begun to worry whether the top notes were exactly where they should be. At the rehearsals for *Tristan and Isolde*, she had hit the second high C fairly well, and the first had been very good. The insomnia that plagued her did not help—her whole body was tired. Flagstad's flawless ear for music would also be far from content with any imperfection. At the rehearsals for the EMI recording, she found that the highest notes were not quite as she thought they should be. When she listened to the test recording, she was not happy. The top notes were not resonant enough, and after she conferred with Furtwängler, they decided to call in Elisabeth Schwartzkopf, whose top notes were not fuller than Flagstad's but at extreme height were relatively similar in color and tone, making it possible to mix the two very different voices.[12]

At first, this was kept secret, but the sharpest professional listeners discovered that it was not Flagstad's voice singing the two high Cs that occur directly after Tristan's entrance at the beginning of the second act. They wrote to the record company asking for an explanation. Consequently, it emerged that it had been Schwartzkopf who had sung these notes. In the duet from the final act of the opera *Siegfried*, released at almost the same time, Sylvia Fisher inserts the one high C. Flagstad had made it a condition for a subsequent recording of *Götterdämmerung* that the two top Cs should also be dubbed. This element constitutes one second of the four hours and sixteen minutes of the opera recording. She felt it was better to avoid being nervous about those notes so that she could concentrate on everything else. Schwartzkopf stood beside her and jumped in at the right moment.[13] All of this reminded Flagstad more and more that her time with Wagner was over.

## Mediator between Furtwängler and Legge

They also had other problems. Legge and Furtwängler disagreed so much that they refused to go on with the recording together. They were engaged in a bitter conflict, in part because Legge had preferred Herbert von Karajan as conductor for two operas in Vienna in 1950. Furtwängler had conducted them that same year in Salzburg, and Legge had then made some disparaging remarks about aging musicians. Furtwängler had heard of this and wrote

# Part 4: Postlude (1951–62)

to the director of British music and entertainment retailer, HMV, Brenchley Mittell, to say quite plainly that he refused to have Legge supervise his work ever again.

Legge approached Flagstad to say that he did not want to continue if Furt-wängler was to conduct. After that, Furtwängler came and said that he would not continue if Legge was to be the artistic director. They both wanted to work with her, and this made her extremely stressed. Flagstad realized that the project could go off the rails and called on Miles for help. One evening, they drafted a letter to Mittell, the HMV director. Flagstad wrote that she was unhappy about the turn the recording of *Tristan and Isolde* had taken. She could scarcely describe how much she relied on Legge's outstanding abilities and his judgment where music was concerned. She would never dare to make a recording of Isolde without his assistance. At the same time, Dr. Furtwängler was her absolute first choice as conductor. Through years of working together, they had reached such a close understanding of the work that it would be impossible to make a recording with any other conductor. She had been so looking forward to this, and it would be her last chance to record this opera. She dearly hoped that all these difficulties could be ironed out as quickly as possible.[14]

They sent a copy of the letter to both antagonists, and this worked miracles. Legge even apologized, and the next day, the recording proceeded without a problem. Miles and Flagstad may have spent a convivial evening together at the fireside in her London apartment while they devised the plan. The con-flict also reflected a generational change in music history—an old and more medial interpretation was about to pass into the annals. The more technical and faster approach was on the way in.

## The Royal Family—the Last of Flagstad's Adversaries

The year 1953 was a painful period in Kirsten Flagstad's life. She called it the winding-up year, but it was not her work that presented difficulties. She was suffering from nerves and physical afflictions and was admitted to the Na-tional Hospital's dermatology department in the middle of April. Her doctor relates that she had several bad eruptions of psoriasis that required special treatment in the hospital.[15]

The festival in Bergen was to launch that summer. The conductor Olav Kiel-land had approached her and invited her to sing there. At first, Flagstad had turned him down. The festival director, Hilmar Reksten, tried again, writing her a letter in which he made an appeal to her "responsibility" to the cultural life of Norway. In the end, she accepted, in order to be used as an advertising poster for Norway. The concerts were to be broadcast, and in Bergen, they certainly knew the market value Kirsten Flagstad possessed abroad and the publicity she would bring to the festival. Through Stake, she had given a clear message that she did not want any filming before, during, or after the concert. She preferred not to have any press photographs or interviews either.[16] She was considering waiving her fee for the concert. However, the feeling of being used, in addition to her intuition probably telling her that other things were going on around her and the festival, made her demand the same fee as Leopold Stokowski, $2,000 for two days. Incidentally, Stake was now taking care of all her business correspondence.

It had filled Flagstad with nervous bewilderment that she had not been asked to sing at the actual opening ceremony. She was Norway's preeminent vocal artist. Intuitively, she understood what was happening behind the scenes, even though the Bergen Festival management attempted to conceal the truth from her. Her old admirer King Haakon had refused to open the Bergen Festival if Kirsten Flagstad was going to sing there. When Reksten, the director, had an audience at the palace and asked King Haakon to be the festival's patron, he had accepted, but only on one condition: that Kirsten Flagstad would not sing in his presence.[17]

And so Flagstad sang at two concerts on the second and third days of the festival, on June 12 and 13, 1953. These concerts were broadcast throughout the world. She spent that summer at Amalienborg, where she was smothered in ointment and coal tar over her entire body and walked around in light clothing because she could not bear fabric on her skin. Her torso and arms were worst. From time to time, it was so painful that she could no longer tolerate bandages and thought it best to walk naked in the fresh sea air of Kristiansand.

## Fleeing to Zurich

In early autumn of 1952, Flagstad's biography was published in London. Some of the content was subsequently reported in the Norwegian press, especially the parts in which she had told the story of the postwar years and her experiences with Sundfør and Morgenstierne. *Aftenposten* had invited these two gentlemen to comment on the story. Their answers were printed on August 17, 1953, with them mainly repeating what they had said previously. At this time, the Norwegian press was not aware of the organized campaign that had been waged against Flagstad through the Foreign Office. Morgenstierne once again wrote about the time she had sung only German songs at a concert in

Part 4: Postlude (1951–62)

Washington and about her journey home to Norway. Sundfør, for his part, re-iterated her lack of oversight of the situation regarding her income and assets.

This tore open old wounds. Kirsten Flagstad was urged to give a reply in the newspaper. She refrained from doing so, but her psoriasis responded by flaring up viciously. That she was once again being subjected to the circum-stances that had arisen during the war caused her great anxiety. She did the same now as she had done just after the war: fled into exile in Zurich, where she had always felt comfortable and safe. She considered leaving Norway for good. From her corner room at the Dolder Grand Hotel, Flagstad wrote to a friend, Mrs. Esberg in San Francisco, on October 9, 1953:

> You're probably wondering about my continued silence. I'm sorry to have to say that I've had a bad time and not felt up to communicating with any-one. Now I'm away from home for a while and feel calmer and less unhappy.
>
> Firstly, I'd like to thank you from the bottom of my heart for coming to visit me. You're so understanding and friendly and I like that about you. I'm afraid I wasn't a particularly good hostess, and for that I can only blame my nerves that were so bad all summer. I couldn't understand the reason for my restlessness, but the explanation finally came to me.
>
> I was still in Kristiansand when Stake phoned to tell me about a dreadful attack on me in our best and most important newspaper in Oslo. It was a London correspondent who had reviewed my book that was recently published there. He misquoted a few things and the newspaper had asked Ambassador Morgenstierne and herr Sundfør to answer my accusations. They came out with their responses in the evening edition in which they were given plenty of column space to tell lies about me and defend them-selves. It was awful.
>
> In the end, the newspaper wrote to say that it would be interesting to see my reply. Well, I have never before answered my accusers, and of course I haven't answered this time either. But I feel it terribly and I'm greatly distressed....
>
> I've spoken to my lawyer who was eager to answer, but I persuaded him not to do anything. I can prove the things I've said in my book about those two people. I'm almost sorry I didn't say even worse things about them!...
>
> I'd planned to leave the country for good and settle down somewhere else—and sell everything up. But as Stake says: revenge is a dish best served cold. He persuaded me to change my mind.
>
> I wanted to cancel my three Oslo concerts in December and again after a great deal of discussion I gave in and now I will only give the last of these, on 12 December. I wrote to Edwin and Peggy that they should not come to

276                    THE VOICE OF THE CENTURY

Norway as planned, and I received a very sympathetic reply. I've asked all
my friends from outside Norway not to come and I hope they will stay away.
I'm still very nervous but I've been better since I left Oslo on 30 September.
My skin problem is bad again. It shows that I mustn't get worked up.
Everything is so painful when you're so sensitive.[18]

On November 26, Flagstad had to go back into the hospital again for two
weeks; she had fears for her farewell concert at the National Theatre in Oslo
on December 12, 1953. This was one of the year's greatest cultural events in
Norway, but Flagstad was struggling with anxiety that there might not be a
capacity audience. She was afraid that dreadful things would happen again.
At the same time, the concert would be her fortieth anniversary as an opera
singer. She had stood on the same stage for the first time on December 12, 1913.

The concert was a fantastic experience for all who came to a packed National Theatre that night. Flagstad was cheered to the rafters, but she wrote to
her friend that her heart felt cold. The theater's royal box loomed like a large,
frightening, empty hole that evening. No representative of the Norwegian
royal family was present to say farewell to one of Norway's most distinguished
artists of all time.

Just after the New Year, she wrote to her friend about her nervous complaints, saying that she found it impossible to relax. She had to return to the
hospital again. From what she wrote, it appears she understood that her psoriasis and her mental state were connected. The flare-ups came when she was
nervous.

## A Quiet Home Life

In April 1955, she was again admitted to the hospital after having been in
New York and having held yet another farewell concert in Carnegie Hall. She
celebrated her sixtieth birthday on July 12 at Amalienborg. Eventually, she
dropped her plans to make her home outside Norway, and in time she settled
down to a quiet life with her highly trusted staff.

Flagstad gave a number of church concerts in Norway in the second half
of the 1950s, and each time, she feared that no one would come to hear her.
The churches were always crammed full, but her anxiety from the days of
persecution was deeply ingrained. Her completely predictable day-to-day life
at Amalienborg soothed her nerves. Her housekeeper, Beret Stabben, gives
a detailed account of her mistress's daily life. She was served a cup of tea at
eight o'clock in the morning, and then she lay on, waiting until her chauffeur,
Nilssen, arrived with her copy of *Aftenposten* around half past eight. Then she

Part 4: Postlude (1951–62)                    277

had a modest breakfast tray and went through her mail before going downstairs around twelve or half past. After that, she wrote letters and sat down at the piano, where she remained until dinnertime, singing and accompanying herself. She ate dinner around four o'clock. Beef stew was her favorite. After dinner, she sat on a chair in the music lounge with her sewing or knitting or with letters. She did not receive many phone calls and often listened to music on the radio. Sometimes she went down into the garden, but that was not often. She did not enjoy going for walks, but she often played solitaire. Most of all, she sat in the living room, with her housekeeper sitting beside her with her sewing, and they liked to drink a glass or two of champagne. The mistress sat up until midnight, when she padded upstairs to bed.[19]

When Flagstad came home from her many trips, they went through a whole suitcase full of fan mail. They normally spent a week at a time on this correspondence, which mainly meant Flagstad sending photos with brief greetings, while her housekeeper stuck on the stamps and delivered the letters to Stake or Nilssen, the chauffeur. A somewhat unusual correspondence, which they had kept going for several years, was with a cattle farmer by the name of Walter I. McKinnon. He lived on a farm called Lammermoor in Upper Ontario and was a passionate opera lover. He had told Flagstad in his first letter that his cows were called Aida, Mimmi, Tosca, Nedda, Elsa, and Norma. Now a particularly lovely calf had been born that would in time become a great breeding cow, and he humbly asked for Flagstad's permission to call the beast Isolde. It would grow up at Lammermoor, and he assured her, "And for the next fifteen or sixteen years, she will be a reminder of the artistry of your singing."[20]

## Flagstad's Final Great Recordings

Miles was sufficiently farsighted to understand how important it was to document as much as possible of Flagstad's voice while she was still able to sing. He fought against her depression and anxiety, which caused her to withdraw from the world. The recording manager at Decca, John Culshaw, met Flagstad in 1954, after Miles had managed to persuade her to undertake some gramophone recordings. After this, she recorded some discs for Decca in the years up to 1959. Culshaw relates that to begin with they made a series of recordings of romances. Romantic songs may not have been her strongest suit, but she felt that the intimacy provided by a studio with a piano rather than an orchestra would be the beginning of a way out again. And she made some fine recordings of Brahms, Schumann, and Grieg, as well as others. The next year, the recordings also included Sibelius.

Culshaw was afraid before his first meeting with her. He had seen her in all the *Ring* cycles and all her performances of *Tristan and Isolde* after the war. He was a great Wagner admirer, and so Flagstad was something of a nonpareil for him. When he entered the studio, he was confronted with a woman who was nothing but friendly and extremely human. Sensitive as she was, she spotted his uneasiness.

A few years later, she said to him, "When we met for the first time in London, I got the impression that you were scared of me!"

"You're damn right I was. I've seen you too many times in the second act of *Götterdämmerung*," he replied.[21]

From 1954 onward, Decca's team attempted to persuade her to record as much of Wagner as possible, but her voice was still unable to cope with it. Initially, she was opposed to doing so, but they persuaded her to agree to record Wagner's *Wesendonck-Lieder* in Vienna in 1956, with the Vienna Philharmonic under the baton of Hans Knappertsbusch. In 1957, she recorded the third act of *Die Walküre*. They chose not to record the whole opera since Flagstad no longer had the top C notes. However, in the third act, she sang brilliantly. The following year, she sang, at her own request, Sieglinde's part in the first act, a role she loved passionately. Next in line were recordings of Mahler's *Kindertotenlieder* (Songs on the death of children) and *Lieder eines fahrenden Gesellen* (Songs of a wayfarer), and this time, the Vienna Philharmonic was conducted by Sir Adrian Boult.

## Old Lady with a Strange Hat

In the autumn of 1958, Kirsten Flagstad was sixty-three years old and had once again agreed to go to Vienna to do some recordings. This time, it was to be the entire *Ring* with the Vienna Philharmonic and with Georg Solti as conductor. Flagstad sang Fricka's part in *Das Rheingold*. The role lasts no more than thirteen or fourteen minutes altogether, though the entire *Ring* cycle has a playing time of just over thirteen hours. All the same, it was quite inspirational to have an old master involved. At that time, Decca had a young recording team, and Flagstad sat knitting waistcoats for them all when she was not singing. She called them "the boys." To start with, they probably thought she was a bit odd, compared to other great singers they had met. At the end of 2001, the Danish radio station, P2, traveled to England to interview one of "the boys," Erik Smith, who had been the record producer in Vienna.

# Part 4: Postlude (1951–62)

Smith recalls that some of the younger singers were taken aback by this lady with the strange big hat, who was getting on in years and who sat behind the orchestra, knitting. "Is she going to sing?" they blurted out to their colleagues in a slightly supercilious tone. When it was her turn, she quietly laid down her knitting. The 110-strong orchestra was playing Wagner at full blast when she stood up and covered the entire orchestra with the most amazing stream of sound, which made even the Vienna Philharmonic seem small.

During the recording of *Das Rheingold*, the singers lined up behind the orchestra. When she sang her first line, "Wotan! Gemahl! Erwache!" (Wotan! Husband! Awake!), the musicians in the orchestra abruptly turned around and stared at her in surprise.[22] The power and authority in her voice was extraordinary. Gordon Perry was responsible for the technical aspect of the recordings. He developed Decca's famous stereo technique, but he was also the team's most significant Wagner expert. Perry considered Flagstad's vocal range to be incredible. He took out the voice microphones, but still the volume of her voice came over the orchestra microphones. He says that Flagstad had the ability to project her voice all the way out, an ability that another great Wagner interpreter, the Swede Birgit Nilsson, did not possess. The perfection of Flagstad's voice was a phenomenon, and he had never heard anything like it in his life.[23]

Rehearsals started at 10:00 a.m. each morning. The disadvantage of this was that no one, except for one of the singers, could sing at that time of day. This exception was Kirsten Flagstad. Solti, the conductor, speaks of her in his expressive Italian style:

> "An unbelievable element, like an iceberg. A natural voice that was totally indestructible. In my life I have not heard this Stradivarius quality in anyone else. In every single register the voice sounded like that. The great Wagner roles have deep notes, high notes and middle notes that run counter to the enormous body of sound from the orchestra. And this incredible voice, it always flowed across the orchestra and could ride up on the back of any wave. There was no need to rebalance the orchestra so much after her. She was an orchestra in herself, and so you had two orchestras.
>
> But her voice was not only big; it could also be soft and tender. She was an amazingly dramatic soprano, probably the greatest of the century. She smiled a lot and had a loud laugh, she seemed like a happy person, or maybe she was not so happy? Solti concluded.[24]

## The Opera Director

Kirsten Flagstad spent November to December 1957 in the hospital. Just after the New Year, she was asked if she could step into the post of director of Norway's new opera company. The Norwegian National Opera was founded on November 19, 1957. She consulted her doctor, as she was far from well. At the same time, this work would be an honor close to her heart, and so she accepted. On February 3, 1958, she was formally appointed. That same afternoon, she visited her old mother, who was living, terminally ill, in a care home. Maja had heard that her daughter had become the opera director, but she had also learned that "the girl" was to travel to London to make some recordings. Maja's condition deteriorated while Kirsten was in London. However, the work went ahead; not even death would stop her. Maja forbade her to come home, and it was the housekeeper, Beret Stabben, who was the last person to see Maja Flagstad alive. Kirsten had never had an intimate personal relationship with her mother, so it was actually understandable that she did not keep vigil at her mother's deathbed. Nor did Maja wish for any such closeness, and she was the one, as already mentioned, who told Kirsten not to come. When Maja Flagstad was buried on February 21, 1958, Kirsten Flagstad was on a flight to Los Angeles. And so their pattern of living was maintained until they were parted by death.

On April 1, 1958, Flagstad landed at Fornebu airport in Oslo to start work as Norway's first opera director, at the age of sixty-two. She had absolutely zero administrative experience and a limited grasp of financial matters. However, she had dabbled with this thought ever since she had discussed the possibility of a Norwegian opera company with Egil Nordsjø in November 1946. In a letter to him, she wrote that something had to be done, not simply demanded, on the opera question. She had at one time requested to have the National Theatre accounts released, listing what they earned from opera, and she enclosed these, asking Nordsjø to find a solution to the idea of having an opera company in Norway. They were to meet for further discussion when she went to Oslo.[25] This discussion with him, as a leading member of the Norwegian Society of Music Artists and the Opera Association, was one of the catalysts for the establishment of the National Opera Company with Flagstad as its first director.

A new chapter in the history of Norwegian opera began in 1950, when the brothers Jonas and Gunnar Brunvoll, along with the conductor István Pajor, founded the Norwegian Opera Company. The Norwegian Ballet, which had

Opera director Kirsten Flagstad welcomes King Olav to the Norwegian National Opera's opening night on February 16, 1959. They both had much experience fulfilling their roles. Flagstad broke down in the elevator on her way to the reception after accompanying King Olav out of the building after the end of the premiere performance.
*Source: Flagstad Museum.*

begun staging performances as early as 1948, chose to join forces with the opera company. Their performances provided an artistic foundation for the establishment of a limited company (Den Norske Opera A/S), with support from Oslo City Council, the Norwegian state, the Norwegian Opera Fund, and the Norwegian Opera Company. The following year, the limited company rented the People's Theatre (Folketeateret) at Youngstorget in Oslo.[26]

In May 1958, Flagstad wrote that her head was full of plans for the opera. Everything was in the initial stages, and she had a whole string of things to attend to. Her psoriasis was so bad that she had to be admitted to the hospital for a few days, even though she really had no time for that.[27] Flagstad enjoyed the work, although it was difficult to start something from scratch. She had been on tour in the US, and when she came home, nothing had been done.

This work had taught her many new things and genuinely gave her a feeling of having started an opera company. There had been many disappointments and critical voices, but she paid them no heed. Until now, no office staff had been appointed: a secretary, as well as a bookkeeper and a few others, would not arrive until August 18. In the meantime, she had used the office workers in her deceased husband's businesses, including Leif Stake, to help her. On September 1, they were all to meet up, and the budget was extremely tight.[28] Flagstad herself never took a salary, and she paid a number of singers in the opera company out of her own pocket. The artists received only 18,000 kroner per year, so she gave them as much time off as possible so that they could find other jobs. Another worry was that the opera company had no chorus, and besides, she intended to not only set up opera productions but also foster a love of opera in the Norwegian public. She regarded this as a double task. The aim, to start with, was to secure a lease for the opera company for the next year, an orchestra of fifty musicians, their own opera chorus, and a repertoire. She believed that if they achieved all this, the future of the opera company would be secure.[29] It is no exaggeration to conclude that the opera company was partly privately financed at the start. How much of her own personal capital Flagstad donated to the opera company in these early years is a well-kept secret.

## Overtaken by Illness

Another significant gift to the opera company was Flagstad's own fame. This alone meant that the institution was noticed even beyond Norway's borders. On February 16, 1959, the Norwegian Opera Company gave their opening performance. Flagstad was struggling with severe physical pain on the day of the opening. She dreaded having to escort King Olav from the entrance and up the stairs to his seat in the balcony. Perhaps she also dreaded meeting him, even though they both put on brave faces—the past was forgotten. It was a great, proud moment when she finally stood in front of the stage curtain to declare the Norwegian Opera and Ballet open. After the premiere, she took the elevator up to the reception, and as she stood there, her body broke down. She only just managed to take a car home to her apartment, where she remained in bed until she was later transferred to the hospital for cortisone treatments. For several lengthy periods, the opera director's office was in the National Hospital, where she had to be treated continuously. On January 19, 1960, she resigned as opera director. She was suffering from acute psoriasis and severe joint pain. There were also test results that suggested metastasis in her spine. At times, she lived with bandages wrapped around her whole body and had difficulty moving. From time to time, she had periods of respite, and then she was at home at Amalienborg, where Beret Stabben took good care of her.

In a letter to Bernard Miles, Flagstad tells of a last sad farewell to her vocation in life. She had finally informed Decca that she would never be able to record any more discs and that she was no longer able to work at all. The letter became quite tearstained as it lay on her desk. The recognition that her life was now moving toward a brutal end brought her fresh anxiety. Her psoriasis and other complaints caused intense pain, and she wanted to return to the hospital as soon as possible.[30]

## Petition Rejected

Just after Kirsten Flagstad had retired as opera director, a number of music and art organizations, together with a few cultural figures, took the initiative to send a petition to the Honors Committee at the palace requesting that Flagstad be appointed Commander with Star of the Order of St. Olav. She had received the Order of St. Olav previously, but it would be quite natural to reward with such a decoration the work she had done to inaugurate such a prestigious cultural institution as the National Opera Company. It would have rounded off her career in a distinguished manner and provided an opportunity for the palace to draw a line under the royal family's unease about contact with her. On April 30, 1960, the petition was processed by the Honors Committee and rejected. The rejection was notified by telephone to the chairman, Olav Lid. This was a fresh demonstration of the royal family's grudge against Kirsten Flagstad. It is not known whether she found out about this. In any case, she wrote to Nordsjø on July 17 to thank him for the telegram from the Norwegian Society of Music Artists on the occasion of her birthday. She also wrote, "I have felt like an outcast from my colleagues in the last couple of years."[31]

Even if this was not an objective truth, the perception of being an outcast was true of her personal feelings. Another petition suggesting an even higher decoration was sent and of course also rejected. The final rejection from the Honors Committee came on September 3, 1962. Hopefully, Kirsten Flagstad knew nothing of it. She would almost certainly have intensely disliked the idea of such a petition being presented again. She knew very well what her position had been vis-à-vis the royal family, and such repudiation would only have hurt her. The rejections sent a clear signal and gave the Norwegian royal family the less than honorable role of being the last of Flagstad's adversaries.

## Mother and Daughter for the Last Time

By August 1962, Kirsten Flagstad had been confined to bed in the National Hospital for several weeks, and Stake writes in a letter that she suffered greatly with severe pain. She had been given radiotherapy a number of times, which brought some relief, and so she hoped to go home to Kristiansand before long. She knew that this would be her final trip home. She could hardly write or move any longer, so Stake dealt with all her correspondence. On her instructions, he burned all her letters. Flagstad had also asked her friends to destroy all letters from her.

284  THE VOICE OF THE CENTURY

Her last wish of returning home was fulfilled, and she stayed at Amalienborg for just over three weeks. They placed her sickbed in the music room so that she could listen to all the records that Culshaw had sent her. Her housekeeper took care of her day and night since Kirsten Flagstad was now helpless and had become dependent on nursing care.

Well into September, her condition deteriorated, and on the nineteenth of that month, an ambulance took Kirsten Flagstad back to the National Hospital in Oslo, while her chauffeur Nilssen and Beret Stabben drove behind it in her car. During this last stay at the National Hospital, she saw only Stake, who insisted that her daughter should be alerted and should come to say goodbye to her mother. Flagstad did not want this. She repeated the pattern she had inherited from her own mother. Maja Flagstad had also been reluctant to have her daughter by her side when she passed away. Their relationship was not close enough to tolerate such intimacy.

It must have been a terrible strain for Else to follow the smear campaign and threats directed at her mother in America and Norway. With her husband, she had tried to settle in Norway. The little family had moved to the country in the summer of 1952. Her husband obtained work in one of the Johansen family firms in Lillestrøm, where they were accommodated in a drafty house with an outside toilet. Her mother did not see much of Else, as she was not in Norway at the time. She was giving more than fifty concerts throughout Europe and the US, from August 1952 to the New Year of 1953. It all ended with the family moving back to America. This experience led to renewed bitterness and yet another harrowing estrangement of mother and daughter. Kirsten Flagstad was not well at this time, either physically or mentally. She only did as she always had done, traveling around singing. Her mental state and physical absence meant that she was certainly in no condition to show any solicitude for her family while they were living in Norway.

A couple of floors below Flagstad's room at the National Hospital, Else's father was also lying on his deathbed. It is not known whether they were aware of each other. On November 16, 1962, Sigurd Hall died, and Else was informed of his passing. She went to his funeral, which took place in Oslo. To her alarm, she discovered that her mother was at death's door, drowsy and unable to talk. Only Leif Stake had access to her before Else arrived. Nevertheless, something miraculous happened. On the morning of December 3, 1962, Kirsten Flagstad awoke. She was clearheaded and able to speak. And so Else and Stake each had a brief, confidential conversation with her. Else was able to say farewell to her mother before she drifted off again.[32]

## Kirsten Flagstad, "The Voice of the Century," Died on December 7, 1962: Last Will and Testament

Kirsten Flagstad drew up her last will and testament on April 13, 1962. After what she had gone through, including her assets being illegally confiscated by the Norwegian state for more than five years, she had no faith in the country's judicial authorities. Her will therefore contained several passages stating that Leif Stake alone, rather than the Probate Court, was to ensure that her will was executed. He was to receive assistance in this from a chartered accountant by the name of Egil Grimsrud. If Stake for any reason had to withdraw, then Astrid Sjønnesen was to take over as executor. The will named Else as sole heir, an inheritance that was to be given into her sole ownership. At the same time, a statement was sent to Else in America. She signed it on April 27, agreeing that it would be Stake in cooperation with Grimsrud, and not the Probate Court, who would implement the will. This was an important point for Flagstad.

The will had been signed by Kirsten Flagstad in Kristiansand. Her Norwegian biographer, Aslaug Rein, and the factory manager Bjarne Lie, from the Johansen manufacturing firm Lumber, were the witnesses. In her will, Flagstad writes: "I expect my wishes to be respected." Point VII goes on to state:

286 THE VOICE OF THE CENTURY

"I wish no death announcement until after my cremation and no gathering at the funeral. My ashes are not to be preserved."[33]

King Olav and a number of other individuals and institutions sent wreaths, floral tributes, and messages to a funeral they should not have known about. The ashes were collected in an urn. This urn was kept for three years in the new crematorium at the Vestre Cemetery in Oslo. On November 23, 1965, it was buried in a memorial garden there.

This was an infringement of Kirsten Flagstad's last will and testament of April 13, 1962. She may have feared that her grave might also become a source of strife. Flagstad left this world in the knowledge that the recordings of her voice lived on. They would be a far more significant affirmation than a tomb.

Fly home, ye ravens! Tell your lord the tidings that here on the Rhine ye have learned! To Brünnhilde's rock first wing your flight! There burneth Loge.[34]

## Notes

1. Art, *New York Times*, March 27, 1951.
2. Solbrekken (2003), p. 381.
3. Astrid Varnay, in discussion with the author, May 2003.
4. Sir Bernard Miles, lecture, sound b/692, Norwegian National Library sound collection.
5. Monica Groop, *Edvard Greig: The Complete Songs*, https://www.eclassical .com/shop/17115/art31/4933231-a1f5f0-BIS-1607-09_booklet.pdf.
6. Miles, lecture.
7. Øivind Fjeldstad, lecture, sound b/698, Norwegian National Library sound collection.
8. "When I Have Sung My Songs," *Nordiske Tidende*, February 7, 1952.
9. Biancolli (1952), p. 198.
10. McArthur (1965), pp. 280–81.
11. "Kirsten Flagstad er kommet hertil" [Kirsten Flagstad has come here], *Berlingske Tidende*, July 21, 1936.
12. "Flagstad laaner høje toner af Schwartzkopf" [Flagstad borrows top notes from Schwartzkopf], *Berlingske Tidende*, March 6, 1954.
13. "Kirsten Flagstads høje toner" [Kirsten Flagstad's top notes], *Berlingske Tidende*, March 8, 1954.
14. Kirsten Flagstad to Mr. Mittell, April 24, 1952, Flagstad Museum archive.

Part 4: Postlude (1951–62)

15. Professor Niels Christian Gauslaa Danbolt, lecture, sound b/694, Norwegian National Library sound collection.

16. Leif Stake to the Bergen Festival, January 12, 1953, Flagstad Museum archive.

17. Frank Meidell Falk, former Bergen Festival director, in discussion with the author, July 25, 2003.

18. Kirsten Flagstad to Mrs. Esberg, October 9, 1953, Flagstad Museum archive.

19. Beret Stabben, interview, sound 705, Norwegian National Library sound collection.

20. Tobroken (2003), pp. 411–12.

21. Kirsten Flagstad, in conversation with Torstein Gunnarson, Radio archive 1994/22375.

22. *Das Rheingold*, scene 2.

23. Kirsten Flagstad in Vienna, recording from Danish Radio, P2, Mogens Bentin.

24. Georg Solti, interview, in the documentary film Århundrets *stemme* [Voice of the century], by Marta Breen, 1994, https://www.youtube.com/watch?v =qf4oj5NQRyM&t=3515s.

25. Kirsten Flagstad to Egil Nordsjø, November 4, 1946, H. Herresthal's personal archive.

26. H. Herresthal, email, August 6, 2020.

27. Kirsten Flagstad to Kathrine, May 23, 1958, Flagstad Museum archive.

28. Kirsten Flagstad to Carol, August 2, 1958, Flagstad Museum archive.

29. "Hon vet inte var hon ska spela!" [She doesn't know where to play], *Svenska Dagbladet*, May 3, 1959.

30. Kirsten Flagstad to Bernard Miles, November 17, 1961, Flagstad Museum archive.

31. Kirsten Flagstad to Egil Nordsjø, July 17, 1960, H. Herresthal's personal archive.

32. Gunnarson (1985), p. 275.

33. Kirsten Flagstad's will, April 13, 1962, Helge Atle Rønningsen's personal archive.

34. "Brunnhilde: Flieg Heim," Ihr Raben, Ending scene Götterdammerung.

# ACKNOWLEDGMENTS

This author's first thanks must go to the late Torstein Gunnarson. He was a journalist reporting on cultural affairs for the Norwegian Broadcasting Corporation for a number of years and a great Flagstad admirer and enthusiast. He knew her personally and was involved in some of her late recordings of psalms. His knowledge of her international career was extensive. In the 1960s and 1970s, he traveled throughout Europe and America, interviewing people who had known her and collecting newspaper cuttings and articles about her life and career. His collection, comprising a total of thirty ring binders, gives an invaluable insight into the way music critics of the time perceived and judged Flagstad's voice. These draw the truest picture we can form of her vocal artistry. Subsequent critics, and those of the present day, can only assess this phenomenon from old recordings of variable sound quality. That is quite different from experiencing the swelling sound of a voice and an orchestra in person in a space with good acoustics.

Gunnarson fought an untiring battle against the injustice that was perpetrated against Flagstad. He wrote a book on the subject, but no publishing company would print it at that time. Nevertheless, it was published with the help of private enterprise. Gunnarson also established a fund and collection for the erection of a monument to Flagstad. This was created by the sculptor Joseph Grimeland, but when it was completed, he had great problems arranging its placement. Several public institutions turned down the opportunity to have a statue of Flagstad either outside or inside their buildings. In the end, the principal of the Norwegian Academy of Music, Professor Harald

Herresthal, had the statue erected in front of the academy's rented premises at Wergelandsveien 21, an address that has the Royal Palace as a close neighbor.

The monument was unveiled on May 5, 1982. Gunnarson had persuaded the police to stop all traffic in Wergelandsveien during the speeches and unveiling ceremony. When the statue was revealed, Brunhild's battle cry, "Ho jo to ho," rang out from the loudspeakers and was heard all through the Palace Park. Kirsten Flagstad stood facing the Royal Palace in her famous pose.[1] The monument is now situated outside the Norwegian Opera House at Bjørvika in Oslo, in what is now called Kirsten Flagstad's Square.

Huge thanks also go to the former manager of the Flagstad Museum Ragnhild Nyhus. Her years of research resulted in a complete, chronological overview of Flagstad's appearances and recordings and laid a foundation stone for every subsequent Flagstad researcher.

Next, I wish to thank Knut Harris, Old Norse philologist, historian, and music expert. His inexhaustible knowledge of all things Old Norse, of music and language, has greatly benefited this author and biographer.

Thanks also go to the former director of Norwegian Opera Bjørn Simensen, for his support and assistance with contacts in international settings and individuals who have supported the translation projects. In connection, thanks are also due to Peter Gelb, the general manager of the Metropolitan Opera, as well as their chief archivist Peter Clark.

Annika E. Engelhart, who is in charge of the Flagstad Museum, has helped the project in numerous ways, and I thank her for her efforts to have the book brought into being.

Jon Otterbeck of the Opera Publishing House (Opera Forlag) is thanked as my loyal and dependable publisher and for taking on this work of cultural importance.

The author grew closer to Kirsten Flagstad the human being through friendship with her late niece Stefi Tyrihjell. As a young girl, she spent summers with her aunt Kirsten. Stefi conveyed a vivid picture of her aunt and of the entire Flagstad family. She once said to me, "Aunt Kirsten would have liked you!" "And I, her," was my response.

## Notes

1. H. Herresthal, email, August 7, 2020.

# SOURCES

## Literature List

Åmli mållag og Åmli historielag (2010) *Jol i Åmli, årbok 2010* [Åmli Language Association and Åmli Historical Association yearbook 2010]. Åmli: Laget.

Ardoin, John (1994) *The Furtwängler Record*. Oregon: Amadeus.

Biancolli, Louis (1952) *The Flagstad Manuscript*. New York: G. P. Putnam's Sons.

Bomann-Larsen, Tor (2013) *Svaret* [The answer]. Oslo: Cappelen Damm.

Bruland, Bjarte (2017) *Holocaust i Norge* [The Holocaust in Norway]. Oslo: Dreyer.

Dorenfeldt, Lauritz J. (1978) "Kan ekstraordinære etterforskningsmetoder aksepteres i visse saker?" [Can unusual investigation methods be accepted in certain cases?]. *Lov og Rett*, pp. 291–303.

Drüner, Ulrich (2016) *Richard Wagner: Die Inzenierung eines Lebens* [The staging of a life]. Munich: Blessing.

Gellert, Christian Fürchtegott (1757) *Geistliche Oden und Lieder* [Spiritual odes and songs]. Leipzig: Weidmann.

Gilliam, Bryan (1992) *Richard Strauss and His World*. Princeton, NJ: Princeton University Press.

Gisvold, Annie, and Knut Harris, trans. (2020) *The Poetic Edda, Part I—The Gods*. Oslo.

Gunnarson, Torstein (1985) *Sannheten om Kirsten Flagstad* [The truth about Kirsten Flagstad]. Oslo: Flagstadselskapet [Flagstad Society].

Hamann, Brigitte (2002) *Winifred Wagner oder Hitlers Bayreuth* [Winifred Wagner or Hitler's Bayreuth]. Munich: Piper.

## SOURCES

Herresthal, Harald (2019) *Propaganda og Motstand, Musikklivet i Oslo 1940–1945* [Propaganda and resistance; music life in Norway, 1940–1945]. Oslo: Ad Notam.

Jefferson, Alan (1996) *Elisabeth Schwarzkopf*. Munich: Langen Müller.

Jensen, Jørgen Arnold, ed. (1942) *Henry Johansen Lumber Co. A/S gjennem 25 år: 1917–1942: Norsk kryssfinerfabrikasjon i 25 år* [25 years of Henry Johansen's Lumber Co.: 1917–1942: Norwegian plywood manufacturing]. Vågsbygd: Fabrikken.

Karlsen, Ola (2020) *Den norske nazieliten* [The Norwegian Nazi elite]. Oslo: Gyldendal.

Kraus, René (1942) *Europe in Revolt*. New York: MacMillan.

Lund, Eve-Marie (2008) *La meg være i fred* [Leave me alone]. Oslo: Arneberg.

McArthur, Edwin (1965) *A Personal Memoir*. New York: Alfred A. Knopf.

Mortensson-Egnund, Ivar, trans. (2017) *Edda-kvedet* [The Poetic Edda]. Oslo: Det Norske Samlaget.

Newman, Ernest (1949) *The Wagner Operas*. London: Alfred A. Knopf.

Newman, Ernest (1976) *The Life of Richard Wagner I–IV*. Cambridge: Cambridge University Press.

*Norsk Sakførerblad* [Norwegian lawyers' journal] 4, no. 10 (1934).

Pryser, Tore (1994) *Fra varm til kald krig* [From hot to cold war]. Oslo: Universitetsforlaget.

Rein, Aslaug (1967) *Kirsten Flagstad*. Oslo: Ernst G. Mortensen.

Ringdal, Nils Johan (2008) *Georg Valentin af Morgenstiernes forunderlige liv og reiser* [The amazing life and travels of Georg Valentin af Morgenstierne]. Oslo: Aschehoug.

Rosenberg, Jonathan (2019) *Dangerous Melodies: Classical Music in America from the Great War through the Cold War*. New York: Norton.

Rosenthal, Herold (1958) *Two Centuries of Opera at Covent Garden*. Putnam: University of Michigan.

Schive, Jens, and Hans Olav (1939) *Med Kronprinsparet—for Norge! 70 dagers ferd gjennem stjernebannerets land* [With the royal couple—for Norway! A 70-day journey through the land of "The Star-Spangled Banner"]. Oslo: Aschehoug.

Schmid-Bloss, Karl, ed. (1943) *Züricher Stadttheater Jahrbuch 1942/43* [Zurich State Theatre yearbook 1942/43]. Zurich: Züricher Stadttheater.

Solbrekken, Ingeborg (2003) *Stemmen: Kirsten Flagstad—verdensstjerne og Syndebukk* [The voice: Kirsten Flagstad—international star and scapegoat]. Oslo: Genesis.

Solbrekken, Ingeborg (2007) *Galskap og rettergang* [Madness and court proceedings]. Oslo: Transit.

SOURCES

Solbrekken, Ingeborg (2015) *Landssvikoppgjørets hemmelige historie* [The secret history of the postwar treason settlement]. Oslo: Opera.

Solbrekken, Ingeborg (2016) *Konspirasjonen mot Kirsten Flagstad* [The conspiracy against Kirsten Flagstad]. Oslo: Opera.

Solhjell, Dag og Hans Fredrik Dahl (2013) *Men viktigst er æren* [But most important of all is honor]. Oslo: Pax.

St. meld. nr. 17 [Norwegian parliamentary report no. 17] (1962–63) Om Landssvikoppgjøret. Innstilling fra et utvalg nedsatt for å skaffe tilveie materiale til en innberetning fra Justisdepartementet til Stortinget 1962. [On the postwar treason settlement. Findings of a commission appointed to produce material for a report from the Ministry of Justice to the Norwegian Parliament, 1962].

St. meld. nr. 64 [Norwegian parliamentary report no. 64] (1950) Angrepene på rettsoppgjøret med landssvikerne. Tilråding fra Justis- og politidepartementet 8. september 1950. Bilag 1: Beretning fra riksadvokaten om undersøkelser som er foretatt i anledning av beskyldninger mot politiet, vaktmannskaper ved fangeleirene m.v. for bruk av ulovlige metoder under rettsoppgjøret mot landssvikerne. Bilag 2: Innberetning til Det Kgl. Justis- og Politidepartement fra konstituert riksadvokat Ø. Thommessen om undersøkelser foretatt i anledning av O. H. Langelands bøker «Dømmer ikke» og «Forat I ikke skal dømmes» og Arne Bergsviks skrift «We are no Criminals» [Attacks on the postwar judicial settlement with traitors. Recommendations of the Ministry of Justice and Police dated August 8, 1950. Appendix 1: Statement by the director of public prosecution regarding investigations taken with respect to accusations against the police, guards at prison camps, etc., on the use of illegal methods during the judicial settlement with traitors. Appendix 2: Statement to the Royal Ministry of Justice and Police from acting director of public prosecution Ø. Thommessen on investigations conducted in the light of O. H. Langeland's books *Do Not Condemn* and *That They Be Not Judged* and Arne Bergsvik's paper "We Are No Criminals"].

Storeide, Anette H. (2014) *Norske krigsprofitører: Nazi-Tysklands velvillige Medløpere* [The Norwegian war profiteers: Nazi Germany's willing helpers]. Oslo: Gyldendal.

Stravinskij, Igor (1962) *An Autobiography*. New York: Norton.

Sturlason, Snorre (2017) *Edda*. Translated into New Norwegian by Erik Eggen. Oslo: Det Norske Samlaget.

Svendsen, Trond Olav (2013) *Flagstad—et kunstnerliv* [Flagstad: Life of an artist]. Oslo: Opera.

Tunbridge, Laura (2018) *Singing in the Age of Anxiety*. Chicago: University of Chicago Press.

Vederlag til politiets kilder og provokasjon som etterforskningsmetode—Riksadvokatens rundskriv nr. 2—2000. Ra 00–25 [Remuneration to police sources and

294 SOURCES

provocation as a method of investigation—the director of public prosecution's circular no. 2—2000].

Wasiutynski, Jeremi (1996) *Creation and Annihilation of the External Pseudo-reality.* Oslo: Wasiutynski.

Westlie, Bjørn (2011) *Oppgjør i skyggen av Holocaust* [Settlement in the shadow of the Holocaust]. Oslo: Aschehoug e-book.

## National Library of Norway

Kirsten Flagstad to Berit Cleve, April 29, 1946. Brevsamling, brev nr. 366 [letter collection, letter no. 366].

*Nordmandsforbundet* [The Norse Federation] (1911) hefte 1, Kristiania [Christiania].

## Sound Collection

Elisabeth Schwarzkopf i minneprogram om Flagstad, sendt av BBC [Elisabeth Schwartzkopf in memorial program about Flagstad, broadcast by BBC].

Flagstad forteller om sitt arbeid med karakterer. I: Radioarkivet Id: 1994/22375:P Operasangerinne Kirsten Flagstad i samtale med Torstein Gunnarson, NRK [Flagstad talks of her work on characters. In Radio Archive Id: 1994/22375: P Opera singer Kirsten Flagstad in conversation with Torstein Gunnarson, NRK].

Intervju med Beret Stabben, lyd/ 705 (Beret Stabben, interview, sound file/705).

Musikksamling lyd b/689. Kåseri Eva Gustavson [Music collection, sound file b/689. Talk by Eva Gustavson].

Musikksamling lyd b/694. Kåseri Karen-Marie Flagstad [Music collection, sound file b/694. Talk by Karen-Marie Flagstad].

Musikksamling lyd b/692. Kåseri Sir Bernard Miles [Music collection, sound file 692. Talk by Sir Bernard Miles].

Musikksamling lyd b/698. Kåseri Øivind Fjeldstad [Music collection, sound file b/698. Talk by Øivind Fjeldstad].

Musikksamling lyd b/698. Kåseri professor Niels Christian Gauslaa Danbolt [Music collection, sound file 698. Talk by Professor Niels Christian Gauslaa Danbolt].

Musikksamling lyd b/693. Kåseri Egil Nordsjø [Music collection, sound file b/693. Talk by Egil Nordsjø].

Torstein Gunnarson intervju med Birgit Nilsson 5. mai 1979, NRK [Torstein Gunnarson's interview with Birgit Nilsson, May 5, 1979, NRK].

SOURCES 295

## National Archives of Norway

Archive code 38.8.15, vols. 1–2, file: Kirsten Flagstad, Ministry of Foreign Affairs archive. Morgenstierne, Wilhelm Thorleif von Munthe af: 1910–1949 RA/ PA 1274.

Finn Støren to Oberführer Fehlis, February 9, 1945.

Norwegian Relief, Embassy in Washington, Ministry of Foreign Affairs archive, Oslo.

Oslo Police Station: Copy judgments dnr. A no. 2679—Arthur Einarsen.

Oslo Police Station: Copy judgments dnr. A no. 4489—Bernt Gustav Somdalen.

Oslo Police Station: Judgments dnr. 3298—Arthur Einarsen.

Oslo Police Station: Misc., Anr. 3194—Henry Thomas Ingvald Johansen.

Oslo Police Station: Treason case against Henry Thomas Ingvald Johansen: H 3194.

Romerike Police Station: cases, pnr. 360/45—Hans Ottar Westby.

S-1555 Director of Public Prosecution's archive, series D—case file, box 51, folder 6—search of Oslo Prison.

S-1555 Director of Public Prosecution's archive, series D—case file, box 52.

St. Olav's Medal, Embassy in Washington, box 374, Ministry of Foreign Affairs archive, Oslo.

## NRK, Radio Archive

Kirsten Flagstad, in conversation with Torstein Gunnarson. ID: 1994/22375.

Lauritz Melchior, Kirsten Flagstad in memoriam, December 30, 1962.

## Flagstad Museum Archive

Chronological overview of all Kirsten Flagstad's performances: https://dms-cf-02 .dimu.org/file/022wazLzTnja

Letter from Kirsten Flagstad to Maja 15/1 1935

Letter from Kirsten Flagstad to Kathrine 10/2 1946

Letter from Royal Norwegian Information Service, New York office, Royal Norwegian embassy, Washington DC to Mrs. K. M. Hall 7/3 1945

Letter from Kirsten Flagstad to Kathrine and Jack 5/9 1945

Letter from Kirsten Flagstad to Peggy and Edwin 22/7 1945

Letter from Kirsten Flagstad to Edwin McArthur 28/9 1945

Letter from Kirsten Flagstad to Kathrine 14/10 1945

Letter from Kirsten Flagstad to Edwin McArthur 24/10 1945

Letter from Kirsten Flagstad to Kathrine 10/2 1946

Letter from Kirsten Flagstad to Kathrine 1/12 1946

Letter from Kirsten Flagstad to Norbert 10/2 1947

Letter from Kirsten Flagstad to Karen-Marie 10/11 1947
Letter from Kirsten Flagstad to Ellen 23/2 1948
Letter from Kirsten Flagstad to Miles 16/4 1948
Letter from Richard Strauss to Kirsten Flagstad 13/5 1949
Letter from Kirsten Flagstad to Miles 20/3 1950
Letter from Kirsten Flagstad to Miles 9/6 1950
Letter from Rudolf Bing to Bernice Nece 9/4 1950
Letter from Kirsten Flagstad to Mr. Mittell 24/4 1952
Letter from Leif Stake to Festspillene i Bergen 12/1 1953
Letter from Kisten Flagstad to Mrs. Esberg 9/10 1953
Letter from Kirsten Flagstad to Kathrine 23/5 1958
Letter from Kirsten Flagstad to Carol 2/8 1958
Letter from Kirsten Flagstad to Miles 17/11 1961 Sir Bernard Miles, notes
Torstein Gunnarson's collection of newspaper cuttings, 30 ring binders

## Personal Archives

Harald Herresthal's archive:
Kirsten Flagstad to Egil Nordsjø, November 4, 1946.
Kirsten Flagstad to Egil Nordsjø, July 17, 1960.
Robert Tuggle's archive:
War against Flagstad.
Belmont Harriman essay.
Helge Atle Rønningsen's archive:
Kirsten Flagstad's last will and testament, April 13, 1962.

## Internet Resources

Apollon (2011) "Kjønnsforsker & matriark." https://www.apollon.uio.no
/portretter/2011/portrett.html.
*Black History Magazine* (n.d.) https://bkhonline.com/marian-anderson-and-the
-dar-controversy/.
Britannica (n.d.) S.v. "Marian Anderson." https://www.britannica.com/biography
/Marian-Anderson.
Cabrera, Donato (2020) "The Music Plays On—Strauss Four Last Songs." *Me-dium*, May 9, 2020. https://donatocabrera.medium.com/the-music-plays-on
-strauss-four-last-songs-49e6bc855f7.
Drake, James A. (1991) "Kipnis Speaks: An Interview with Alexander Kipnis."
*Opera Quarterly* 8, no. 2 (Summer): 74–94. https://doi.org/10.1093/oq/8.2.74.
Frida Leider Society (n.d.) "Biography." http://www.frida-leider.de/en/biography
.html.

SOURCES                                                    297

Groop, Monica (n.d.) *Edvard Greig: The Complete Songs.* https://www.eclassical
.com/shop/17115/art31/4933231-a1f5f0-BIS-1607-09_booklet.pdf.

Guttormsen, T. S. (2018) "Valuing Immigrant Memories as Common Heritage:
The Leif Erikson Monument in Boston." *History and Memory* 30 (2): 79–115.
https://www.niku.no/2018/10/valuing-immigrant-memories-as-common
-heritage/.

Horowitz, Joe (2014) "Remembering Artur Bodanzky." ArtsJournal, July 17, 2014.
https://www.artsjournal.com/uq/2014/07/remembering-artur-bodanzky.html.

Interview with Horenstein (1969) Wilhelm Furtwängler, BBC Documentary.
https://www.youtube.com/watch?v=NnXn9wwQeXQ.

Karlsen, Ola (2015) "Norway's Strangest National Betrayal Case." ABC Nyheter,
June 28, 2015. https://www.abcnyheter.no/nyheter/2015/06/28/194407471
/norges-merkeligste-landssviksak?nr=1.

Kipnis, Igor (1991) "Alexander Kipnis: A Son Remembers His Father." *Opera
Quarterly* 8, no. 2 (Summer): 59–73. https://doi.org/10.1093/oq/8.2.59.

Metropolitan Opera (n.d.) "This Month in Met History." https://www.metopera
.org/discover/archives/notes-from-the-archives/january/.

Oxford International Song Festival (n.d.) https://www.oxfordlieder.co.uk/song
/1815.

Rushprint (2015) "Det er nødvendig å omskrive norsk krigshistorie." http://
rushprint.no/2015/11/det-er-nodvendig-a-omskrive-norsk-krigshistorie/.

"Sigrdrifumál in the *Poetic Edda*" (1961) "Edda-Kvede," Det Norske Samlaget,
Oslo. http://www.voluspa.org/sigrdrifumal.htm.

Statistics Norway (n.d.) https://www.ssb.no/a/histstat/aarbok/ht-0901-lonn
.html.

Voluspå.org (n.d.) http://www.voluspa.org/voluspa56-60.htm.

*Wilhelm Furtwängler* (1964) BBC Radio Documentary. https://www.youtube.com
/watch?v=9NTO1VItLmE.

**Ingeborg Solbrekken** is a Norwegian author and playwright. She has written three books in Norwegian on Kirsten Flagstad.

FOR INDIANA UNIVERSITY PRESS

Lesley Bolton  *Project Manager/Editor*
Tony Brewer  *Artist and Book Designer*
Allison Chaplin  *Acquisitions Editor*
Anna Garnai  *Production Coordinator*
Sophia Hebert  *Assistant Acquisitions Editor*
Samantha Heffner  *Marketing and Publicity Manager*
Katie Huggins  *Production Manager*
Pamela Rude  *Senior Artist and Book Designer*